MW00581319

THE HODAYOT (THANKSGIVING PSALMS)

Society of Biblical Literature

Early Judaism and Its Literature

Rodney A. Werline, Editor

Mark J. Boda
George J. Brooke
Esther G. Chazon
Steven D. Fraade
Martha Himmelfarb
James S. McLaren
Jacques van Ruiten

Number 36

THE HODAYOT (THANKSGIVING PSALMS)

A Study Edition of 1QH^{a}

THE HODAYOT (THANKSGIVING PSALMS)

A STUDY EDITION OF 1QH[a]

Eileen M. Schuller and Carol A. Newsom

Society of Biblical Literature
Atlanta

THE HODAYOT (THANKSGIVING PSALMS)
A Study Edition of 1QH[a]

Copyright © 2012 by the Society of Biblical Literature

All rights reserved. No part of this work may be reproduced or transmitted in any form or by any means, electronic or mechanical, including photocopying and recording, or by means of any information storage or retrieval system, except as may be expressly permitted by the 1976 Copyright Act or in writing from the publisher. Requests for permission should be addressed in writing to the Rights and Permissions Office, Society of Biblical Literature, 825 Houston Mill Road, Atlanta, GA 30329 USA.

Library of Congress Cataloging-in-Publication Data

Schuller, Eileen M., 1946–.
The Hodayot (Thanksgiving Psalms) : a study edition of 1QH[a] / Eileen M. Schuller and Carol A. Newsom.
p. cm. — (Society of Biblical Literature : early Judaism and its literature ; no. 36)
Text in Hebrew with English translation.
Includes bibliographical references.
ISBN 978-1-58983-692-1 (paper binding : alk. paper) -- ISBN 978-1-58983-693-8 (electronic format)
1. Thanksgiving Psalms—Criticism, interpretation, etc. 2. Dead Sea scrolls. I. Newsom, Carol A. II. Title.
BM488.T5S38 2012
296.1'55—dc23 2012019072

Printed on acid-free, recycled paper conforming to
ANSI/NISO Z39.48-1992 (R1997) and ISO 9706:1994
standards for paper permanence.

To the memory of Hartmut Stegemann (1933–2005),
eminent scholar and generous mentor

Contents

Preface

This impetus for this book goes back to Eibert Tigchelaar and a series of conversations during the summer of 2010 at the International SBL meeting in Tartu, Estonia, and the International Organization of Qumran Studies meeting in Helsinki. The recent publication of the reconstructed scroll of 1QH[a] in DJD 40 was an important step forward in the study of this major collection of poetry from the Dead Sea Scrolls. Eibert noted that graduate students in particular, but also scholars who are not Qumran specialists, would benefit by having access to this text in a more accessible and much cheaper format than the full DJD volume.

Both of us readily agreed with this assessment and set about to see how such a volume could become a reality as expeditiously as possible. Although a number of different possibilities were proposed and considered, in the end we are very pleased that the Society of Biblical Literature took this on as an SBL-Brill co-publication. Given that the SBL Texts and Translation Series is now defunct, the volume was given a home in the Early Judaism and Its Literature series; perhaps other of the major texts from the Dead Sea Scrolls will eventually be included in a similar format in this series.

One of the main reasons for doing this volume is the confusion that continues to abound around the ordering and numbering of the columns and lines of the 1QH[a] manuscript. Some people continue to use the "old" system, often labeled the "Sukenik" system. Various interim arrangements are to be found in translations and editions that were produced over the last two decades, most before the reconstructed scroll was fully accessible. Now there is the "new" or "reconstructed" or "Stegemann/Puech" system that was presented in DJD 40. In much secondary literature, it is often unclear which system of numbering for columns and lines is being followed. It is hoped that making the reconstruction of the 1QH[a] manuscript more readily available will facilitate the adoption of the column and line numbers as presented in DJD 40.

The Hebrew text that is presented here as well as the English translation is basically taken from DJD 40. In the Hebrew transcription, the readings are those of Harmut Stegemann. In the English translation prepared by Carol Newsom, there are some minor revisions of what was in DJD 40, often for the sake of consistency and clarification. We are grateful to Oxford University Press for the requisite permissions for the OUP copyrighted materials.

Thanks are due to many people who helped to bring this project to fruition. A special debt is owed to Bob Buller, Editorial Director of the SBL, who prepared the manuscript for the press. Anne Whitaker Stewart, graduate student at Emory University, adapted the DJD Concordance to the Word List format with great care, accuracy, and attention to detail. Eric Montgomery, graduate student at McMaster University, did extensive proofreading and preparation of the charts in the introduction. Judith Newman as editor of the Early Judaism and Its Literature series and Rod Werline as her successor offered advice and accepted the volume into their series.

We hope that this edition of the Hodayot will serve graduate students and many other scholars who want to work with the Hebrew text. For specialized study, of course, one will still need to consult DJD 40 with its photographic plates, detailed analysis of the reconstruction, extensive notes, and a full concordance. But it is our hope that this study edition can make a contribution within its own limited parameters. May the availability of the text in this format encourage many more scholars in the years ahead to take up the study of this fascinating and challenging collection of religious poetry.

Eileen M. Schuller
Carol A. Newsom
Spring 2012

Sigla

In the Hebrew Text

◦◦◦	traces of letters that cannot be read
א̊	damaged letter (the open circle indicates that there is damage, whether the reading is certain or uncertain; that is, there is no distinction between probable and possible readings of damaged letters)
[א]	reconstructed letter
כ^{יא}	superlinear insertion
{ }	letter(s) erased by the scribe and space left on the leather
א̣̇	deletion dots written by the scribe
·אאא·	alternate word

In the English Translation

◦◦◦	traces of letters in the Hebrew that cannot be read
letters in italics	individual letters in the Hebrew
[...]	lacunae of any length in the Hebrew text
( )	word(s) added for the sake of clarity
< >	word(s) marked for deletion
{ }	word(s) indicated by scribe as alternative

Abbreviations

DJD	Discoveries in the Judaean Desert
DSSR	*Dead Sea Scrolls Reader*
DSSSE	*Dead Sea Scrolls Study Edition*
EDSS	*Encyclopedia of the Dead Sea Scrolls*
col(s).	column(s)
frg(s).	fragment(s)

Introduction

The Hodayot Manuscripts

One of the scrolls that was found by the Bedouin in Cave 1 and purchased in November 1947 by Eleazar Sukenik for the Hebrew University was a collection of approximately thirty poems similar to the biblical psalms. Since the majority of them begin with the phrase "I thank you, Lord" (אודכה אדוני), Sukenik designated this "The Thanksgiving Scroll" (מגילת ההודיות), and the poems themselves came to be called "Hodayot" (in English, Thanksgiving Psalms or Thanksgiving Hymns). The photos and a transcription of this scroll, designated 1QH^{a}, were published in *The Dead Sea Scrolls of the Hebrew University*.[1] When archaeologists excavated Cave 1 in 1949, two fragments were found that contained text that overlaps with the large scroll. These fragments were all that remained of a scroll designated 1Q35/1QH^{b}, another copy of the same collection; they were published in 1955 by J. T. Milik in DJD 1. In Cave 4 six more very fragmentary manuscripts were found that contained text that overlaps with 1QH^{a} and, in a few places, fills in material missing from that manuscript (4Q427–432, 4QH^{a-e}, and 4QpapH^{f}). They were allotted to John Strugnell, who did extensive work on identifying and analyzing these very fragmentary scrolls; they were eventually published by Eileen Schuller in DJD 29 in 1999.

The fact that there are eight copies preserved and that 1QH^{a} was a large and elegantly crafted scroll indicates that these psalms had importance and authority for the community that wrote them and preserved them in the caves near the Dead Sea. They reflect the distinctive vocabulary and religious ideas that marked the type of Judaism found in other core works such as the Rule of the Community and the War Scroll, and at least some poems may have been composed by the Teacher of Righteousness, the founder of this sect. Although there are still many unanswered questions about the origin and use of these poems, they serve as an important resource for understanding the piety and religious devotion of those who composed them and those who continued to copy and recite them.

The 1QH^{a} Manuscript

The 1QH^{a} manuscript is the largest, the most complete, and still the most important copy for working with this collection of poems; that is why this is the manuscript presented in this volume. There are some places where the 1QH^{b} and the 4QH^{a-f} copies can be used to fill in lacunae in 1QH^{a}, often only a few words but more extensively near the end of the scroll. When these copies are incorporated, columns 4–26 of 1QH^{a} are approximately three-quarters complete; unfortunately, very little remains from the first three and what were probably the last two columns. On the basis of the paleography, the scroll is dated to the early Herodian period, circa 30–1 B.C.E.

The "Sukenik Edition"

When 1QH^{a} came into Sukenik's possession, he described it as "a badly damaged scroll" preserved in two separate parts, "three sheets, each one with four columns, or a total of twelve columns … and a crumpled mass of about 70 detached fragments of various sizes" (Sukenik 1955). Sukenik recognized immediately that two scribes were involved in copying the manuscript: one scribe wrote up until column 11 line 22 (column 19 line 25 in the reconstructed scroll), then another scribe took over in the middle of the line and completed the scroll. (It has sometimes

1. Hebrew edition, 1954; English edition, 1955. Bibliographic details of works mentioned in this introduction are given in the bibliography, 10–11.

been suggested that there was a third scribe who wrote a few lines at the point of transition, but this is far from certain.) As a result of this change of hand, it can be determined whether a detached fragment, even a very small one, came from the beginning or the end section of the scroll.

Although Sukenik had hoped to produce a full and complete study of the scroll, after his death in 1952 the committee appointed by Hebrew University determined that an edition should be published quickly, without any attempt to reconstruct the original order of the scroll. Sukenik designated the twelve columns on the three sheets as columns 1–12; he organized some of the larger fragments from the first scribe (scribe A) into columns that he numbered columns 13–17 and some fragments from the second scribe (often called scribe C) into column 18. Many of the smaller fragments could not be placed; he simply numbered them from one to sixty-six, according to their size and the scribal hand. Over the years, the impression was sometimes given that the numbering of the columns reflected the real order of how the original scroll looked, that is, that the scroll began with Sukenik's column 1. In fact, of course, it was obvious that columns 13–17 must have come from the beginning of the scroll (before columns 1–12), since they were written entirely by the first scribe. Some of the fragments written by the second scribe were quite large (especially frgs. 1–9), but there was no way of knowing how they related to each other and in what order they came, so little could be said about them without a context.

Much study of the scroll in the 1960s concentrated on a form-critical analysis and on the question of who might have authored some or all of these poems. Based on the work of a number of German scholars (Morawe 1961; Jeremias 1963; Kuhn 1966), the poems were divided into two groups. One group, clustered in Sukenik's columns 2–9 (now cols. 10–17 in the reconstructed scroll) was designated the "Teacher Hymns." They were distinguished by distinctive linguistic features and vocabulary; where the opening formula is preserved, it is consistently "I thank you, O Lord," although in one place (col. 13:22) an editor deleted this phrase and replaced it with the formula "Blessed are you." The "I" voice seems very personal and to be speaking of the experience of an individual who was chosen by God to receive special knowledge of divine mysteries, who suffered persecution and opposition, and who served as a medium of revelation for a community; this individual is usually identified with the Teacher of Righteousness, who seems to have been the founder and leading figure of this community. The second group of poems, the "Community Hymns," are a more nebulous category. They vary in length and contain much more wisdom vocabulary; only a few incipits are preserved with the "Blessed are you" formula, and sometimes there are also a series of blessings toward the end of a psalm (in 19:30–35 and probably at the end of col. 26). The "I" voice speaks less about personal experience and suffering and more about general declarations of the knowledge and salvation received, combined with confession of profound human weakness and sinfulness. Some scholars assume that these poems were authored by multiple members of the community, though other scholars (e.g., Émile Puech in *EDSS*) argue for the authorial unity of the whole collection.

The Reconstructed 1QH^a Scroll

Relatively little attention was paid to the Hodayot in the 1970s and 1980s, in part because the copies from Cave 4 had not yet been published. However, two scholars, Hartmut Stegemann and Émile Puech, worked on the 1QH^a scroll over many years in order to reconstruct its original arrangement. On the basis of the recurring shapes and the patterns of the damaged pieces and by a series of holes that decrease and increase in size as the scroll was rolled, they were able to establish the original order of the columns and to put many of the smaller pieces into place. Although Stegemann and Puech worked independently, they arrived at basically the same results; this, in itself, speaks to the accuracy of their reconstruction. Stegemann did much of his work for his 1963 dissertation, but he did not publish a full description of his method and results until 2000 ("The Material Reconstruction of 1QHodayot"); Puech published an article in 1988 ("Quelques aspect de la restauration") describing his reconstruction in broad outline and a few selected passages in 1993 (*La croyance des Esséniens)*. A complete text of the reconstructed scroll was first published in DJD 40 in 2009 by Hartmut Stegeman with Eileen Schuller, along with a translation by Carol Newsom. It is this reconstruction of the scroll that is presented in this study edition. The columns and lines have been numbered according to their place in the reconstructed scroll; for many letters that Sukenik had not attempted to decipher, Stegemann introduced new readings based on a close examination of the original scroll itself and on some new photographs.

As reconstructed, the original scroll was made up of seven sheets with four columns in each for a total of twenty-eight columns. It was about four and a half meters in length. The three joined sheets that are the best preserved, Sukenik's columns 1–12, come from the middle of the reconstructed scroll, that is, columns 9–20. The placement of many of the smaller fragments written by scribe A, on the basis of their shapes, allow for the reconstruction of much of columns 4–8; there are a few larger fragments that must have come in columns 1–3, but it is very unclear exactly how they are to be placed. The preservation of overlapping text in 4QH[b] and 4QH[e] allows for the placement of some of the bigger fragments written by the second scribe and hence the reconstruction of much of columns 21–26; indeed, this produces some "new" psalms. There are a couple of fragments that must have been in column 27 or in columns 27 and 28; it is theoretically possible that there was still another sheet, but there is no positive evidence, and very few fragments from it would have remained. Of the sixty-six fragments, all but sixteen have been placed. In addition, six more very small fragments that Puech identified as being 1QH[a] fragments (though they had not been published by Sukenik) have also been incorporated.

One of the most important results of the reconstruction is that the "shape" of the 1QH[a] scroll is now clear. The Teacher Hymns (cols. 2–9 according to Sukenik, 10 –17 in the reconstructed scroll) came in the middle of the scroll, with a collection of Community Hymns at the beginning (cols.1–8) and another collection of Community Hymns at the end (cols. 18–28). The reconstruction, along with some evidence that can be incorporated from various 4Q copies, has clarified in many places where individual psalms begin and end, although there are still some places of uncertainty or where the evidence can be interpreted in different ways. There are between twenty-eight and thirty-four psalms in the collection (see appendix C and Stegemann 2003).

1QH[b]

Only two fragments remain from this manuscript (1Q35), corresponding to 1QH[a] 15:30–16:1 and 16:13–14. The second fragment has very narrow lines and only two lines of writing, followed by a section of leather that is ruled but not inscribed. It is not at all clear why the scribe did not continue writing or even whether this was ever a complete copy of the entire collection.

The 4QHodayot Manuscripts

The six copies from Cave 4 are all fragmentary and badly damaged. Five are written on leather (4QH[a–e]) and one on papyrus (4QpapH[f]). Of the approximately 125 fragments in total, about forty preserve text that overlaps with passages in 1QH[a]. In this study edition, the Cave 4 manuscripts with overlapping text have been incorporated into the 1QH[a] manuscripts and marked by underline (regular underline, dotted underline, and broken underline are used to distinguish when there are different manuscripts overlapping in the same column). In some places, a Cave 4 copy can supply letters and words that were missing from the 1QH[a] manuscript.

There is one psalm that is partially preserved in 4QH[a] frg. 8 i 13–ii 19 that is not found in any of the preserved columns of 1QH[a] (though it is possible that it was part of cols. 1–3 or cols. 27–28). A few other fragments of significant size in the 4Q copies have not yet been identified with any text in 1QH[a], and there are many tiny fragments with only a letter or partial letter so that it is impossible to say if they overlap or not. For all these fragments, it is necessary to consult the complete publication of the 4Q manuscripts in DJD 29.

4QH[a] is a manuscript of about sixteen fragments, written in a semi-cursive hand from possibly as early as 75 B.C.E. The order of the psalms is different from that in 1QH[a], as is clear from one of the larger fragments (8), where the transition between three psalms is preserved. All of the psalms belong to the category of the Hymns of the Community and contain a large number of liturgical elements (the use of the plural, series of blessings, the calendar of the times); this may indicate something about the distinctive nature of this collection.

4QH[b] is the earliest copy of the Hodayot, written in the first quarter of the first century B.C.E., circa 100–75 B.C.E. Some seventy-five fragments are preserved, though many are very tiny and cannot be identified. In the sections where transitions are preserved and in the latter part of the scroll where the shapes of the fragments give us some indication of how they were originally ordered, it seems as if this copy was identical with 1QH[a] in the content and order of the psalms. Very little is preserved from the first part of the scroll, but it seems to have corresponded with

1QH[a] (alternatively, Harkins 2010 proposes that this copy did not contain the first collection of Community Hymns corresponding to 1QH[a] cols. 1–8).

4QH[c] is a very small manuscript with narrow columns and only twelve lines per column; perhaps it was a copy for personal use. It could not have contained all the material found in 1QH[a], since that would have required a scroll of some fourteen or fifteen meters (and with its small height, such a scroll would have been impossible to roll). Four fragments remain from this scroll, and the sections that are preserved all overlap with columns 13–14 of 1QH[a]. It is probable that this scroll contained only the Teacher Hymns.

4QH[d] is a single fragment that overlaps with 1QH[a] 12:15–19. It is impossible to say if this one fragment is all that survived from a complete Hodayot copy or whether this was originally a smaller collection.

4QH[e] is preserved by two fragments, though the first fragment has sometimes been published separately as a distinct manuscript, 4Q471b. Both fragments overlap with the so-called "Self-Glorification Hymn" that is preserved most extensively in 4QH[a] fragment 7, along with a few very small fragments from 1QH[a] (from col. 26) and from 4QH[b]. In this scroll, the Self-Glorification Hymn seems to come at the beginning, as indicated by the wide margin on the right of fragment 1.

4QpapH[f] is a badly damaged papyrus scroll of which twenty-nine pieces survive. The identifiable fragments overlap with 1QH[a] 9:13–16:10. It can be established on material grounds that the scroll began with the psalm of 1QH[a] column 9, the so-called "Creation Hymn," and continued with the Teacher Hymns.

In addition to filling in some of the lacunae in 1QH[a], the 4Q copies are important as we seek to understand how the collection(s) were put together. 4QH[a] and 4QH[e] clearly have a different order of psalms than that of 1QH[a]. 4QH[c] and 4QpapH[f] seem to indicate that the Teacher Hymns or the Teacher Hymns plus the Creation Hymn functioned as blocs of material that circulated independently. However, much more study is required before all the evidence (including orthographic variations between copies and within 1QH[a] in particular) can be compiled and analyzed and a comprehensive hypothesis of compositional development can be proposed.

Appendix A: Converting Columns/Fragments and Line Numbers from the Sukenik System to the Reconstructed Scroll

Citations of the Hodayot in books and articles written in past decades used the column/fragment number and line number from Sukenik's edition (1954/1955). These can be converted to the column number and the line number of the reconstructed scroll according to the chart below.

Sukenik's Edition	DJD 40 / Study Edition
col. 1:1–39	col. 9:3–41
col. 2:1–39	col. 10:3–41
col. 3:1–39	col. 11:2–40
col. 4:1–40	col. 12:2–41
col. 5:1–39	col. 13:3–41
col. 6:1–36	col. 14:4–39
col. 7:1–36	col. 15:4–41
col. 8:1–40	col. 16:2–41
col. 9:1–36	col. 17:1–36
col. 9:37–40	col. 17:38–41
col. 10:1–39	col. 18:3–41
col. 11:1–38	col. 19:4–42
col. 12:1–36	col. 20:4–39
col. 13:1–21	col. 5:18–38
col. 14:1–28	col. 6:12–41
col. 15:1–26	col. 7:14–39
col. 16:1–20	col. 8:18–38

col. 17:1–28	col. 4:12–41
col. 18: 1–16	col. 23:2–17
col. 18:16–33	col. 21:2–19
col. 19:1–7	col. 24:9–15
col. 19:8, 9, 10–12	col. 22:7, 11, 13–15

Fragments in the Hand of the First Scribe

Sukenik's Edition	DJD 40 / Study Edition
frg. 10	col. 7:11–21
frg. 11	col. 3:23–33
frg. 12	col. 8:12–20
frg. 13	col. 8:8–16
frg. 14	col. 4:13–22
frg. 15a	col. 5:12–17
frg. 15b i	col. 5:12–20
frg. 15b ii	col. 6:17–21
frg. 16	col. 2:24–32
frg. 17	col. 5:15–21
frg. 18	col. 6:12–18
frg. 19	col. 6:39–41
frg. 20	col. 5:23–28
frg. 21	col. 3:15–19
frg. 22	col. 6:16–22
frg. 23	col. 2:12–16
frg. 24	col. 9:2–6
frg. 25	col. 11:40–41
frg. 26	col. 14:40–41
frg. 27	unplaced, renamed frg. A8
frg. 28	unplaced, renamed frg. A3
frg. 29	col. 13:31–33
frg. 30	col. 18:16–19
frg. 31	col. 5:13–15
frg. 32	col. 7:40–41
frg. 33	col. 5:38–40
frg. 34	col. 7:16–19
frg. 35	unplaced, renamed frg. A4
frg. 36	unplaced, renamed frg. A7
frg. 37	unplaced, renamed frg. A5
frg. 38	unplaced, renamed frg. A6
frg. 39	unplaced, renamed frg. A1
frg. 40	unplaced, renamed frg. A2
frg. 42	col. 7:12–16
frg. 43	col. 12:18
frg. 44	col. 6:20–24

Fragments in the Hand of the Second Scribe

frg. 1	col. 22:3–17
frg. 2 i	col. 23:21–38
frg. 2 ii	col. 24:27–39
frg. 3	col. 21:21–38
frg. 4	col. 22:20–39
frg. 5	col. 25:3–17
frg. 6	col. 24:24–37
frg. 7 i	col. 25:29–37
frg. 7 ii	col. 26:26–38
frg. 8	col. 25:25–36
frg. 9	col. 24:4–17
frg. 41	unplaced, renamed frg. C8
frg. 45	col. 24:21–28
frg. 46 i	col. 25:8–14
frg. 46 ii	col. 26:10–14
frg. 47	col. 22:24–28
frg. 48	col. 28:11–15
frg. 49	unplaced, renamed frg. C1
frg. 50	col. 24:5–10
frg. 51	col. 25:11–16
frg. 52	col. 22:17–19
frg. 53	unplaced, renamed frg. C2
frg. 54	col. 20:4–7
frg. 55 i	col. 25:15
frg. 55 ii	col. 26:15–17
frg. 56 i	col. 25:7
frg. 56 ii	col. 26:6–10
frg. 57 i	col. 23:6
frg. 57 ii	col. 24:5–9
frg. 58	unplaced, renamed frg. C3
frg. 59	unplaced, renamed frg. C4
frg. 60	col. 20:40–42
frg. 61	col. 27:12–14
frg. 62	col. 27:12–14
frg. 63	col. 25:25–27
frg. 64	unplaced, renamed frg. C7
frg. 65	unplaced, renamed frg. C6
frg. 66	unplaced, renamed frg. C5

"Interim Editions"

Citations of the Hodayot in books and articles written from the 1990s on are sometimes complicated and confusing. Often the column numbering of the reconstructed scroll is used but the line numbers of Sukenik's edition. This system is found in such "interim editions" of 1QH^a as *DSSSE* (García Martínez and Tigchelaar 1997); *DSSR* (Parry and Tov 2005); *The Complete Dead Sea Scrolls in English* (Vermes 1997); *The Dead Sea Scrolls, A New Translation* (Wise, Abegg, and Cook 1996); *Die Texte vom Toten Meer* (Maier 1995).

For the most part, these line numbers differ by one, two, or three lines from that in the reconstructed scroll. However, in columns 4–8 there is a larger disparity between the Sukenik line numbers and those of the Stegemann reconstruction. The chart below outlines how to make the conversion in these columns.

Interim Editions	DJD 40 / Study Edition
col. 4:1–28	col. 4:12–41
col. 5:1–29	col. 5:12–40
col. 6:1–30	col. 6:12–41
col. 7:1–31	col. 7:11–41
col. 8:1–28	col. 8:8–38

Appendix B: Converting from the Reconstructed Scroll to Sukenik's Columns and Fragments

This chart gives an overview of the reconstructed scroll and where Sukenik's columns and fragments have been placed. For more details and the rationale for the reconstruction, see the full discussion in DJD 40, especially 13–53.

DJD 40 / Study Edition		Sukenik's Edition
col. 2	12–16 (left)	frg. 23 1–5
	24–32 (left)	frg. 16 1–9
col. 3	15–19 (center)	frg. 21 1–5
	23–33 (center)	frg. 11 1–11
col. 4	12–41	col. 17:1–28
	13–22 (left)	frg. 14 1–10
col. 5	18–38	col. 13:1–21
	12–17 (right)	frg. 15a 1–6
	12–20 (left)	frg. 15b i 1–9
	13–15 (center)	frg. 31 1–3
	15–21 (center)	frg. 17 1–7
	21–22 (center)	frg. on SHR 4277
	23–28 (left)	frg. 20 1–6
	38–40 (center)	frg. 33 1–3
col. 6	12–41	col. 14:1–28
	12–18 (right)	frg. 18 1–7
	16–22 (right)	frg. 22 1–7
	17–21 (right)	frg. 15b ii 1–5
	20–24 (right)	frg. 44 1–5
	20–22 (right)	frg. on SHR 4284
	39–41 (right)	frg. 19 1–3

col. 7	14–39	col. 15:1–26
	11–21 (center)	frg. 10 1–11
	12–16 (left)	frg. 42 1–5
	16–19 (left)	frg. 34 1–4
	36–39 (center)	frg. on SHR 4276
	40–41 (right)	frg. 32 1–2
col. 8	18–38	col. 16:1–20
	8–16 (left)	frg. 13 1–9
	12–20 (right)	frg. 12 1–9
col. 9	3–41	col. 1:1–39
	2–6	frg. 24 1–5
col. 10	3–41	col. 2:1–39
col. 11	2–40	col. 3:1–39
	40–41 (center)	frg. 25 1–2
col. 12	2 –41	col. 4:1–40
	18 (center)	frg. 43 1
col. 13	3–41	col. 5:1–39
	31–33 (left)	frg. 29 1–3
col. 14	4–39	col. 6:1–36
	40–41 (right)	frg. 26 1–2
col. 15	4–41	col. 7:1–36
col. 16	2–41	col. 8:1–40
col. 17	1–41	col. 9:1–40
col. 18	3–41	col. 10:1–39
	16–19 (left)	frg. 30 1–4
col. 19	4–42	col. 11:1–38
	42	frg. 60 3
col. 20	4–39	col. 12:1–36
	4–7 (right)	frg. 54 1–4
	40–42 (right)	frg. 60 1–3
col. 21	2–19 (left)	col. 18:16–33
	21–38 (right)	frg. 3 1–18
col. 22	3–17 (left)	frg. 1 1–15
	7, 11, 13–15	col. 19:8, 9, 10–12
	17–19 (left)	frg. 52 1–3
	20–39 (left)	frg. 4 1–20
	24–28 (right)	frg. 47 1–5
col. 23	2–17 (right)	col. 18:1–16
	6 (left)	frg. 57 i 1
	21–38 (left)	frg. 2 i 1–18
col. 24	4–17 (left)	frg. 9 1–14
	5–10 (left)	frg. 50 1–6
	5–9 (right)	frg. 57 ii 1–5
	9–15 (right)	col. 19:1–7
	21–28 (center)	frg. 45 1–8
	24–37 (left)	frg. 6 1–14
	26–39 (right)	frg. 2 ii 1–14

col. 25	3–17 (right)	frg. 5 1–15
	7 (left)	frg. 56 i 1
	8–14 (left)	frg. 46 i 1–8
	11–16 (left)	frg. 51 1–6
	15 (left)	frg. 55 i 1
	25–27 (left)	frg. 63 1–3
	25–36 (right)	frg. 8 1–12
	29–37 (left)	frg. 7 i 1–9
col. 26	6–10 (right)	frg. 56 ii 1–5
	10–14 (right)	frg. 46 ii 1–5
	15–17 (right)	frg. 55 ii 1–3
	26–38 (right)	frg. 7 ii 1–13
col. 27	12–14 (right)	frg. 61 + 62
col. 28	11–15 (center)	frg. 48 1–5

Appendix C: Dividing 1QH[a] into Individual Psalms

In some places the beginnings and ends of individual psalms are clear and undisputed, but in a number of places it is not obvious where one psalm ends and another begins, and different divisions can and have been proposed.

Sometimes a psalm division is indicated by spacing: either an extended *vacat* space at the end of a line or an indentation at the beginning of a line. In other cases an opening formula is fully or partially preserved. The formula אודכה ("I give you thanks") always indicates the beginning of a psalm; sometimes (but not always) the ברוך אתה "Blessed are you" formula begins a new psalm. In some places there are headings similar to those found in the biblical Psalter, with the rubric למשכיל "For the *Maskil*" (in 5:12, 7:21, 20:7, 25:34; probably to be reconstructed in 1:1). In one place, 1QH[a] 20:6, a scribal mark in the margin seems to indicate a new section.

The following chart gives a list of the individual psalms, according to readings and reconstructions proposed in DJD 40. There are a limited number of places where different divisions have been proposed, most often depending whether the "blessed are you" formula is taken as beginning a new psalm or just a subsection of a psalm. Some of these possibilities are noted in the chart.

For fuller discussion, see the section "Divisions of the Psalms" for each column in DJD 40. The divisions are those proposed by Hartmut Stegemann in his 2003 article "The Number of Psalms in *1QHodayot[a]* and Some of Their Sections."

Cols. 1–3	There is insufficient material preserved to divide into psalms—or even to determine the number of psalms in these columns.
4:? –4:40	Sometimes col. 4 is divided into two or three psalms, e.g., 4:?–20, 4:21–27, 4:28–40
5:1–11	
5:12–6:33	or 5:12–6:18; 6:19–33
6:34–7:11	
7:12–20	
7:21–8:41	
9:1–10:4	
10:5–21	
10:22–32	
10:33–11:5	
11:6–19	
11:20–37	

11:38–12:5	
12:6–13:6	
13:7–21	
13:22–15:8	
15:9–28	
15:29–36	
15:37–16:4	
16:5–17:36	
17:38–19:5	or 17:38–18:14; 18:16–19:5
19:6–20:6	or 19:6–17; 19:18–30; 19:30–20:6
20:7–22:42	or 20:7–22:34
23:1–25:33	or 22:34–25:33
25:34–27:3?	
27–28	There is too little material preserved to determine the number of psalms or how to divide.

Bibliography

This is a very selective bibliography, mainly covering works referred to in the introduction, as well as commentaries on the Hodayot and works that may be of particular help to students. Fuller bibliographical resources can be found in:

Schuller, Eileen M., and Lorenzo DiTommaso. "A Bibliography of the Hodayot, 1948–1996." *Dead Sea Discoveries* 4 (1997): 55–101.

Schuller, Eileen M. "Recent Scholarship on the *Hodayot* 1993–2010." *Currents in Biblical Research* 10 (2011): 119–62.

Editions

García Martínez, Florentino, and Eibert J. C. Tigchelaar, eds. *The Dead Sea Scrolls Study Edition.* Leiden: Brill, 1997.

Maier, Johann. *Die Qumran-Essener: Die Texte vom Toten Meer, Band 1.* Munich: Reinhardt, 1995.

Milik, Józef T. "Recueil de cantiques d'action de grâces (1QH)." Pages 136–38 in *Qumran Cave I.* Edited by D. Barthélemy and Józef T. Milik. Discoveries in the Judaean Desert 1. Oxford: Clarendon, 1955.

Parry, Donald W., and Emanuel Tov, eds. *Poetic and Liturgical Texts.* Vol. 5 of *The Dead Sea Scrolls Reader.* Leiden: Brill, 2005.

Qimron, Elisha. *The Dead Sea Scrolls: The Hebrew Writings, Volume One* [Hebrew]. Between Bible and Mishnah. Jerusalem: Yad Ben-Zvi Press, 2010.

Schuller, Eileen M. "4Q427–432." Pages 69–323 in *Qumran Cave 4.XX: Poetical and Liturgical Texts, Part 2.* Edited by Esther G. Chazon et al. Discoveries in the Judaean Desert 29. Oxford: Clarendon, 1999.

Stegemann, Hartmut, and Eileen M. Schuller. *1QHodayot[a], with Incorporation of 1QHodayot[b] and 4QHodayot[a–f].* Discoveries in the Judaean Desert 40. Oxford: Clarendon, 2009.

Sukenik, Eleazar L. *The Dead Sea Scrolls of the Hebrew University.* Jerusalem: Magnes, 1955.

———. *Otzar ha-Megillot ha-Genuzot* [Hebrew]. Jerusalem: Bialik, 1954.

Vermes, Geza. *The Complete Dead Sea Scrolls in English.* New York: Penguin, 1997.

Wise, Michael O., Martin Abegg Jr., and Edward M. Cook. *The Dead Sea Scrolls: A New Translation.* New York: HarperSanFrancisco, 1996 and 2005.

Books and Articles

Chazon, Esther G. "Liturgical Function in the Cave 1 Hodayot Collection." Pages 135–49 in *Qumran Cave 1 Revisited, Texts from Cave 1 Sixty Years after Their Discovery: Proceedings of the Sixth Meeting of the IOQS in Ljubljana*. Edited by Daniel K. Falk, Sarianna Metso, Donald W. Parry, and Eibert J. C. Tigchelaar. Studies on the Texts of the Desert of Judah 91. Leiden: Brill, 2010.

Harkins, Angela Kim. "A New Proposal for Thinking about 1QH^{A} Sixty Years after Its Discovery." Pages 101–34 in *Qumran Cave 1 Revisited, Texts from Cave 1 Sixty Years after Their Discovery: Proceedings of the Sixth Meeting of the IOQS in Ljubljana*. Edited by Daniel K. Falk, Sarianna Metso, Donald W. Parry, and Eibert J. C. Tigchelaar. Studies on the Texts of the Desert of Judah 91. Leiden: Brill, 2010.

Holm-Nielsen, Svend. *Hodayot: Psalms from Qumran*. Acta Theologica Danica 2. Aarhus: Universitetsforlaget, 1960.

Jeremias, Gert. *Der Lehrer der Gerechtigkeit*. Studien zur Umwelt des Neuen Testaments 2. Göttingen: Vandenhoeck & Ruprecht, 1963.

Kuhn, Heinz-Wolfgang. *Enderwartung und Gegenwärtiges Heil: Untersuchungen zu den Gemeindeliedern von Qumran*. Studien zur Umwelt des Neuen Testaments 4. Göttingen: Vandenhoeck and Ruprecht, 1966.

Licht, Jacob. *The Thanksgiving Scroll: A Scroll from the Wilderness of Judaea* [Hebrew]. Jerusalem: Bialik, 1957.

Morawe, Günter. *Aufbau und Abgrenzung der Loblieder von Qumrân: Studien zur gattungsgeschichtlichen Einordnung der Hodajôth*. Theologische Arbeiten 16. Berlin: Evangelische Verlagsanstalt, 1961.

Newsom, Carol A. *The Self as Symbolic Space: Constructing Identity and Community at Qumran*. Studies on the Texts of the Desert of Judah 52. Leiden: Brill, 2004. Repr., Atlanta: Society of Biblical Literature, 2007.

Puech, Émile. *La croyance des Esséniens en la vie future: Immortalité, résurrection, vie éternelle? Histoire d'une croyance dans le judaïsme ancien*. 2 vols. Paris: Gabalda, 1993.

———. "Hodayot." Pages 365–69 in vol. 1 of *Encyclopedia of the Dead Sea Scrolls*. Edited by Lawrence H. Schiffman and James C. VanderKam. 2 vols. New York: Oxford University Press, 2000.

———. "Quelques aspects de la restauration du Rouleau des Hymnes (1QH)." *Journal of Jewish Studies* 39 (1988): 38–55.

Stegemann, Hartmut. "The Material Reconstruction of 1QHodayot." Pages 272–84 in *The Dead Sea Scrolls: Fifty Years after Their Discovery. Proceedings of the Jerusalem Congress, July 20–25, 1997*. Edited by Lawrence H. Schiffman, Emanuel Tov, and James C. VanderKam. Jerusalem: Israel Exploration Society in cooperation with the Shrine of the Book, Israel Museum, 2000.

———. "The Number of Psalms in *1QHodayot^{a}* and Some of Their Sections." Pages 191–234 in *Liturgical Perspectives: Prayer and Poetry in Light of the Dead Sea Scrolls, Proceedings of the Fifth International Symposium of the Orion Center for the Study of the Dead Sea Scrolls and Associated Literature, 19–23 January, 2000*. Edited by Esther G. Chazon, with the collaboration of Ruth Clements and Avital Pinnick. Studies on the Texts of the Desert of Judah 48. Leiden: Brill, 2003.

Hebrew Text and English Translation

Columns I–III

The reconstruction of columns I–III is much more uncertain than that of columns IV–XXVI. No fragments can be placed with any certainty in column I, though it is possible that some of the small unplaced fragments from Scribe A may originate from this column.

Column II

12 נפל]ו֯א֯תיכ֯[ה אי]ן֯ פ֯ה֯
13 ו]ת֯ו֯צ֯א֯ ל֯עולמי
14 ישמי]ע֯ו֯ בהמון רנה
15 אר]ננה °°[ ]ל֯[ ]
16]°°[ ]
[17–23]
24]°[ ]
25]מ֯רות[ ]°[ ]
26 ע]שוקים ו֯מ֯י֯
27]ר֯חמיו על אביונ֯י֯
28]ה֯ ומי מתכן
29] ומי מתכן גבורה֯
30 ע]ד֯ עו֯לם מי חושב֯
31] ער֯ומים ו֯מ֯י֯
32 גב]ו֯רתכה °°[ ]°[ ]

Column III

15]ם֯ °°°[
16]°כ֯ה֯ ות֯ע֯ז֯ו֯ר נדיב֯[י
17 כ]י֯ אתה מ֯נחם אבל [
18] נגע ובברכות °°[
19]כ֯ה א֯ל֯י֯ °°°°ל°°[
[20–22]
23]° מ֯ע֯פ֯ר֯ °°[
24]ע֯מדה לכול שני עו֯ל֯ם֯[
25]כ֯ל֯בד כול חיתם °°°°°ש֯ם֯ ו֯מ֯°[
26]ם כ֯ר֯וחם °°ו איש לפי שכלו ו°°[
27]°פ֯ל מלכותו מי עשה כול אלה °[
28]°°ת֯ם֯ א֯לך ת֯מ֯י֯ד֯ ובצדק תשימני ל°[
29] לפניך °°°ם֯ תהו ויצר חמ֯[ר
30]ל֯ה֯ ואת֯ה נכב֯ד֯ת֯ה֯ מכול אל֯[ים

Columns I–III

Column II

12. [… yo]ur [won]ders [there is n]o speech
13. [… and] you brought forth for ages of
14. […] they [announ]ce with a tumultuous cry
15. [… I will re]joice °°[…]*l*[…]
16. […]°°[…]

[17–23]

24. […]°[…]
25. […]*mrwt*[…]°[…]
26. [… o]ppressed, and who
27. […] his compassion for the poor ones of
28. […]*h*, and who measures
29. […] and who measures the might
30. [… f]or ever. Who calculates
31. […] prudent ones. And who
32. […] your [mi]ght °°[…]°[…]

Column III

15. […]*m* °°°[…]
16. […]° your […] and you help those who are willi[ng…]
17. [… f]or you comfort the mourner […]
18. […] a blow, and with blessings °°[…]
19. […] your[…], O my God, °°°°*l*°° […]

[20–22]

23. […]° from the dust °°[…]
24. […] it stands for all the years of eternity […]
25. […] according to your heart all their desire °°°°*šm* and *m*°[…]
26. […]*m* according to their spirit °°*w* a man according to his insight and °°[…]
27. […]°*pl* his kingdom. Who has done all these things? °[…]
28. […]°°*tm* I will walk continually, and in righteousness you set me *l*°[…]
29. […] before you °°°*m* formlessness and a vessel of cla[y…]
30. […]*lh* and you are honored more than all the god[s…]

31] קו֯דשך֯ וכאשר ב°°°° °[

32 ולהל]ל֯ שמך֯ תבי֯א֯[ני]בעדת קד֯[ושים

33]ל֯[ ]°[

Column IV

Parallel: 4QH^{b} 1 1–3 (underline; lines 39–40)

1 [ ]

2 [ ]

3 [ ]

4 [ ]

5 [ ]

6 [ ]

7 [ ]

8 [ ]

9 [ ]

10 [ ]

11 [ ]

12 [ ]°[ ]°°° °°°[ ]

13 [ ]° ו֯משפלת מדה מ°°[ ]°°°[ ]

14 [ ]מ֯גולה בלוא מש֯פט֯ מרוח

15 [ ]°בים אוכלת בשר֯ ש֯נא֯יה בלוא

16 [מרוח]ת֯ ביבישה ומכש[לת ב]ל֯וא משפט֯

17 [מרוח] פוגעות פתע פתאו[ם בל]ו֯א֯ ב֯ר֯ית֯

18 [מרוח בלו]א֯ משפט מרוח דורש֯ת֯[ ]°ו֯ת °ש°°°°

19 [ ]מ֯תרמה ב°[ב]ל֯[וא] מצוה מרוח כו[ ] מ°°°

20 [ ]ע֯ בנגיעי ב[שר] *vacat*

21 [ברוך אתה אל הדעות]מ֯נסתרות אש֯[ר]°°שר לא השיגום ב֯מצ֯[רף]°°ף

22 [ ] וממשפט קצי֯[מח]ש֯בות רשעה פ֯ע֯מ֯י֯ם֯ [רבות]°°°

23 [ע]ו֯ון וממשפט אח°°°°°[ ]° עבדך מכול פשעיו ב֯[המון]ר֯חמיך

24 [כאשר ד]ברתה ביד מושה ע֯ב֯ד֯[ך לשא]ת֯ ע֯ו֯ו֯ן֯ וחטאה ולכפר בעד֯[פש]ע֯ ומעל

25 [ ]מוסדי הרים ואש [ב]ק֯ע֯ה בשאול תחתיה ואת הנו[ ] במשפטיך

26 [ ]ת֯ה לע֯בדיך באמונה [ל]ה֯יות זרעם לפניך כול הימים ושמ֯[ותיהם] ה֯קימותה

27 [ ]פ֯שע ולהשליך כול עו֯ו֯נ֯ות֯ם ולהנחילם בכול כבוד אדם ל֯רוב ימים

28 [ ] *vacat*

29 [ברוך אתה אל הרחמי]ם֯ מרוחות אשר נתתה בי וא֯[מ]צ֯אה מענה לשון לספר צדקות֯יך וארוך אפים

30 [ ]ך֯ ומעשי ימין עוזך ו֯לה֯ו֯דות על פשעי ראשונים ולה[תנפ]ל ולהתחנן על

31. […] your holiness and just as *b*°°°° °[…]
32. [… and to prai]se your name you bring [me] into the congregation of the ho[ly ones…]
33. […]*l*[…]°[…]

Column IV

1. […]
2. […]
3. […]
4. […]
5. […]
6. […]
7. […]
8. […]
9. […]
10. […]
11. […]
12. […]°[…]°°° °°°[…]
13. […]° and bringing low by measure *m*°°[…]°°°[…]
14. […] removed unjustly by means of a spirit
15. […]°*bym* consuming the flesh of its enemies without
16. [… by means of a spirit …]*t* upon dry land and causing to stum[ble un]justly
17. [by means of a spirit …] striking quite sudden[ly, with]out agreement
18. [by means of a spirit … un]justly by means of a spirit that seeks[…]°*wt* °*š*°°°°
19. […] acting deceitfully with °[… u]nlawfully by means of a spirit of *kw*[…] *m*°°°
20. […]ʻ with afflictions of the fl[esh …] *vacat*
21. [Blessed are you, O God of knowledge]on account of the hidden things th[at …]°°*šr* did not overtake them in the cru[cible …]°°*p*
22. […] and because of the judgment of the times of[…] wicked [pl]ans [many] times°°°
23. [… ini]quity and because of the judgment of *ʼḥ*°°°°°[…]° your servant from all his transgressions through the [abundance of] your compassion
24. [… just as] you [sa]id through Moses [your] servant [to remo]ve iniquity and sin and to atone for [transgress]-ion and unfaithfulness
25. […] foundations of the mountains and fire [bu]rsts forth in the depths of Sheol and *hnw*[…] by your judgments
26. […]*th* for those who serve you loyally [so that] their posterity [may] be before you for all time. And [their] na[mes] you have raised up
27. […] transgression and casting out all their iniquities and giving them an inheritance in all the glory of Adam for long life.
28. […] *vacat*
29. [Blessed are you, O God of compassi]on on account of the spirits that you have placed in me. I will [f]ind a ready response, reciting your righteous acts and (your) patience
30. […]*k* and the deeds of your strong right hand, and confessing the transgressions of (my) previous (deeds), and p[rostr]ating myself, and begging for mercy concerning

31]]°° מעשי ונעוית לב֯ב֯י֯ כי בנדה התגוללתי ומסוד ר֯מ֯[ה י]צ֯א֯תי ולא נ֯לוי֯תי

32]]°°° כי לך אתה הצדקה ולשמך הברכה לעול[ם]כ֯צ֯ד֯קתך ופדה

33]]תמו רשעים ואני הו֯בינותי כי את אשר בחר֯ת֯ה֯ ה֯[כינותה] דרכו ובשכל

34] ת]ח֯שכהו מחטוא לך ול°°ב לו ענותו ביסוריך ובנס[וייך חזק]ת֯ה לבו

35]] עבדך מחטוא לך ומכשול ב֯כ֯ול דברי רצונך חזק מת֯נ֯[יו לעמו]ד על רוחות

36] ולה]ת֯הלך בכול אשר אהבתה ולמאוס ב֯כ֯ול אשר שנאת֯ה֯[ולעשות] ה֯ט֯וב בעיניך

37] ממ]ש֯לתם בתכמו כי רוח בש֯ר֯ ע֯בדך] [*vacat*] [*vacat*

38 [ברוך אתה אל עליון אשר]ה֯ניפותה֯ רוח קודשך֯ על עבדך֯[ות]ט֯הר מ°[ ]ת° לבו

39] א]נ֯ו֯ש ואל כול בר֯ית <u>אד</u>ם אביט [ ]°°°[ ]ה ימצאוה

40] <u>ו]ב</u> משיגיה ואוה֯ב֯יה °°°°°[<u>°יד]ל֯ע֯ולמי</u> עד

41] [*vacat*] [*vacat*

Column V

Parallel: 4QH^{b} 2 1–2 (underline; lines 19–20)

1] [

2] [

3] [

4] [

5] [

6] [

7] [

8] [

9] [

10] [

11] [

12 [מזמור למ]ש֯כ֯י֯ל֯ ל֯התנפל֯ ל֯פ֯נ֯[י אל]מ֯ע֯ש֯י֯ א֯ל֯

13]]ו֯להבין פ֯'תאים [ ]°°[ ]°°[ ]°י עולם

14]]°ת ולהבין אנוש ב֯[ ] בשר וסוד ר֯וחי [ ]° התהלכו

15 [ברוך] אתה אדוני °°[ ]°°ר רוח ב֯שר ב֯ב֯°[ ]ב֯כ֯ו֯ח֯ גבורתך

16 [והמון ח]ס֯ד֯ך עם רוב טובך֯[וכוס]ח֯מ֯ת֯ך וקנאת משפ֯[טיך לאין]ח֯קר כול

17]]°ת כול בינה ו֯מ֯[וסר] ורזי מחשבת וראש֯י֯ת֯[ה]כ֯ינותה

18]]°° קודש מקדם עו֯[לם ו]לעולמי עד אתה הוא֯ל֯[תה]ק֯דושי֯ם֯

19]] וברזי פלאך ה֯ו֯ד֯ע֯[תני בע]ב֯ור כבודך ובעומק °°[מעי<u>ן</u>]ב֯ינתך לא

31. […]°° my deeds and the perversity of my heart, because I have wallowed in impurity. But from the council of wor[ms] I have [de]parted, and I have not joined myself to
32. […]°°° For to you yourself belongs righteousness and to your name belongs blessing for eve[r …]according to your righteousness, and ransom
33. […]*tmw* the wicked. As for me, I understand that (for) the one whom you have chosen [you determi]ne his way and through insight
34. [… you] draw him back from sinning against you. And in order to °°*b* to him his humility through your disciplines and through [your] tes[ts] you have [strengthened] his heart
35. […] your servant from sinning against you and from stumbling in all the matters of your will. Strengthen [his] loi[ns that he may sta]nd against spirits
36. [… and that he may w]alk in everything that you love and despise everything that [you] hate, [and do] what is good in your eyes.
37. […]their [domi]nion in his members; for your servant (is) a spirit of flesh. […] *vacat* […] *vacat*
38. [Blessed are you, God Most High, that]you have spread your holy spirit upon your servant[and you] have purified *m*°[…]*t*° his heart
39. [… hu]mankind, and to the whole covenant of Adam I will look […]°°°[…]*h* they will find it
40. [… *w*]*b* those who attain it and those who love it °°°°°[… °*yk*] for everlasting ages.
41. […] *vacat* […] *vacat*

Column V

1. […]
2. […]
3. […]
4. […]
5. […]
6. […]
7. […]
8. […]
9. […]
10. […]
11. […]
12. [A psalm for the In]structor, that he may prostrate himself befor[e God …]deeds of God
13. […]and that the simple may understand […]°°[…]°°[…]°*y* forever
14. […]°*t* and that humankind may understand concerning […] flesh and the council of the spirits of […]° they walk.
15. [… Blessed are] you, O Lord, °°[…]°°*r* a spirit of flesh *bb*°[…]through your mighty strength
16. [and the abundance of]your [kind]ness together with your great goodness[and the cup of]your wrath and [your] zealous judgeme[nts … unsea]rchable. All
17. […]°*t* all insight and in[struction] and the mysteries of the plan and the beginning[…]you [es]tablished
18. […]°° holiness from a[ges] of old [and] to everlasting ages you yourself resolved […]holy ones
19. […] and in your wonderful mysteries [you] have instructed [me for the s]ake of your glory, and in the depth °°[… source of] your insight not

20 [ ]אתה גליתה דרכיׄ אׄמׄתׄ וׄמעשי רע חוכמה ואולתׄ[ ] צׄדׄקׄ

21 [ ] מעשיהם אמת [ ]°[ ]הׄ ואולת כולׄ התהלכ[ו]

22 [ ]םׄ וחסדי עולם לכׄוׄלׄ קׄצׄ[י]הׄםׄ לשלום ושחת כׄוׄלׄ °[ ]

23 [מש]פׄטיהם כבוד עולם וׄחׄמׄדׄהׄ וׄשׄמחת עד למעשה[ ]°שים לׄ°[ ]

24 [ ]ע *vacat* ואלה אשר הכׄ[ינותה מקדם]עׄוׄלׄםׄ לשפוט בם

25 אׄת כול מעשיך בטרם בראתם עם צבא רוחיך ועדת [אלים ע]םׄ רקיע קודשך וׄכׄוׄלׄ

26 צבאותיו עם הארץ וכול צׄאׄצׄאׄיׄה בימים ובתהומות [כ]כׄול מחשבותׄםׄ לכול קצי עׄוׄלׄםׄ

27 ופקודת עד כי אתה הכינותמה מקדם עולם ומעשׄה [ ]°°° בם בעבור

28 יׄספרו כבודך בכול ממשלתך כי הראיתם את אשר לא י[ ]אׄשׄר קדם ולברוא

29 חדשות להפר קימי קדם ולׄ[הק]ים נהיות עולם כי אׄתׄהׄ הׄ[כינות]מׄהׄ ואתה תהיה

30 לעולמי עד וברזי שכלכה פלגׄ[תה] כול אלה להודיע כבודךׄ [כי מה ה]יאׄ רוח בשר להבין

31 בׄכׄול אלה ולהשכיל בס°[ ] גדול ומה ילוד אשה בכולׄ [ג]דׄ[ו]לׄ[י]ךׄ הנוראים והוא

32 מבנה עפר ומגבל מים אׄ[שמה וחט]אה סודו ערות קלוׄןׄ וׄמׄ[קור הנ]דה ורוח נעוה משלה

33 בו ואם ירשע יהיהׄ[לאות עד]עׄולם ומופת דורות רחוקׄ[י]םׄ לׄבשר רק בטובך

34 יצדק איש וברׄוׄב רחׄ[מיך] בהדרך תפארנו ותמשׄיׄלׄנׄ[ו ב]רׄוב עדנים עם שלום

35 עולם ואורך ימים כי [ו]דברך לא ישוב אחור ואני עבדך ידעתי

36 ברוח אשר נתתה בי [ ]וצדק כול מעשיך ודבׄרׄךׄ לׄאׄ ישוב אחוׄרׄ וׄכׄוׄלׄ

37 קציך מועדׄ[ים] לׄ[ס]דׄורים לחפציהם ואדעהׄ [כי]לׄ[ ]

38 ורשע ש°[ ]°ק להתבונן [ ]

39 [ ]°° רוחיך ולׄ[ ]

40 [ ]°הלׄ[ ]

41 [ ]

Column VI

1 [ ]

2 [ ]

3 [ ]

4 [ ]

5 [ ]

6 [ ]

7 [ ]

8 [ ]

9 [ ]

10 [ ]

20. [...]you yourself have revealed the ways of truth and the works of evil, wisdom and folly[...] righteousness
21. [...] their works, truth [...]°[...]*h* and folly. All have walke[d ...]
22. [...]*m* and eternal mercies for all their time[s] for peace or (for) destruction. All °[...]
23. their [jud]gments, eternal glory, loveliness and everlasting joy for the work[...] *sym l*°[...]
24. [...]ʿ *vacat* And these are what [you] es[tablished from]ages [of old] to judge through them
25. all your creatures, before you created them together with the host of your spirits and the congregation of [the heavenly beings together wi]th your holy firmament and all
26. its hosts, together with the earth and all that springs from it, in the seas and in the deeps, [according to] all the plans for them for all the eternal epochs
27. and the everlasting visitation. For you yourself established them from ages of old and the work [...]°°° among them in order that
28. they might make known your glory in all your dominion, for you showed them what not *y*[...] which was of old, and creating
29. new things, destroying what was established of old, and [raising] up what will be forever. For you yourself have [established] them, and you yourself exist
30. for everlasting ages. In the mysteries of your understanding [you] apportioned all these in order to make known your glory. [But how i]s a spirit of flesh to understand
31. all these things and to discern *bs*°[...] great [...]? What is one born of woman amid all your [gre]at fearful acts? He
32. is a thing constructed of dust and kneaded with water. Sin[ful gui]lt is his foundation, obscene shame, and a so[urce of im]purity. And a perverted spirit rules
33. him. If he acts wickedly, he will become[a sign for]ever and a portent for dis[ta]nt generations of flesh. Only through your goodness
34. can a person be righteous, and by [your] abundant compas[sion ...]. By your splendor you glorify him, and you give [him] dominion [with] abundant delights together with eternal
35. peace and long life. For [... and] your word will not turn back. And I, your servant, know
36. by means of the spirit that you have placed in me [...] and all your deeds are righteousness. And your word will not turn back. And all
37. your ages are appoin[ted] *l*[... ar]ranged with respect to their affairs. I know [that ...]*l*[...]
38. and wicked *š*° [...]°*q* to understand [...]
39. [...]°° your spirits and *l*[...]
40. [...]°*hl*[...]
41. [...]

Column VI

1. [...]
2. [...]
3. [...]
4. [...]
5. [...]
6. [...]
7. [...]
8. [...]
9. [...]
10. [...]

11] [

12 [ ]תׄעוׄדׄוׄתׄםׄ[ ] בעמד והיׄהׄ °°[ ]°°°

13 וׄאׄ[תה גליתה]אׄוזננו לׄ[רזי פלא]אׄנשי אמת ובׄחׄיׄרׄיׄ צ[דק דורש]יׄ

14 שׄכׄל ומבקשי בינה ב°°[או]הׄבי רחמים וענׄוׄיׄ רׄוׄח מזוקקי

15 עׄוני וברורי מצרף °°°[מ]תׄאפקים עד לעׄתׄ מׄשׄפׄטיכה

16 וׄצׄופים לׄישועתך וׄאתהׄ[ ] וחזקתה חוקיך בׄיׄדׄםׄ לעשות

17 מׄשפׄט תבל ולנחול בכול צׄ[דקותיך ולהיות בס]וׄדׄ קודש לדורות עׄוׄלׄםׄ וכול

18 °°שי מעשיהם עם תענוׄ[ג]° אנשי חזונכה *vacat*

19 [ ] *vacat* [ברוך אתה]אׄדוני הנותן בלב עבדךׄ בׄיׄנה

20 להשׄכׄיל בכוׄל אלה ולהתׄ[בונן ב]° ולהתאפק על עׄלׄיׄלׄוׄתׄ רשע ולברך

21 בׄצׄדׄק כׄוׄל בוחרי רצונׄךׄ[לבחור בכול א]שׄר אהבתה ולתעב אׄתׄ כׄוׄלׄ אשר

22 [שנאתה] ותשכל עׄבדך[ב גור]לׄוׄת אנוש כי לפי רוחות תׄפׄיׄלם בין

23 טוב לרשע [ו]תׄכן [ ]°°תם פעולתם ואני ידעתי מבינתך

24 כי ברצונכה באׄ[י]שׄ הׄרׄבׄ[יתה נחלתו]בׄרׄוׄח קודשך וכן תגישנו לבינתׄךׄ ולפי

25 קׄורבו קנאתו על כול פועלי רשע ואׄנשי רמיה כי כול קרוביך לא יׄמרו פיך

26 וׄכׄוׄל יודעיך לא ישנו דבריך כי אתה צדיק ואמת כול בחיריך וכׄוׄל עולה

27 וׄרׄשע תשמיד לעד ונגלתה צדקתך לעיני כול מעׄשיך *vacat*

28 וׄאׄנׄי ידעתי ברוב טובך ובשבועה הקימותי על נפׄשי לבלתי חטוא לך

29 [ו]לׄבלתי עשות מכול הרע בעיניך וכן הוגשתי ביחד כול אנשי סודי לפי

30 שׄכלוׄ אגישנו וכרוב נחלתו אהבנו ולא אשא פני רׄעׄ וש[וח]דׄ ברׄ[ש]עׄהׄ לא אכיר

31 [ו]לׄ[א] אמיר בהון אמתך ובשוחד כול משפטיך כי אם לפיׄ °°[אי]ש

32 [אה]בׄנו וכרחקך אותו כן אתעבנו ולא אביא בסוד אׄ[מתך כול]שבי

33 [מב]רׄיתך *vacat* [ ] [

34 [אוד]ך אדוני כגדול כוחך ורוב נפלאותיך מעולם ועד עׄוׄלׄ[ם רב הרחמי]ם וגדול

35 [החס]דים הסולח לשבי פשע ופוקד עו{ו}ן רשעים °°°°°[ ]° בנדבת

36 [לבב]םׄ ותשנא עולה לעד ואני עבדך חנותני ברוח דעה לׄ[בחור בא]מׄת

37 [וצד]קׄ ולתעׄב כול דרך עולה וׄאהבכה נדבה ובכול לבׄ[ ]°ד

38 [ ]° וׄבׄמׄשׄפׄטׄך כי מידך היתה זאת ובלוא רׄצׄ[ונ]ךׄ לׄ[וא יעשה כ]וׄלׄ

39 [ ]°°כה ימשול בש°°[ ]שׄיׄדׄ ותטׄ°°°°°[כי אנוש ר]קׄ שב

40 [לעפר]וׄ הוא ותכן בשׄ°° את לׄ°°[ ]°°°

41 [ ]° רקיע עׄל כנפי רׄוׄח ויפׄלׄ[ ]°

11. [...]
12. [...]their testimonies[...] with your people and was °°[...]°°°
13. and yo[u yourself revealed]in our hearing [wonderful mysteries ...]persons of truth and the elect of ri[ghteousness, those who see]k
14. insight and those who search for understanding *b*°°[... those who l]ove compassion, and the humble in spirit, and those purified
15. by affliction, and those refined in the crucible °°°[... who per]severe still to the time of your judgments,
16. and watch for your salvation. And you[...] and you have strengthened your statutes in their hand that they may do
17. justice (in) the world and obtain an inheritance in all [your] ri[ghteous deeds and to exist in a cou]ncil of holiness for eternal generations. And all
18. °°*šy* their deeds together with delig[ht ...]° persons (who have received) your vision. *vacat*
19. [...] *vacat* [Blessed are you,]O Lord, who places understanding in the heart of your servant
20. so that he may have insight into all these things, and under[stand ...]° and persevere against evil deeds, and bless
21. with righteousness all who choose what pleases you, [to chose all t]hat you love, and abhor all that
22. [you hate]. And you have caused your servant to have insight [... lo]ts of humankind. For according to (their) spirits you cast (the lot) for them between
23. good and evil, [and] you have determined [...]°°*tm* their recompense. And as for me, I know from the understanding that comes from you
24. that through your goodwill toward a p[er]son you mul[tiply his portion] in your holy spirit. Thus you draw him closer to your understanding. And according to
25. his closeness, so is his zeal against all evildoers and people of deceit. For all who are near to you do not rebel against your command,
26. and all who know you do not pervert your words. For you are righteous and all your chosen ones are trustworthy. All injustice
27. and wickedness you will destroy forever, and your righteousness will be revealed in the sight of all your creatures. *vacat*
28. And as for me, I have knowledge by means of your abundant goodness and by the oath I pledged upon my life not to sin against you
29. [and] not to do anything evil in your sight. And thus I was brought into association with all the men of my counsel. According to
30. his insight I will associate with him, and according to the amount of his inheritance I will love him. But I will not regard evil, and a b[rib]e (given) in wi[cked]ness I will not acknowledge.
31. [And] I will no[t] exchange your truth for wealth nor any of your judgments for a bribe. But according as °°[... a per]son,
32. [I will l]ove him, and according as you place him far off, thus I will abhor him. *vac* And I will not bring into the council of [your] tr[uth any]who turn away
33. [from] your [co]venant. *vacat* [...]
34. [I thank] you, O Lord, in accordance with your great strength and your abundant wonders from age to ag[e, abundant in compassi]on and great in
35. [mer]cies, who forgives those who repent of transgression but visits the guilt of the wicked °°°°°[...] in the generosity of
36. their [heart.] But you hate iniquity for ever. As for me, your servant, you have favored me with the spirit of knowledge to [choose tr]uth
37. [and righteous]ness and to abhor every iniquitous way. And (so) I love you freely, and with all (my) heart[...]°*k*
38. [...]° and in your judgment, for from your hand this comes and without your wi[ll] n[oth]ing [happens]
39. your [...]°° will rule *bš*°°[...] your [...]*š* and *ṭṭ*°°°°°[... for a human on]ly one who returns
40. [to] his [dust] is he. And you have determined *bš*°° *'t l*°°[...]°°°
41. [...]° firmament upon the wings of the wind and *ypl*[...]°

Column VII

Parallel: 4QHª 8 i 6–12 (underline; lines 14–20)

1] [
2] [
3] [
4] [
5] [
6] [
7] [
8] [
9] [
10] [
11]]סׄ[[
12 [ברוך אתה אל עליון אשר ב]מׄעׄיׄן גׄבׄוׄרׄתׄכה הׄשכלתנׄוׄ [ ]נׄוׄ [ ]
13] ועל מעשי פ]לׄאכה מה נשיב כי גמלתנו הׄמׄ[ון רחמים ל]הׄפליא
14 ות°[ ]° לא יעצרו כוח לדעת בׄכבוד[כה ולס]פׄר נפלאׄ[ותיכה]
15 °°[ ]לׄעׄ[ול]םׄ כׄיׄ יׄהׄללׄוׄכה לפׄיׄ שכלם וכפי דעתׄםׄ[בכ]בודכה כׄ[י אתה]
16 פׄתחתהׄ[ ]כׄהׄ לאין השׄ[ב]ת מׄקׄץׄ לקץ ישמיעו ומועׄדׄ[ל]מׄוׄעׄדׄ[יברכו]
17 בׄקׄוׄלׄ[ ] ואנחנו ביחד נועדׄיׄםׄ ועם ידעים נׄ[וס]רׄה^לכה ונרׄ[ננה ברוב]
18 רחמיכׄ[ה]ח עם גבוריכה ובהפלא נספרהׄ יחד בדע[ת אל]וׄעד °[ ]
19 בעדתׄ[ ]הׄ וצאצאינו הודעׄ[תה ע]םׄ בני איש בׄתׄוׄךׄ[בני]אדם [ ]
20 כי^א[ב]הׄפלא מאדה [ ] *vacat* [ ]
21 ברׄוׄ[ך אתה אל הרחמים ב]שׄיׄרׄ^מזמור למשׄ[כיל] °°°[ ]דׄ רׄנה [ ]
22] י]אׄהבו אותך כול הימים ואׄנׄיׄ °[ ]
23 אמׄ[ת] ואהבכה בנדבה ובכול לב ובכול נפש בררתי מׄעׄוׄוׄןׄ[ועל נפ]שׄיׄ
24 הקׄיׄ[מותי לבלת]יׄ סור מכול אשר צויתה ואחז'קה על רבים מוׄעׄדׄיׄםׄ לׄ[יום הרגה לבלת]יׄ
25 עזׄוב מכוׄלׄ חׄוקיך *vacat* ואני ידעתי בבינתך כיאלא ביד בשר [יוכל להתם]אדם
26 דרכו ולא יוכל אנוש להכין צעדו ואדעה כי בידך יׄצׄר כול רוח [וכול פעול]תׄו
27 הכינותה בטרם בראתו ואיכה יוכל כול להשנות את דבריכה רק אתהׄ בׄ[רא]תה
28 צדיק ומרחם הכינותו למועד רצון להשמר בבריתך ולתהלך בכול ולהגׄיׄשׄ עליו
29 בהמון רחמיך ולפתוח כול צרת נפשו לישועת עולם ושלום עד ואין מחסור ותרם
30 מבשר כבודו ורשעים בראתה ל[י]צׄרׄ חׄרׄוׄנכה ומרחם הקדשתם ליום הרגה
31 כי הלכו בדרך לא טוב וימאסו בברׄיׄתׄכׄ[ה וחוקי]ך תעבה נפשם ולא רצו בכול אשר

Column VII

1. [...]
2. [...]
3. [...]
4. [...]
5. [...]
6. [...]
7. [...]
8. [...]
9. [...]
10. [...]
11. [...]*m*[...]
12. [Blessed are you, God Most High, who by] the spring of your power gave us insight [...]*nw*[...]
13. [... and on account of]your [wo]nderful [deeds.] What shall we reply when you show us abun[dant compassion in order to] act wondrously
14. and *t*°[...]° they will not have the power to understand [your] glory [and to re]cite [your] wonder[ful deeds]
15. °°[...]for[eve]r, for they praise you according to their insight and according to their knowledge[in] your [gl]ory, f[or you]
16. have opened[...]*kh* without ces[sa]tion. From age to age they proclaim, and (from) appointed time[to] appointed time [they bless]
17. with a voice[...] And as for us, in the community of those gathered and with those who have knowledge we are inst[ruc]ted by you and we ex[ult in the abundance of]
18. yo[ur] compassion [...]*ḥ* with your warriors. And when (you) act wondrously we will recount (it) together in the know[ledge of God]and until °[...]
19. in the assembly of[...]*h* and our offspring [you] have caused to understand together with the children of men in the midst of[the children of]Adam [...]
20. for [... when] (you) act exceedingly wondrously. [...] *vacat* [...]
21. Bless[ed are you, God of compassion, with a]song, a psalm for the Ins[tructor] °°°[...]*d* glad cry [...]
22. [... th]ey love you forever. And as for me, °[...]
23. tru[th ...] and I love you freely. With all (my) heart and with all (my) soul I have purified (myself) from iniquity. [And upon] my [li]fe
24. [I] have sw[orn no]t to turn aside from all that you have commanded. I will stand firm against the many appointed for the [day of slaughter, no]t
25. abandoning any of your statutes. *vacat* And as for me, I know, by the understanding that comes from you, that it is not through the power of flesh [that] an individual [may perfect]
26. his way, nor is a person able to direct his steps. And I know that in your hand is the inclination of every spirit, [and all] its [activi]ty
27. you determined before you created it. How could anyone change your words? You alone [crea]ted
28. the righteous, and from the womb you prepared him for the time of favor, to be attentive to your covenant and to walk in all (your way,) and to advance (him) upon it
29. in your abundant compassion, and to relieve all the distress of his soul for eternal salvation and everlasting peace, without lack. And so you raise
30. his honor higher than flesh. But the wicked you created for the [pur]pose of your wrath, and from the womb you dedicated them for the day of slaughter.
31. For they walk in the way that is not good, and they despise yo[ur] covenant, [and] their soul abhors your [statutes]. They do not take pleasure in anything that

32 צויתה ויבחרו באשר שנאתה כיא לק[צי חרו]נך הכינותם לעשות בם שפטים גדולים
33 לעיני כול מעשיך ולהיות לאות ומופ[ת דורות]עולם לדעת כול את כבודך ואת כוחך
34 הגדול ומה אף הוא בשר כי ישכיל [באלה ויצ]ר עפר איך יוכל להכין צעדו *vacat*
35 אתה יצרתה רוח ופעולתה הכינות[ה מעולם] ומאתך דרך כול חי ואני ידעתי כיא
36 לא ישוה כול הון באמתך ואין בת[בל כמלאכי]קודשך ואדעה כי בם בחרתה מכול
37 ולעד הם ישרתוך ולא תקבל שוחד [למעשי רע]ולא תקח כופר לעלילות רשעה כיא
38 אמת אתה וכול עולה תשמיד ל[עד וכול]רשעה לא תהיה לפניך ואני ידעתיך
39 כי לך ד[רך]כ[ו]ל חי וברצונך ◦◦◦[כול]מעשה ואד[עה כיא]ל[ ]
40 קודשך ב◦[ ]
41 כי ב◦◦◦◦◦◦[ ]

Column VIII

1] [
2] [
3] [
4] [
5] [
6] [
7] [
8]]◦◦◦◦ם וכול ◦◦[ ]◦◦
9] אנשי מ]ופת תביא במספר
10] ואין כרזי פ]לאו בשמים ובארץ
11]]◦ות ובידך משפט כולם
12 [ ]◦ ך[ ]◦◦◦ש ◦◦[ואין]לנגדך ומה נחשב וכול
13 [איש]מתקדש בל יטה לאשמה לישר לבבו[איכה]יבין ולא יעשה כול
14 [מבלע]דיך עד עולם ומקור אור פתחתה[ ] ולעצתך תקראני
15 להלל קודשך מפי כל מעשיך כיא פעלת[ה להו]חד עם צבא
16 [ג]בורי עולם ורוח עורף קשה לדממה[ ]הואלת[ה]ל[עשות]
17 [בם מ]שפט ולהאזין קול נכבד למעש[י [
18 [ור]וח נעוה משל[ה]ביצר עפר ◦◦[ ]◦ ו◦[ ]
19 [ ]◦◦ מ◦◦◦◦◦◦◦◦◦◦ש[ ]◦◦◦[ ]◦יך מעפ[ר צ]דיק וכב◦[ ]
20 ברוח קו[ד]שך[אשר נתת]ה בי ◦◦◦◦ ◦◦[ ]◦◦ ולא יוכל א[נוש לבקש]
21 רוח קוד[ש]ך ◦◦[ ]מלוא השמים והארץ [כ]בודך מלוא כול[תבל]
22 ואדעה כי ברצונ[ך] באיש הרביתה נחלתו בצדקות[יך]◦◦ר אמתך בכול [ ]

32. you have commanded, but they choose what you hate. For you determined them for the a[ges of] your [wra]th in order to execute great judgments upon them
33. in the sight of all your creatures, and to be a sign and a por[tent for] everlasting [generations], so that all may know your glory and your great strength.
34. But what is flesh that it should have insight into [these things? And] how is [a creat]ure of dust able to direct its steps? *vacat*
35. You yourself have formed the spirit and determined its activity [from of old]. And from you (comes) the way of every living being. And as for me, I know that
36. no wealth can compare with your truth, and there are none in the w[orld like] your holy [angels]. I know that you have chosen them above all (others),
37. and they will serve you forever. You do not accept a bribe [for evil acts,]nor do you take a ransom for guilty deeds. For
38. you are a God of truth, and all iniquity you will destroy for[ever] and no wickedness will exist in your presence. And I myself know
39. that to you belongs the w[ay] of ev[er]y living being and by your will °°°[… every]deed. I kn[ow that]*l*[…]
40. your holiness *b*°[…]
41. for *b*°°°°°°[…]

Column VIII

1. […]
2. […]
3. […]
4. […]
5. […]
6. […]
7. […]
8. […]°°°°*m* and all °°[…]°°
9. [… men of po]rtent you bring in by number
10. [… and there is nothing like] his [won]drous [mysteries] in the heavens and upon the earth
11. […]°*wt* and in your hand is the judgment of them all
12. […]°*k* °[…]°°°*š̊* °°[… And there is none] to compare with you. And how shall he be regarded? And every
13. [person] who sanctifies himself will not turn to guilt, in order to make his heart right[… how] can he understand? And nothing is done
14. [apart] from you forever. A source of light you have opened[…] and for your council you have called me
15. to praise your holiness by the mouth of all your creatures, for you have don[e … to be un]ited with the host of
16. the eternal [wa]rriors. And a stubborn spirit into calmness[…] yo[u] decided to [make]
17. [ju]dgment [upon them] and to make the glorious voice heard by the creature[s of …]
18. [… and] a perverted [sp]irit has rule[d] over a vessel of dust °°[…]° and °[…]
19. […]°° *m*°°°°°°°°°°°*š̊*°[…]°°°[…]°*yk* from dus[t … ri]ghteous and *kb*°[…]
20. by means of your ho[l]y spirit [which yo]u [placed] in me °°°° °°[…]°° And hu[mankind] is not able [to search out]
21. your ho[l]y spirit °°[…]the fullness of the heavens and the earth […] your [g]lory, the fullness of all[the world].
22. And I know that by [your] goodwill toward a person you have multiplied his inheritance in [your] righteous deeds […]°°*r* your truth in all […]

23 ומשמר צדק על דברך אשר הפקדתה בו פן ישגה [ממצוותיך ול]בלתי כשול בכול מע[שיו כי]
24 בדעתי בכול אלה אמצאה מענה לשון להתנפל ולהת[חנ]ן[תמיד] על פשעי ולבקש רוח בינ[ה]
25 ולהתחזק ברוח קודשך ולדבוק באמת בריתך ולעובדך באמת ולב שלם ולאהוב את דבר פ[יך]
26 ברוך אתה אדוני גדול העצה ורב העליליה אשר מעשיך הכול הנה הואלתה לעשות בי ר[וב]
27 חסד ותחונני ברוח רחמיך ובעבור כבודך לך אתה הצדקה כי אתה עשיתה את כול אלה
28 ובדעתי כי אתה רשמתה רוח צדיק ואני בחרתי להבר כפי כרצו[נ]ך ונפש עבדך תעבה כול
29 מעשה עולה ואדעה כי לא יצדק איש מבלעדיך ואחלה פניך ברוח אשר נתתה בי להשלים
30 חסדיך עם עבדך ל[עו]לם לטהרני ברוח קודשך ולהגישני ברצונך כגדול חסדיך [א]שר עשיתה
31 עמדי ול[ה]עמ[יד פעמי ב]כול מעמד רצו[נך] אשר בח[ר]תה לאוהביך ולשומרי מצוותי[ך להתיצב]
32 לפניך לעולם ו[לכפר עוון]ולהדש[ן]ברצון ולהתערב ברוח עבדך ולשכיל מעש[י]ך ל[ ]
33 °°°°° אל י°[ ]°ו ואל יב[ו]א לפניו כול נגע מכשול מחוקי בריתך כי °°[ ]
34 פניך ואדע[ה כי אתה אל]חנון ורחום ארוך אפים ורב חסד ואמת ונושא פשע ומע[ל]
35 ונחם על כ[ול עוון אוהב]יך ושומרי מצוות[יך ה]שבים אליך באמונה ולב שלם [ ]
36 לעובדך [ב לעשות ה]טוב בעיניך אל תשב פני עבדך [וא]ל תזנח בן אמתך [ ]
37 [ ]אה ואני על דבריך קרבתי ל[ ]
38 [ ]ל[ ]°°°°[ ]
39 [ ]
40 [ ]
41 [ ]

Column IX

Parallels: 4QpapH^{f} 1 1–3 (underline; lines 13–15)
4QpapH^{f} 2 1–2 (underline; lines 36–37)

1 [ ]
2 [ ] בשובך מתוהו [ ]
3 °°[ ]די קדוש[י]ם °[ ]
4 וכול [ ]°°°°[ ]°° בין טוב לרש[ע עד]
5 עולם א°[ ]°°° °°°ים [ ]°עים ו°°°°° °°[ ]
6 בם ומש[ ]°°ם כיא[אתה אלי מקור ד]עת ומקוה המ°°°°
7 ומעין הגבור[ה]גדול העצה [ ] אין מספר וקנאתכה
8 לפני חכמתכה[ ] וארוך אפים במשפטיך צדקתה בכל מעשיכה

23. and a righteous guard over your word that you have entrusted to him lest he stray [from your commandments and so as n]ot to stumble in any of [his] dee[ds. For]
24. through my knowledge of all these things I will find the proper reply, falling prostrate and be[gging for me]rcy [continuously] on account of my transgression, and seeking a spirit of understand[ing],
25. and strengthening myself through your holy spirit, and clinging to the truth of your covenant, and serving you in truth and (with) a perfect heart, and loving the word of [your] mou[th].
26. Blessed are you, O Lord, great in counsel and mighty in deed, because all things are your works. Behold you have determined to do me gr[eat]
27. kindness, and you have been gracious to me in your compassionate spirit and for the sake of your glory. Righteousness belongs to you alone, for you have done all these things.
28. Because I know that you have recorded the spirit of the righteous, I myself have chosen to cleanse my hands according to your wil[l.] The soul of your servant abhors every
29. malicious deed. I know that no one can be righteous apart from you, and so I entreat you with the spirit that you have placed in me that you make
30. your kindness to your servant complete [for]ever, cleansing me by your holy spirit and drawing me nearer by your good favor, according to your great kindness [wh]ich you have shown
31. to me, and causing [my feet] to sta[nd in] the whole station of [your] good fa[vor], which you have cho[sen] for those who love you and for those who keep [your] commandments [that they may take their stand]
32. before you forever, and [atone for iniquity], and savo[r] what is pleasing, and mingle myself with the spirit of your work, and understand your deed[s] *l*[…]
33. °°°°° not *y*°[…]°*w* and let there not c[o]me before him any affliction (that causes) stumbling from the precepts of your covenant, for °°[…]
34. your face. And I kno[w that you are a God]gracious and compassionate, patient and abounding in kindness and faithfulness, one who forgives transgression and unfaithful[ness …],
35. moved to pity concerning a[ll the iniquity of those who love] you and keep [your] commandments, [those] who have returned to you in steadfastness and (with) a perfect heart […]
36. to serve you [in … to do what is] good in your sight. Do not turn away the face of your servant [and do no]t reject the son of your handmaid. […]
37. […]*'h* And as for me, on account of your words I have drawn close to[…]
38. […]*l*[…]°°°°[…]
39. […]
40. […]
41. […]

Column IX

1. […]
2. […] at your turning back from chaos […]
3. °°[…]*dy* holy on[e]s °[…]
4. and all […]°°°°[…]°° between good and wicked[ness for-]
5. ever ’°[…]°°° °°°*ym* […]°‘*ym* and°°°°° °°[…]
6. in them and *mš*[…]°°*m* for[you, O my God, are a source of kno]wledge and a reservoir of *hm*°°°°
7. and a spring of pow[er …]great in counsel […] innumerable, and your zeal
8. before your wisdom[…] and patient in your judgments. You are righteous in all your deeds.

9 ובחכמתכה ◦[ ]עׄולם ובטרם בראתם ידעתה כׄוׄלׄ מעשיהם
10 לעולמי עד וׄ[מבלעדיך לא] יעשה כו[ו]ל ולא יודע בלוא רׄצׄונכה אתה יצרתה
11 כול רוח ופׄעולׄתׄ[ם הכינות]הׄ ומשפט לכול מעשיהם ואתה נטיתה שמים
12 לכבודכה וׄכול ◦[ה]כׄיׄנׄותה לרצונכה ורוחות עוז לחוקיהם בטרם
13 היותם למלאכי קׄ[ודש ו]םׄ לרוחות עולם בממשלׄותׄםׄ מאורות לרזיהם
14 כוכבים לנתיבותׄיׄ[הם ורוחות סער]הׄ למשאם זקים וברקים לעבודתם ואוצרות
15 מחשבת לחפציה[ם]◦ לרזיהם אתה בראתה ארץ {ב}בכוחכה
16 ימים ותהומות עׄשׄיׄ[תה בעוזכה ומח]שׄביהם הכינותה בחוכמתכה וכׄל אשר בם
17 תכ[נ]תׄה לרצונכׄ[ה] לׄרוח אדם אשר יצרת בתבל לכׄל ימי עולם
18 ודורות נצח למ[ ]לׄ וׄבקציהם פלגתה עבודתם בכול דוריהם ומשׄ[פ]ט
19 במועדיה לממשׄלׄ[ת וד]רׄכׄיהם הׄכׄיׄנׄותׄהׄ לדור ודור ופקודת שלומם עם
20 עם כול נגיעיהם[ ]ה ותפלגׄ לכול צאצׄאׄיׄהׄם למספר דורות עולם
21 ולכול שני נצח ◦◦◦[ ]הׄ ובחכמת דעתכה הכׄ[י]נׄותה תע[ו]דתם בטרם
22 היותם ועל פי רׄצׄ[ונ]כׄהׄ[נ]הׄיה כול ומבלעדיך לא יעשה *vacat*
23 אלה ידעתי מבינתכה כיא גליתה אוזני לרזי פלא ואני יצר החמר ומגבל המים
24 סוד הערוה ומקור הנדה כור העוון ומבנה החטאה רׄוח התועה ונעוה בלא
25 בינה ונבעתה בׄמׄשפטי צדק מה אדבר בלא נודע ואשמיעה בלא סופר הכול
26 חקוק לפניכה בחרת זכרון לכול קצי נצח ותקופות מספר שני עולם בכול מועדיהם
27 ולוא נסתרו ולא נעדרו מלפניכה ומה יספר אנוש חטאתו ומה יוכיח על עוונותיו
28 ומה ישיב עׄל על משפט הצדק לכה אתה אל הדעות כול מעשי הצדקה
29 וסוד האמת ולבני האדם עבודת העוון ומעשי הרמיה אתה בראתה
30 רוח בלשון ותדע דבריה ותכן פרי שפתים בטרם היותם ותשם דברים על קו
31 ומבע רוח שפתים במדה ותוצא קוים לרזיהם ומׄבׄעׄיׄ רׄוׄחות לחשבונם להודיע
32 כבודכה ולספר נפלאותיכה בכול מעשי אמתכה ומׄ[ש]פׄ[ט]יׄ צׄדקכה ולהלל שמכה
33 בפה כול יודעיכה לפי שכלם יברכוכה לעולמי עׄ[ולמי]םׄ ואתה ברחמיכה
34 וגדול חסדיכה חזקתה רוח אנוש לפני נגע וׄנׄפׄשׄ[אביון] טהרׄתׄהׄ מרוב עוון
35 לספר נפלאותיכה לנגד כול מעשיכה ואׄספׄרׄ[ה תמיד]בׄקׄרׄבׄםׄ משפטי נגיעי

9. And in your wisdom °[...]eternity, and before you created them, you knew {all} their deeds
10. for everlasting ages. And [without you no]thing is done, and nothing is known without your will. You formed
11. every spirit, and [their] work [you determin]ed, and the judgment for all their deeds. You yourself stretched out the heavens
12. for your glory, and all °[...] you [de]termined according to your will, and powerful spirits according to their laws, before
13. they came to be ho[ly] angels [and ...]*m* eternal spirits in their dominions: luminaries according to their mysteries,
14. stars according to [their] paths, [stor]m [winds] according to their task, shooting stars and lightning according to their service, and storehouses
15. devised for th[eir] purposes [...]° according to their mysteries. You yourself created the earth through your strength,
16. the seas and the deeps [you] made [through your might and] their [de]signs you established through your wisdom, and all that is in them
17. you set in or[der] according to your will [...] for the human spirit that you fashioned in the world for all the days of eternity
18. and everlasting generations for *m*[...]*l* And according to their seasons, you allotted their service throughout all their generations and the jud[g]ment
19. in the times appointed for it, according to the domini[on ... and] their [w]ays you determined for every generation, and a visitation for their recompense together with
20. with all their punishments[...]*h*. And you allotted it to all their offspring according to the number of the generations of eternity
21. and for all the everlasting years °°°[...]*h* And in the wisdom of your knowledge you determ[i]ned their des[t]iny before
22. they existed. According to your wi[ll] everything [comes] to pass; and without you nothing is done. *vacat*
23. These things I know because of understanding that comes from you, for you have opened my ears to wondrous mysteries. Yet I am a vessel of clay and a thing kneaded with water,
24. a foundation of shame and a well of impurity, a furnace of iniquity, and a structure of sin, a spirit of error, and a perverted being, without
25. understanding, and terrified by righteous judgments. What could I say that is not already known, or what could I declare that has not already been told? Everything
26. is engraved before you in an inscription of record for all the everlasting seasons and the numbered cycles of the eternal years with all their appointed times.
27. They are not hidden nor missing from your presence. And how should a person explain his sin, and how should he defend his iniquities?
28. And how should an unjust person reply to righteous judgment? To you, yourself, God of knowledge, belong all righteous deeds
29. and true counsel. But to mortal beings belongs iniquitous service and deceitful deeds. You yourself created
30. breath for the tongue. You know its words, and you determine the fruit of the lips before they exist. You set the words according to the measuring line,
31. and the utterance of the breath of the lips by measure. And you bring forth the lines according to their mysteries and the utterances of the breath according to their calculus, in order to make known
32. your glory and to recount your wonders in all your faithful deeds and your righteous j[ud]gm[ents], and to praise your name
33. with the mouth of all who know you. According to their insight they bless you for ev[erlasti]ng ages. And you, in your compassion
34. and your great kindness, you have strengthened the human spirit in the face of affliction and [the poor] soul you have cleansed from great iniquity
35. so that it might recount your wonders before all your creatures. And I will recit[e continually] in their midst the judgments which have afflicted me,

36 ולבני אנוש כול נפלאותיכה אשר הגברתה ב[י לנגד ב]ני אדם שמעו

37 חכמים ושחי דעת ונמהרים יהיו ליצר סמוך[כל ישרי ד]רך הוסיפו ערמה

38 צדיקים השביתו עולה וכול תמימי דרך החזיק[ו נד]כא עני האריכו

39 אפים ואל תמאסו במשפט[י צדק ו]ילי לב לא יבינו

40 אלה ו°°°°ד אמ°[ ]

41 [ער]יצים יחרוקו[ ] שנים]

Column X

Parallels: 4QpapH[f] 3 1–5 (underline; lines 5–8)
4QpapH[f] 4 1 (underline; line 19)
4QH[b] 3 1–9 (dotted underline; lines 35–41)

1 [ ]

2 [ ]

3 [ ]°°[ ]°דו [ ]

4 [ ]°°°, °°°[ ]°°°°°[ ]

5 [ ] אודכה אדוני כיא ישרתה בלב]בי כול מעשי עולה ותטה[רני]

6 [ו]תשם ש[ומרי אמת נגד עוני ומ]וכיחי אמת (צדק) בכל חמ[סי] (ט[ ]°[)

7 [ ]למחץ מכתי[מנחמי כוח]ומשמיעי שמחה לאבל יג[וני]

8 [מבשר]שלום לכול הוות שמוע[תי] חזקים למוס לבבי ומאמצי רו[ח]

9 לפני[נ]גע ותתן מענה לשון לער[ול] שפתי ותסמוך נפשי בחזוק מותנים

10 ואמוץ כוח ותעמד פעמי בגבול רשעה ואהיה פח לפושעים ומרפא לכול

11 שבי פשע ערמה לפתיים ויצר סמוך לכול נמהרי לב ותשימני חרפה

12 וקלס לבוגדים סוד אמת ובינה לישרי דרך ואהיה על עון רשעים

13 דבה בשפת עריצים לצים יחרוקו שנים ואני הייתי נגינה לפושעים

14 ועלי קהלת רשעים תתרגש ויהמו כנחשולי ימים בהרגש גליהם רפש

15 וטיט יגרושו ותשימני נס לבחירי צדק ומליץ דעת ברזי פלא לבחון

16 [אנשי] אמת ולנסות אוהבי מוסר ואהיה איש ריב למליצי תעות ובעל

17 [מד]נים לכול חוזי נכוחות ואהיה לרוח קנאה לנגד כל דורשי חל[קות]

18 [וכול]אנשי רמיה עלי יהמו כקול המון מים רבים ומזמות בליעל [כול]

19 [מ]חשבותם ויהפוכו לשוחה חיי גבר אשר הכינותה בפי ותלמד{נ}ו[1] בינה

20 שמתה בלבבו לפתוח מקור דעת לכול מבינים וימירום בערול שפה

21 ולשון אחרת לעם לא בינות להלבט במשגתם *vacat*

22 *vacat* אודכה אדוני כי שמתה נפשי בצרור החיים

23 ותשוך בעדי מכול מוקשי שחת כ[י]א עריצים בקשו נפשי בתומכי

1. The scribal correction and erasure indicates some confusion. The first *waw* is to be read with the previous word and the second *waw* with the next word

36. and to humankind all your wonders by which you have shown yourself strong through [me before hu]mankind. Hear,
37. O sages, and those who ponder knowledge. May those who are eager become firm in purpose. [All who are straight of wa]y become more discerning.
38. O righteous ones, put an end to injustice. And all you whose way is perfect, hold fast [... O you who are cru]shed by poverty, be patient.
39. Do not reject [righteous] judgment[s. ... But the ...]*yly* of mind do not understand
40. these things and °°°°*d 'm*°[...]
41. [the ruth]less grind [(their) teeth ...]

COLUMN X

1. [...]
2. [...]
3. [...]°°[...]°*dw* [...]
4. [...]°°°*y* °°°[...]°°°°°[...]
5. *vacat* [I thank you, O Lord, that you have made straight in] my [hea]rt all the deeds of iniquity, and you have purifi[ed me]
6. [... and] you placed faithful gu[ardians in the face of (my) distress], righteous [re]provers for all the violen[ce done to me.]
7. [...]for the wound of the blow inflicted on me, [strong comforters, ...] and those who announce joy for [my] sor[rowful] mourning,
8. [a messenger of]peace for all the disasters reported [to me], strong [...] for the melting of my heart, and strengtheners of spir[it]
9. in the face of [afflic]tion. You have given the proper reply to my uncircum[cised] lips, and you have supported my soul with a potent strength
10. and powerful might. You have maintained my steps in the realm of wickedness. And so I became a snare to transgressors but healing to all
11. who repent of transgression, discernment for the simple, and a resolute purpose for the hasty. You made me an object of reproach
12. and derision to the treacherous, (but) a foundation of truth and understanding to those whose way is upright. Because of the iniquity of the wicked, I have become
13. a slander on the lips of the ruthless; the scornful gnash (their) teeth. And I have become a mocking song for transgressors.
14. Against me the assembly of the wicked rages, and they roar like stormy seas when their waves crash, heaving up slime
15. and mud. But you have made me a banner for the elect of righteousness and an expert interpreter of wonderful mysteries in order to test
16. [persons of] truth and to prove those who love moral discipline. And I have become an adversary to erring interpreters, and a
17. conten[der] for all who see what is right. I have become a zealous spirit to all who seek smo[oth things,]
18. [so that all] the deceitful ones roar against me like the sound of the roaring of mighty waters. Devilish schemes are [all]
19. their [th]oughts, and they cast into the pit the life of the man in whose mouth you established instruction,
20. and in whose mind you placed understanding, in order to open the source of knowledge for all who are able to understand. But they have changed them by means of uncircumcised lips
21. and an alien tongue into a people without understanding, so that they might be ruined by their error. *vacat*
22. *vacat* I thank you, O Lord, that you have placed my soul in the bundle of the living
23. and that you have protected me from all the snares of the pit; f[o]r ruthless people have sought my life when I held fast

24 בבריתךה והמה סוד שוא ועדת בליעל לא ידעו כיא מאתכה מעמדי
25 ובחסדיכה תושיע נפשי כיא מאתכה מצעדי והמה מאתכה גרו
26 על נפשי בעבור הכבדכה במשפט רשעים והגבירכה בי נגד בני
27 אדם כיא בחסדכה עמדי ואני אמרתי חנו עלי גבורים סבבום בכל
28 כלי מלחמותם ויפרו חצים לאין מרפא ולהוב חנית כאש אוכלת עצים
29 וכהמון מים רבים שאון קולם נפץ וזרם להשחית רבים למזורות יבקעו
30 אפעה ושוא בהתרומם גליהם ואני במוס לבי כמים ותחזק נפשי בבריתך
31 והם רשת פרשו לי תלכוד רגלם ופחים טמנו לנפשי נפלו בם ורגלי עמדה במישור
32 מקהלם אברכה שמכה *vacat*
33 אודכה אדוני כיא עינכה על[י]בשכול נפשי ותצילני מקנאת מליצי כזב
34 ומעדת דורשי חלקות פדיתה נפש אביון אשר חשבו להתם דמו
35 לשפוך על עבודתכה אפס כי [לא]ידעו כי מאתך מצעדי וישימוני לבוז
36 וחרפה בפי כל דורשי רמיה ואתה אלי עזרתה נפש עני ורש
37 מיד חזק ממנו ותפד נפשי מיד אדירים ובגדפותם לא החתותני
38 לעזוב עבודתכה מפחד הוות רשעים ולהמיר {ב}בהולל יצר סמוך אשר
39 נתתה °°°°°° °°°° [ ]°° °°°מי חוקים ובתעודות [כו]ננתני להחזיק
40 [ב]שר[ ]°°°°° °°°° שחת לכול צאצאי עם
41 [לש]ון כלמודיכה ובמש[פט]

Column XI

Parallels: 4QH[b] 4 1–2 (underline; line 13)
4QpapH[f] 5 1–7 (dotted underline; lines 14–19)
4QpapH[f] 6 1–6 (dotted underline; lines 27–31)
4QH[b] 5 1–7 (underline; lines 28–32)
4QpapH[f] 7 1–2 (dotted underline; lines 40–41)

1 [ ]
2 [ ]ם בכי מ°°°[ ]
3 [ ]°ם והב°°ל°°° °°°°°°[ ]
4 [אתה]אלי האירותה פני לבריתכה °°[ ]
5 [ ]ה לכה בכבוד עולם עם כול [ ]°° °°°[ ]
6 [ ] *vacat* אודכה אדוני כיא אמ]ת פיכה ותצילני מ[סוד שוא] ומ[ ]ים
7 [הוש]עתה נפש[י כיא לחרפה וקל]ס יחשבוני וישימו נפש[י] כאוניה במצולות ים

24. to your covenant. They are a council of deception and a congregation of Belial. They do not know that my station comes from you
25. and that by your kindness you save my life, for from you come my steps. And because of you they have threatened
26. my life, so that you may be glorified in the judgment of the wicked and manifest your strength through me before
27. mortal beings, for by your kindness do I stand. And I myself said, "Warriors have encamped against me; they have surrounded (me) with all
28. their weapons of war. Arrows for which there is no cure destroy, and the blade of the spear is like fire that devours trees.
29. Like the roar of mighty waters is the tumult of their shout, a cloudburst and tempest to destroy a multitude.
30. When their waves mount up, deception and vanity burst forth toward the constellations." But as for me, even when my heart melted like water, my soul held fast to your covenant.
31. And as for them, the net they spread against me seized their feet, and the snares they hid for my life, they themselves fell into them. But my feet stand upon level ground.
32. Far away from their assembly I will bless your name. *vacat*
33. I thank you, Lord, that your eye (watches) over [me]in the bereavement of my soul, and you have saved me from the jealousy of the lying interpreters;
34. and from the congregation of those who seek smooth things, you have redeemed the soul of the poor one whom they thought to destroy,
35. pouring out his blood because of service to you. Yet they did [not] know that my steps come from you, and so they made me an object of scorn
36. and reproach in the mouths of all who seek deceit. But you, O my God, have saved the life of the humble and poor one
37. from the hand of the one who was stronger than he. You ransomed my life from the hand of the mighty, and you did not let me be dismayed by their slanders
38. so as to abandon your service out of fear of destruction by the wicked or to exchange in delusion the resolute purpose that
39. you gave °°°°°° °°°° [...]°° °°°*my* statutes and in the testimonies that you [es]tablished for me to strengthen
40. [fl]esh [...]°°°°° °°°° pit to all my offspring with
41. [... ton]gue like your disciples and in judg[ment]

Column XI

1. [...]
2. [...]*m* weeping *m*°°°[...]
3. [...]°*m whb*°°*l*°°° °°°°°°[...]
4. [... you], O my God, have made my face shine for your covenant °°[...]
5. [...]*h* for yourself in eternal glory with all [...]°° °°°[...]
6. [*vacat* I thank you, O my Lord, that] your command is [tru]th and that you delivered me from [a worthless council] and from[...]*ym*
7. you have [sav]ed [my] life, [for] they regard me [as a reproach and a deris]ion and make [my] life like a ship on the depths of the sea

8 וכעיר מבצר מלפני[צר]ואהיה בצוקה כמו אשת לדה מבכריה כיא נהפכו צירים
9 וחבל נמרץ על משבריה להחיל בכור הריה כיא באו בנים עד משברי מות
10 והרית גבר הצרה בחבליה כיא במשברי מות תמליט זכר ובחבלי שאול יגיח
11 מכור הריה פלא יועץ עם גבורתו ויפלט גבר ממשברים בהריתו החישו כול
12 משברים וחבלי מרץ במולדיהם ופלצות להורותם ובמולדיו יהפכו כול צירים
13 בכור הריה והרית אפעה לחבל נמרץ ומשברי שחת לכול מעשי פלצות ויריעו
14 אושי קיר כאוניה על פני מים ויהמו שחקים בקול המון ויושבי עפר
15 כיורדי ימים נבעתים מהמון מים וחכמיה° למו כמלחים במצולות כי תתבלע
16 כול חכמתם בהמות ימים ברתוח תהומות על נבוכי מים ויתרגשו לרום גלים
17 ומשברי מים בהמון קולם ובהתרגשם יפתחו ש[או]ל[וא]בד[ון ו]כול חצי שחת
18 עם מצעדם לתהום ישמיעו קולם ויפתחו שערי[עולם תח]ת מעשי אפעה
19 ויסגרו דלתי שחת בעד הרית עול ובריחי עולם בעד כול רוחי אפעה
20 *vacat* אודכה אדוני כי פדיתה נפשי משחת ומשאול אבדון
21 העליתני לרום עולם ואתהלכה במישור לאין חקר ואדעה כיא יש מקוה לאשר
22 יצרתה מעפר לסוד עולם ורוח נעוה טהרתה מפשע רב להתיצב במעמד עם
23 צבא קדושים ולבוא ביחד עם עדת בני שמים ותפל לאיש גורל עולם עם רוחות
24 דעת להלל שמכה ביחד רנה ולספר נפלאותיכה לנגד כול מעשיכה ואני יצר
25 החמר מה אני מגבל במים ולמי נחשבתי ומה כוח לי כיא התיצבתי בגבול רשעה
26 ועם חלכאים בגורל ותגור נפש אביון עם מהומות רבה והוות מדהבה עם מצעדי
27 בהפתח כל פחי שחת ויפרשו כול מצודות רשעה ומכמרת חלכאים על פני מים
28 בהתעופף כול חצי שחת לאין השב ויורו לאין תקוה בנפול קו על משפט וגורל אף
29 על נעזבים ומתך חמה על נעלמים וקץ חרון לכול בליעל וחבלי מות אפפו לאין פלט
30 וילכו נחלי בליעל על כול אגפי רום באש אוכלת בכול שנאביהם להתם כול עץ לח
31 ויבש מפלגיהם ותשוט בשביבי להוב עד אפס כול שותיהם באושי חמר תאוכל
32 וברקיע יבשה יסודי הרים לשרפה ושורשי חלמיש לנחלי זפת ותאוכל עד תהום

8. and like a city fortified before[the enemy]. I was in distress like a woman giving birth to her firstborn, when pangs
9. and painful labor have come upon her womb opening, causing spasms in the crucible of the pregnant woman. For children come to the womb opening of death,
10. and she who is pregnant with a manchild is convulsed by her labor pains. For in the breakers of death she delivers a male, and in the cords of Sheol there bursts forth
11. from the crucible of the pregnant woman a wonderful counselor with his power, and the manchild is delivered from the breakers by the one who is pregnant with him. All
12. wombs hasten, and there are severe labor pains at their births and shuddering for those pregnant with them. And so at his birth all (these) pains come upon
13. the crucible of the pregnant one. But she who is pregnant with venomous vanity (will be subject) to painful labor, and the womb opening of the pit to all the works of terror. And
14. the foundations of the wall groan like a ship upon the surface of the waters and the clouds thunder with tumultuous noise. The dwellers in the dust
15. are like those who go down to the seas, terrified by the roar of the waters. And their sages are for them like sailors on the deeps, for
16. all their wisdom is reduced to confusion by the tumult of the seas. When the deeps boil up over the sources of the waters, the waves and the breakers of the waters surge up on high
17. with their noisy roar. And as they surge, Sh[eo]l [and A]badd[on] open up [and] all the arrows of the pit together with their retinue.
18. They make their sound heard to the deep, and break open the [eternal] gates [benea]th the works of venomous vanity.
19. And the doors of the pit close behind the one who is pregnant with iniquity, and the eternal bars behind all the spirits of venomous vanity.
20. *vacat* I thank you, Lord, that you have redeemed my life from the pit and that from Sheol-Abaddon
21. you have lifted me up to an eternal height, so that I walk about on a limitless plain. I know that there is hope for one whom
22. you have formed from the dust for an eternal council. And a perverted spirit you have purified from great sin that it might take its place with
23. the host of the holy ones and enter into community with the congregation of the children of heaven. And you cast for a person an eternal lot with the spirits
24. of knowledge, that he might praise your name in a common rejoicing and recount your wonderful acts before all your works. But I, a vessel
25. of clay, what am I? A thing kneaded with water. And as what am I regarded? What strength do I possess? For I have stationed myself in a wicked realm
26. and with the vile by lot. The soul of the poor one dwells with tumults in abundance, and disastrous calamities dog my steps.
27. When all the snares of the pit are open, and all the nets of wickedness are spread, and the seine of the vile ones is upon the surface of the waters;
28. when all the arrows of the pit fly without cease and are shot, leaving no hope; when the line is cast for judgment, and the lot of anger
29. is upon the forsaken, and the outpouring of fury upon the hypocrites, and the time of wrath comes upon all devilishness, and the cords of death encompass, leaving no escape—
30. then the torrents of Belial pour over all the steep banks in a devouring fire on all their vegetation, destroying every tree, green
31. and dry, from their channels. And it sweeps on with flaming fire until there is nothing left that drinks from them. It eats away at the foundations of clay
32. and at the expanse of the dry land. The bases of the mountains become an inferno, and the flinty roots become torrents of pitch. It consumes as far as the great deep.

33 רבה ויבקעו לאבדון נ֯חלי בליעל ויהמו מחשבי תהום בהמון גורשי רפש וארץ

34 תצרח על ההווה הנ֯ה֯יה בתבל וכול מחשביה יריעו ויתהוללו כול אשר עליה

35 ויתמוגגו בהווה ג֯ד֯[ו]ל֯ה כיא ירעם אל בהמון כוחו ויהם זבול קודשו באמת

36 כבודו וצבא השמים יתנו בקולם ו֯יתמוגגו וירעדו אושי ע֯ולם ומלחמת גבורי

37 שמים תשוט בתבל ולא תשוב עד כלה ונחרצה לעד ואפס כמוה *vacat*

38 *vacat* אודכה אדוני כיא הייתה לי לח֯ומת עוז

39 ב֯◦[ ]ל משחיתים וכול [ ] כ֯י תסתירני מהוות מ֯ה֯ו֯מ֯ה֯ אש֯ר ד֯◦◦◦[ ]

40 [ד]ל֯ת֯י֯[מגן ובריח]י ברזל בל יבוא֯ גדוד מ֯ש֯[מר גבורים]

41 [בהלוות]מ֯ם בסביביה פ֯ן י֯ו֯ר֯ה֯ ג֯ב֯[ור]

Column XII

Parallels: 4QpapH[f] 7 3–5 (underline; lines 1–3)
4QH[b] 6 1–2 (dotted underline; lines 1–2)
4QpapH[f] 8 1 (underline; line 11)
4QH[d] 1–7 (broken underline; lines 15–19)
4QpapH[f] 9 1 (underline; line 23)
4QpapH[f] 10 1–2 (underline; lines 36–37)

1 [ ] גמולי גבורתם ויפולו מגבורתם [

2 [ ] חכמים בערמת]ם ואני ב֯ת֯ומכי [ב]ב֯[ריתכה [

3 [ ]◦]◦ק֯ ◦◦◦◦◦◦◦◦◦◦◦י מ◦◦[ ]◦◦◦[ ] [

4 [ו]ת֯כ֯ן ע֯ל סלע רגלי ו֯ת֯ס֯י֯ר֯ פ֯ע֯מי מ֯ד֯[רך [

5 [ ]ב֯ד֯ר֯ך עולם ובנתיבות אשר בחרתה מצ֯ע֯ד֯י ◦◦◦[[

6 [ ] *vacat* אודכה אדוני כיא האירותה פני לבריתכה ומ[[

7 [ ]◦ אדורשכה וכשחר נכון לאור֯[תי]ם֯ הופעתה לי והמה עמכה [ ]

8 ב֯ת֯ע֯[ותם ו]ב֯ד֯ב֯רים החליקו למו ומליצי רמיה ה֯ת֯ע֯ו֯ם וילבטו בלא בינה כיא֯ [ ]

9 בהולל מעשיהם כי נמאסי למו ולא יחשבוני בהגבירכה בי כיא ידיחני מארצי

10 כצפ֯ור מקנה וכול רעי ומודעי נדחו ממני ויחשבוני לכלי אובד והמה מליצי

11 כזב וחוזי רמיה זממו עלי {כז}בליעל להמיר תורתכה אשר שננתה בלבבי בחלקות

12 לעמכה ויעצורו משקה דעת מצמאים ולצמאם ישקום חומץ למע הבט אל

13 תעותם להתהולל במועדיהם להתפש במצודותם כי אתה אל תנאץ כל מחשבת

14 בליעל ועצתכה היא תקום ומחשבת לבכה תכון לנצח והמה נעלמים זמות בליעל

15 יחשובו וידרשוכה בלב ולב ולא נכונו באמתכה שורש פורה רוש ולענה במחשבותם

16 ועם שרירות לבם יתורו וידרשוכה בגלולים ומכשול עוונם שמו לנגד פניהם ויבאו

17 לדורשכה מפי נביאי כזב מפותי תעות והם [ב]ל֯[ו]ע֯ג שפה ולשון אחרת ידברו לעמך

18 להולל ברמיה כול מעשיהם כי לא ב֯חרו בדר[ך לב]כ֯ה ולא האזינו לדברכה כי אמרו

19 לחזון דעת לא נכון ולדרך לבכה לא היאה כי אתה אל תענה להם לשופטם

33. And the torrents of Belial break through to Abaddon, and the structures of the deep roar at the noise of those who cast up mire. And the land
34. cries out on account of the destruction that has come upon the world, and all its structures scream, and all who are upon it go mad
35. and shake to pieces in the g[re]at destruction. For God thunders with his powerful roar, and his holy dwelling resounds with his glorious truth.
36. The host of heaven raise their voice, and the eternal foundations shake and tremble. The war of the champions of
37. heaven sweeps through the world and does not turn back until full consummation. It is determined forever; and there is nothing like it. *vacat*
38. *vacat* I thank you, Lord, that you have been a strong wall to me
39. *b*°[...]*l* the destroyers and all [...] for you hide me from terrifying calamities that *d*°°°[...]
40. [... shielding d]oors [and ba]rs of iron, so that no marauding troop may enter, a gu[ard of warriors]
41. [when they join themselves ...]*mm* in its environs, lest a war[rior] shoot[...]

Column XII

1. [... recompense of their might. And they will fall on account of their might ...]
2. [... the wise in] their [discernment.] And I, when I hold [on to your] co[venant ...]
3. [... ° ...]°*q*°°°°°°°°°°°*y m*°°[...]°°° [...]
4. [... and] you set my feet upon a rock and you have turned my steps from the w[ay ...]
5. [...]in the eternal way, and upon the paths that you have chosen my steps °°°[...]
6. [...] *vacat* I thank you, Lord, that you have illumined my face for your covenant and *m*[...]
7. [...]° I seek you, and as sure as dawn, you appear to me as early [li]ght. But they, your people, [...]
8. in [their] stra[ying, and] they used slippery words on them. Deceitful interpreters led them astray, and they came to ruin without understanding, for [...]
9. with delusion their deeds, for I have been rejected by them. They have no regard for me when you show your strength through me, for they drive me away from my land
10. like a bird from its nest. All my friends and my relatives are driven away from me, and they regard me as a broken pot. But they are lying interpreters
11. and deceitful seers. They have planned devilry against me to exchange your law, which you spoke repeatedly in my heart, for slippery words
12. for your people. They withhold the drink of knowledge from the thirsty, and for their thirst they give them sour wine to drink so that they may gaze on
13. their error, acting like madmen on their feast days, snaring themselves in their nets. But you, O God, despise every devilish plan,
14. and it is your counsel that will stand and the plan of your mind that will be established forever. But they, the hypocrites, concoct devilish plans
15. and seek you with a divided heart. And so they are not steadfast in your truth. A root that grows poison and wormwood is in their thoughts,
16. and in the stubbornness of their heart they explore, and they seek you among idols. The stumbling block of their iniquity they have placed before themselves, and they come
17. to inquire of you by means of the mouth of lying prophets, who are themselves seduced by error. And they, [with] m[o]cking lips and an alien tongue speak to your people,
18. deceitfully ridiculing all their deeds. For they have not chosen the wa[y of] your [heart], and they have not listened to your word, for they say
19. of the vision of knowledge, "It is not certain," and of the way of your heart, "It is not that." But you, O God, will answer them, judging them

20 בגבורתכהׄ[כ]גלוליהם וכרוב פשעיהם למען יתפשו במחשבותם אשר נזורו מבריתכה
21 ותכרת במׄ[שפ]ט כול אנשי מרמה וחוזי תעות לא ימצאו עוד כי אין הולל בכול מעשיך
22 ולא רמיהׄ בׄמזמת לבכה ואשר כנפשכה יעמודו לפניכה לעד והולכי בדרך לבכה
23 יכונו לנצחׄ[ו]אׄני בתומכי בכה אתעודדה ואקומה על מנאצי וידי על כול בוזי כיא
24 לא יחשבונׄ[י]עׄד הגבירכה בי ותופע לי בכוחכה לאורתים ולא טחתה בבושת פני
25 כול הנדרשׁ[י]םׄ לי הנועדים יחד לבריתכה וישומעוני ההולכים בדרך לבכה ויערוכו לכה
26 בסוד קדושים ותוצא לנצח משפטם ולמישרים אמת ולא תתעם ביד חלכאים
27 כזומם למו ותתן מוראם על עמכה ומפץ לכול עמי הארצות להכרית במשפט כול
28 עוברי פיכה ובי האירותה פני רבים ותגבר עד לאין מספר כי הודעתני ברזי
29 פלאכה ובסׄוד פלאכה הגברתה עמדי והפלא לנגד רבים בעבור כבודכה ולהודיע
30 לכול החייםׄ גבורותיכה מי בשר כזאת ומה יצר חמר להגדיל פלאות והוא בעוון
31 מרחם ועד שבה באשמת מעל ואני ידעתי כי לׄא לאנוש צדקה ולׄא לבן אדם תום
32 דרך לאל עׄליון כול מעשי צדקה ודרך אנוש לׄא תכון כי אם ברוח יצר אל לו
33 להתם דרך לבני אדם למען ידעו כול מעשיו בכוח גבורתו ורוב רחמיו על כול בני
34 רצונו ואני רׄעׄד ורתת אחזוני וכול גרמי ירועו וימס לבבי כדונג מ{לׄ}פני אש וילכו ברכי
35 כמים מוגרים בׄמורד כי זכרתי אשמותי עם מעל אבותי בקום רשעים על בריתך
36 וחלכאים על דברכה ואני אמרתי בפשעי נעזבתי מבריתכה ובזוכרי כוח ידכה עם
37 המון רחמיכה התעודדתי ואקומה ורוחי החזיקה במעמד לפני נגע כי נשענתׄיׄ
38 בחסדיכה וׄכׄהמון רחמיכה בי תכפר עוון ולטהׄ[ר]אׄנׄוׄש מאשמה בצדקתכה לׄכׄהׄ[א]לׄ[י]
39 ולא לאדםׄ כׄוׄלׄ אׄשׄרׄ עׄשיתה כי אתה בראתה צדיק ורשע °°°[ ]
40 [ ]°°°°°°°° אתחזקה בבריתכה עד [ ]
41 [ ]°°°°° כׄיׄ אמת אתה וצדק כולׄ מׄ[עשיכה]

20. in your strength [according to] their idols and the magnitude of their transgressions, so that those who have deserted your covenant will be caught in their own machinations.
21. You will cut off in ju[dgm]ent all deceitful people, and erring seers will be found no longer. For there is no delusion in all your works,
22. and there is no deceit in the plan of your mind. Those who are in harmony with you will stand before you forever, and those who walk in the way of your heart
23. will be established everlastingly. [And] as for me, when I hold fast to you, I stand strong and rise up against those who despise me. My hand is against all who have contempt for me, for
24. they have no regard for [me], as long as you show your strength through me and appear to me in your strength as early light. You have not covered in shame the faces of
25. all who have been examined by me, who have gathered together for your covenant. Those who walk in the way of your heart listen to me, and they marshal themselves before you
26. in the council of the holy ones. You bring forth their justice successfully and truth with ease. You do not let them be led astray by the hand of the vile
27. when they scheme against them. But you put a dread of them upon your people, and (bring) destruction to all the peoples of the lands, in order to cut off in judgment all
28. who transgress your command. Through me you have illumined the faces of many, and you have increased them beyond number. For you have made me understand your wonderful
29. mysteries, and in your wonderful council you have shown yourself strong to me, doing wondrously before many for the sake of your glory and in order to make known
30. to all the living your mighty deeds. What being of flesh is like this? And what vessel of clay is able to do wondrous great deeds? It (exists) in iniquity
31. from the womb, and until old age in faithless guilt. But as for me, I know that righteousness does not belong to humankind nor perfection of way to a mortal.
32. To God Most High belong all the works of righteousness. The way of humanity is not established except by the spirit God has fashioned for it,
33. in order to perfect a way for mortal beings, so that they may know all his works through his mighty strength and his abundant compassion toward all the children of
34. his goodwill. But as for me, trembling and quaking have seized me, and all my bones shatter. My heart melts like wax before the fire, and my knees give way
35. like water hurtling down a slope. For I remember my guilty acts together with the unfaithfulness of my ancestors, when the wicked rose against your covenant
36. and the vile against your word. And I said, "In my sin I have been abandoned, far from your covenant." But when I remembered the strength of your hand together with
37. your abundant compassion, I stood strong and rose up, and my spirit held fast to (its) station in the face of affliction. For I am supported
38. by your kindness, and according to your abundant compassion to me, you pardon iniquity and thus clean[se] a person from guilt through your righteousness. For yourself, O [my G]od,
39. and not for the sake of humankind, is all that you have made, for you yourself created the righteous and the wicked °°°[...]
40. [...]°°°°°°°° I will hold fast to your covenant until [...]
41. [...]°°°°° for you are truth and righteous are all [your] de[eds ...]

Column XIII

Parallels: 4QH[c] 1 i 1–3 (underline; lines 9–11)
4QH[c] 1 ii 1–6 (underline; lines 17–20)
4QH[b] 7 1 (broken underline; line 26)
4QH[c] 2 7–12 (underline; lines 28–30)
4QH[c] 3 1–12 (underline; lines 31–40)
4QpapH[f] 11 1–3 (dotted underline; lines 35–37)

1] [
2] [
3 ליום [ז]עם חרון [רוב]
4 סליחותיכה והמון רחמ[י]כה [ ]ב°
5 ובדעתי אלה נחמ[תי] באמתכה °°°[ ]°י
6 על פי רצונכה ובידכה משפט כולם *v]acat* [*vacat*
7 אודכה אדוני כי לא עזבתני בגורי בעם נכר [ ]כאשמתי
8 שפטתני ולא עזבתני בזמות יצרי ותעזור משחת חיי ותתן לי °[פ]לט בתוך
9 לביאים מועדים לבני אשמה אריות שוברי עצם אדירים ושותי דם גבורים ותשמני
10 במגור עם דיגים רבים פורשי מכמרת על פני מים וצידים לבני עולה ושם למשפט
11 יסדתני וסוד אמת אמצתה בלבבי ומזה ברית לדורשיה ותסגור פי כפירים אשר
12 כחרב שניהם ומתלעותם כחנית חדה חמת תנינים כול מזמותם לחת{ו}ף יורבו ולא
13 פצו עלי פיהם כי אתה אלי סתרתני נגד בני אדם ותורתכה חבתה ב[י]עד קץ
14 הגלות ישעכה לי כי בצרת נפשי לא עזבתני ושועתי שמעתה במרורי נפשי
15 ודנת יגוני הכרתה באנחתי ותצל נפש עני במעון אריות אשר שננו כחרב לשונם
16 ואתה אלי סגרתה בעד {ל}ש{ו}ניהם פן יטרפו נפש{י} עני ורש ותוסף לשונם
17 כחרב אל תערה בלוא[נכר]תה נפש עבדכה ולמען הגבירכה בילנגד בני אדם הפלתה
18 באביון ותביאהו במצר[ף]כזהב במעשי אש וככסף מזוקק בכור נופחים לטהר שבעתים
19 וימהרו עלי רשעי עמים במצוקותם וכול היום ידכאו נפשי *vacat*
20 ואתה אלי תשיב נפשי[2] סערה לדממה ונפש אביון פלטתה כצפו[ר מפח ו]כטרף מפי
21 אריות *vacat*
ברוך אתה
22 אודכה אדוני כי לא עזבתה יתום ולא בזיתה רש כי גבורתכה לא[ין ק]ץ וכבודכה
23 לאין מדה וגבורי פלא משר{י}תיכה ועם ענוים בטאטאיי רגליכ[ה יחד] עם נמהרי
24 צדק להעלות משאון יחד כול {נמה}אביוני חסד ואני הייתי על ע°[ ]דני לריב
25 ומדנים לרעי קנאה ואף לבאי בריתי ורגן ותלונה לכול נועדי ג[ם א]וכלי לחמי
26 עלי הגדילו עקב ויליזו עלי בשפת עול כול נצמדי סודי ואנשי עצתי סוררים
27 ומלינים סביב וברז חבתה בי ילכו רכיל לבני הוות ובעבור הגב[רכה] בי ולמען
28 אשמתם סתרת מעין בינה וסוד אמת והמה הוות לבם יחשובו ודב[רי]בליעל פתחו

2. The overbar and underbar mark deletion of the word.

Column XIII

1. [...]
2. [...]
3. for the day of furious [in]dignation [... the greatness of]
4. your forgiveness and the abundance of your compassion [...]*b*°
5. and when I knew these things [I] was comforted by your truth °°°[...]°*y*
6. according to your goodwill, and in your hand is the judgment of them all. *vacat* [...] *vacat*
7. I thank you, O Lord, that you have not abandoned me when I dwelt with a foreign people [...]according to my guilt
8. did you judge me. You did not abandon me to the devices of my inclination. And you delivered my life from the pit, and you gave me °[... es]cape in the midst
9. of lions appointed for the children of guilt, lions that crush the bones of the mighty and drink the blood of warriors. You placed me
10. in a dwelling place among the many fishers who spread a net over the surface of the waters and among the hunters of the children of iniquity. And there, for judgment,
11. you established me, and the counsel of truth you strengthened in my heart. From this comes a covenant for those who seek it. And you closed the mouth of the young lions whose
12. teeth are like a sword and whose jaw teeth are like a pointed spear. Snake venom—such is all their scheming. They lie in wait for robbery, but they have not
13. opened their mouths against me. For you, O my God, have sheltered me against mortals, and your law you have hidden in [me] until the time
14. when your salvation is revealed to me. For you have not abandoned me in the distress of my soul, you have heard my cry for help in the bitterness of my soul,
15. and the outcry of my misery you have recognized in my groaning. You rescued the life of the poor one in the dwelling of the lions that whet their tongue like a sword.
16. And you, O my God, have shut their teeth, so that they would not rend the life of the poor and destitute, and you drew back their tongue
17. like a sword into its sheath, so that the life of your servant was not [cut] off. And in order to manifest your strength through me before mortal beings you have acted wonderfully
18. toward the poor one. You have brought him into the furna[ce] like gold (subjected to) the action of fire and like silver refined in the crucible of the smelters for sevenfold purity.
19. The wicked among the peoples rushed against me with their torments, and all day they crush my soul. *vacat*
20. But you, O my God, turn the storm into stillness, and the soul of the poor one you have rescued like a bir[d from the snare, and] like prey from the mouth
21. of the lions. *vacat*
22. Blessed are you, O Lord, for you have not abandoned the orphan and you have not despised the destitute one, for your strength is witho[ut en]d and your glory
23. without measure. And wonderful warriors are your servants, but a humble people (has a place) in the mud of yo[ur] feet [together] with those who are eager for
24. righteousness so that all the faithful poor may be lifted up from the mire altogether. But as for me, I have become on account of ‘°[...]*dny* a cause of controversy
25. and quarrels with my neighbors, an object of jealousy and anger to those who enter into covenant with me, an object both of grumbling and murmuring to all who are associated with me. Al[so those] who eat my bread
26. have lifted the heel against me. All who are attached to my council speak ill of me with evil lips, and the people of my council are rebels
27. and murmurers all around. With the secret you have hidden in me they go about with slander to the children of destruction. But in order to show [your] gre[atness] through me, and on account of
28. their guilt, you have hidden the spring of understanding and the foundation of truth. But as for them, they plot the destruction they have in mind, and (with) devilish wor[ds] they loosen

29 לשון שקר כחמת תנינים פורחת לקצים וכזוחל֯י עפר יורו לחת֯ו֯[ף] מ֯[בלגות] פתנים
30 לא֯ין חבר ותהי לכאוב אנוש ונגע נמאר בתכמי עבדכה להכשי֯ל֯ [רו]ח֯ ולהתם
31 כוח לבלתי החזק מעמד וישיגוני במצרים לאין מנוס ולא בה֯ב֯ד֯ל֯ מ֯מ֯ש֯פ֯חות ויהמ֯ו
32 בכנור ריבי ובנגינות יחד תלונתם עם שאה ומשואה זלעופות א֯חזוני וחבלים כצירי
33 יולדה ויהם עלי לבי קדרות לבשתי ולשוני לחך{ֽי} תדבק כ֯י֯ ס֯ב֯בו֯נ֯י֯ בהוות לבם ויצרם
34 הופיע לי למרורים ויחשך מאור פני לאפלה והודי בהפך למשחי֯ת֯ ואת אלי
35 מרחב פתחתה בלבבי ויוספוה לצוקה וישוכו בעדי בצלמות ואוכלה בלח֯ם֯ אנח֯ת֯י֯
36 ושקוי בדמעות אין כלה כי עששו מכעס עיני ונפשי במרורי יום א֯נח֯ה֯ ויגו֯ן֯
37 יסובבוני ובושת על פנים ויהפך לי לח֯מ֯י֯ ל֯ריב ושקוי לבעל מדנים ויבוא בעצ֯מ֯י֯
38 להכשיל רוח ולכלות כוח כרזי פשע משנים מעשי אל באשמתם כי נאס֯ר֯ת֯י֯ בעבו֯ת֯י֯ם
39 ל֯א֯ין נתק וזקים ללוא ישוברו וחומ֯ת֯ עו֯ז֯[בעדי]ו֯בריחי ברזל ודלתי[נחושת לאין]
40 [פתוח]כ֯לאי עם תהום נחשב{תי} לאין[ ]°°[[
41 [ונחלי]ב֯ל֯י֯על אפפו נפשי לא֯י֯ן֯[פ]ל֯[ט [

Column XIV

Parallels: 4QH[b] 8 1–5 (dotted underline; lines 17–20)
4QH[c] 4 i 2–12 (underline; lines 20–25)
4QH[c] 4 ii 1–12 (underline; lines 25–31)

1] [
2] [
3] [
4]° °°°[ ]°° °°° [
5 לבי בנאצו֯ת֯ בפ֯י֯ [[
6 ו֯הווה לאין חקר ו֯כלה לא֯י֯ן֯ מ֯ד֯[ה ואתה אלי]
7 גליתה אוזני ב֯מ֯[ו]ס֯ר֯ מוכ֯י֯ח֯י֯ צ֯דק עם[ ] °°°
8 מעדת ש֯ו֯א ו֯מסוד חמס ו֯ת֯ביאני בעצ֯ת֯ ה֯קו֯ד֯ש֯ °°[ ]°°° אשמה
9 ואדעה כי יש מקוה לשבי פשע ועוזבי חטאה בה[ ] ו֯ל֯התהלך
10 בדרך לבכה לאין עול ואנחמה על המון עם ועל שאון מ֯מ֯ל֯כות בהאספם [ליש]ו֯עתי אשר
11 תרים למצער מחיה בעמכה ושארית בנחלתכה ותזקקם להטהר מאשמ֯ה֯ [ומח]ט֯ו֯א כול
12 מעשיהם באמתכה ובחסדיך תשפטם בהמון רחמים ורוב סליחה וכפיכ֯ה֯ להורותם
13 וכי֯ישיר אמ֯ת֯כ֯ה להכינם בעצתכה לכבודכה ולמענכה עשי֯[תה] לג֯ד֯ל תורה ו°[ ]ל °°°°
14 אנשי עצתכה בתוך בני אדם לספר לדורות עולם נפלאותיכה ובגבורותי֯[כה יש]ו֯חחו

29. a lying tongue like the venom of serpents that shoots forth repeatedly, and like creatures that slither in the dust they lie in wait in order to sie[ze] (with) the po[ison of] vipers
30. for which there is no charm. It has become an incurable pain and a malignant affliction in the bowels of your servant, causing [the spi]rit to stumble and bringing an end to
31. strength, so that he could not stand firm. And they overtook me in narrow straits without means of escape, so that there was no separating from the restraining bands. And they sounded forth
32. on a zither their complaint against me and in unison on stringed instruments their slander. Amid ruin and desolation torments seized me, and pains like the spasms of
33. a woman in labor. My mind was in tumult within me. I clothed myself with darkness, and my tongue clung to the roof of my mouth, for they surrounded me with their heart's destructiveness, and their purpose
34. revealed itself to me for bitterness. The light of my face darkened into gloom, and my radiance changed into disfigurement. But you, O my God,
35. you opened a broad place in my heart; but they made it tight with distress, and they hedged me in with deep darkness. And I ate the bread of my sighs,
36. and my drink was endless tears, for my eyes have dimmed from distress and my soul with the bitterness of the day. Sighs and grief
37. surrounded me, and shame was upon (my) face. My bread was changed for me into conflict and my drink into an accuser. It entered my very bones,
38. making the spirit stumble and bringing an end to strength. In accordance with the mysteries of sin they alter the works of God through their guilt, for I was bound with cords
39. that could not be sundered and chains that could not be broken. A strong wall was [around me] and bars of iron and doors of [bronze that could not be]
40. opened]. My prison could be regarded as the deep, without[...]°°[...]
41. [and torrents] of Belial encompassed my soul without [es]ca[pe ...]

Column XIV

1. [...]
2. [...]
3. [...]
4. °°° °°[...]°°° °[...]
5. my heart with slanders in the mouth of [...]
6. and destruction without limit and annihilation without measu[re ... But you, O my God,]
7. you opened my ears with ins[tru]ction. Righteous reprovers with[...] °°°
8. from the assembly of fraud and from the fellowship of violence. You brought me into the council of holiness °°[...]°°° guilt.
9. I know that there is hope for those who repent of transgression and for those who abandon sin *bh*[...] and to walk
10. in the way of your heart without iniquity. And I am reassured [with respect to] my [sal]vation, concerning the tumult of the people and the clamor of kingdoms when they gather together, that
11. you will raise up in a little while, survivors among your people and a remnant in your inheritance. And you refine them in order to purify from guilt [and from s]in all
12. their deeds by means of your truth. And in your kindness you judge them with overflowing compassion and abundant forgiveness, teaching them according to your command
13. and establishing them in your counsel, according to your proper truth for the sake of your glory. And for your own sake [you] have acted to magnify the teaching and [...] *l* °°°°
14. the people of your counsel in the midst of humankind that they may recite for everlasting generations your wonderful deeds, and they [medi]tate on [your] mighty acts

15 לאין השבת וידעו כול גוים אמתכה וכול לׄאומים כבודכה כי הביאותׄהׄ °[ ]סׄודכה
16 לכול אנשי עצתכה ובגורל יחד עם מלאכי פנים ואין מליץ בנים לק[ל]הׄשיב
17 כרוחׄ כי °°ל֯[ ]תד°° בׄ°°° והם ישובו בפי כבודכה ויהיו שריכה בגור[ל עולם וגזע]םׄ
18 פרח כציץׄ[יציץ ל]הׄוׄד עולם לגדל נצר לעופי מטעת עולם ויצל צל על כול תׄבׄלׄ וׄדׄ[ליותי]ו
19 עד שׄחׄקׄיׄםׄ ושרשיו עד תהום וכול נהרות עדן [ת]לׄ[חלחנה ד]לׄ[י]ותיו והיה לימׄיׄם לׄ[אין]
20 חקר וׄהׄתׄאׄזרו על תבל לאין אפס ועׄדׄ שאול [ו]הׄיה מעין אור למקור
21 עולם לאין הסר בשביבי נוגהו יבערו כול בנׄיׄ[עולה והיה] לאש בוערת בכול אנשי
22 אשמה עד כלה והמה נצמדי תעודתי פותו במליׄ[צי תעות ל]הׄבׄיׄאׄ זרׄ בעבודת צדק
23 ואתה אל צויתם להועיל מדרכיהם בדרך קוׄדׄ[ש אשר ילכו] בה וערל וטמא ופריץ
24 בל יעוברנׄה וׄיׄתׄמׄוטטו מדרך לבכה ובהוותׄ פׄ[שעם יכשל]וׄ וכמוא יועץ בליעל
25 עם לבׄבם [ויכי]נׄוׄ מחשבת רשעה יתגוללו באשמה וׄ[אני היי]תי כמלח באוניה בׄזׄעף
26 ימים גליהם וׄכול משבריהם עלי המו רוח עועייםׄ[לאין]דממה להשיב נפש ואין
27 נתיבת לישרׄ דרך על פני מים ויהם תהום לאנחתי ונׄגׄשׄ[ו חיי]עׄד שערי מות ואהיה
28 כבא בעיר מצור ונעוז בחומה נ{ס}גבה עד פלט ואשעׄ[נה]בׄאמתכה אלי כי אתה
29 תשים סוד על סלע וכפיס על קו משפט ומשקלת אמׄ[ת]לׄ[ע]שׄות אבני בחן לבׄניתׄ
30 עוז ללוא תתזעזע וכול באיה בל ימוטו כי לא יבוא זרׄ בׄשׄעׄרׄיה דלתי מגן לאיןׄ
31 מבוא ובריחי עוז ללוא ישוברו בל יבוא גדוד בכלי מלחמתו עם תום כול חׄצׄיׄ
32 מלחמות רשעה ואז תחיש חרב אל בקץ משפט וכול בני אמׄתו יעורו לׄהׄכׄרׄיׄ[ת]
33 רשעה וכול בני אשמה לא יהיו עוד וידרוך גבור קשתו וׄיפתׄח מצוריׄ הׄשׄמׄיׄםׄ
34 למׄרחב אין קץ ושערי עולם להוציא כלי מלחמות ויעצומׄו מקצה עד קׄצׄהׄ וׄחׄצׄיׄ[ם]
35 יורו ואׄיןׄ פׄלט ליצר אשמה לכלה ירמוסו ואין שׄרׄיׄתׄ וׄאׄיׄןׄ תקוה ברׄוב פׄגׄרׄיׄםׄ
36 וׄלכוׄלׄ גבׄוׄרי מלחמ'ת אין מנוס כי לאל עליון הׄ°[ ]° °°° °° °°°° °°°°
37 וׄשׄוׄכׄבי עׄפר הרימו תרן ותולעת מתים נשאו נס ל°°°°[ ]°י°ר°ן °°°°°°°° °°°
38 במלחמות זׄדׄים ובעבור שוט שוטף בל יבוא במבצרׄ[ ]
39 °°°°° °°°°° °[ ]לׄ[ ]לׄ[ ]לתפל וככפיס לא°[ ]
40 מ°°°°°°° °[ ]
41 אמת °°°°°° [ ]

15. without ceasing. Thus all the nations will acknowledge your truth and all the peoples your glory, for you have brought °[...]your secret counsel
16. all the people of your council, and in a common lot with the angels of the presence, without an intermediary between them *lq*[... to] reply
17. according to the spirit. For °°*l*[...]*td*°° *b*°°° and they repent because of your glorious command, so that they become your princes in the [eternal] lo[t and] their [shoot]
18. opens as a flower [blooms, for] everlasting fragrance, making a sprout grow into the branches of an eternal planting. And it will cast shade over all the world, and its br[anches]
19. will reach to the clouds and its roots as far as the deep. All the rivers of Eden [make] its [br]an[ches m]oist, and it will (extend) to the measure[less] seas,
20. and they wrap themselves over the world without end, and as far as Sheol [... and] the spring of light will become an eternal
21. fountain, without lack. In its bright flames all the children of[iniquity] will burn, [and it will become] a fire that burns up all the
22. guilty until they are utterly destroyed. But they, who had attached themselves to my witness, were persuaded by [erring] interpre[ters to] bring a stranger into the service of righteousness.
23. Yet you, O God, have commanded them to seek profit away from their ways, in the way of holin[ess] in [which they may walk]; and the uncircumcised and unclean and violent
24. will not cross over it. But they stagger off from the way of your heart, and in the destructiveness of [their] tr[ansgression] they [stumble]. Belial is like a counselor
25. in their heart, [and so] they [determ]ine upon a wicked scheme and wallow in guilt. And I [was] like a sailor on a ship in raging
26. seas. Their waves and all their breakers roared over me, a whirling wind[with no]respite to restore the soul nor
27. a path to make a straight course upon the surface of the water. And the deep roared to the sound of my groaning, and [my life] reached the gates of death. But I became
28. like one who enters into a fortified city and finds refuge behind a high wall until deliverance (comes). And so I re[ly] on your faithfulness, O my God, for you yourself
29. lay the foundation upon rock and the crossbeam according to the correct measure and accu[rate] level, in order [to ma]ke the tested stones into a strong building
30. that will not be shaken. All who enter it will not waver, for no stranger will enter into its gates, whose shielding doors
31. allow no entry and whose strong bars cannot be shattered. No troop with its weapons of war can enter, until the end of all the arrows
32. of the wars (with) wickedness. And then the sword of God will come quickly at the time of judgment. All the children of his truth will rouse themselves to extermin[ate]
33. wickedness, and all the children of guilt will be no more. The warrior will stretch his bow and open the citadels of heaven
34. upon an endless plain, and (he will open) the eternal gates to bring forth the weapons of war. They will be mighty from one end (of the earth) to the other, and (their) arrow[s]
35. they will shoot, so that there will be no escape for a guilty creature. To utter destruction they will trample (them) down without remnant or hope in a profusion of corpses,
36. and there will be no refuge for all the soldiers of war. For to El Elyon *h*°[...]° °°° °° °°°° °°°°
37. Those who lie in the dust raise up a standard, and the worms of the dead lift up a banner to °°°°[...]°*y*°*r*°*w* °°°°°°°° °°°
38. in the wars against the insolent. And when the scourging flood passes by, it will not enter the fortified place[...]
39. °°°°° °[...]*l*[...]*l*[...]for plaster and as crossbeams for *l*'°[...]
40. *m*°°°°°°° °[...]
41. truth °°°°°° [...]

Column XV

Parallels: 4QH^{b} 9 1–3 (underline; lines 30–31)
1QH^{b} 1 1–13 (dotted underline; lines 30–41)
4QpapH^{f} 12 1–4 (broken underline; lines 33–37)
4QH^{b} 10 1–6 (underline; lines 37–41)

1] [
2] [
3] [
4]]◦םׄ ואׄני נאלׄמתי מׄהׄו[ות]סׄ[ ]◦◦ ◦◦◦◦קׄ אלׄהׄ וׄגׄדׄפׄוׄנׄיׄ
5] זרו]ע נשברת מקניה ותטבע בבבץ רגלי שעו עיני מראות
6 רע ואׄוזניׄ משמוע דמים השם לבבי ממחשבת רוע כי בליעל עם הופע יצר
7 הוותם ויריעו כול אושי מבניתׄי ועׄצמי יתפרדו ותכמי עלי כאוניה בזעף
8 חרישית ויהם לבי לכלה ורוח עועיים תבלעני מהוות פשעם *vacat*
9 *vacat* אודכה אׄדוני כי סמכתני בעוזכה ורוח
10 קודׄשכה הניפותה בי בל אמוט ותחזקני לפני מלחמות רשעה ובכול הוותם
11 לאׄ החת◦◦ה מבריתכה ותשימני כמגדל עוז כׄחומה נשגבה ותכן על סלע
12 מבניתי ואושי עולם לסודי וכול קירותי לחׄומת בחן ללוא ת'ד{ז}עזע
13 ואׄתה אלי נתתי לעפים לעצת קודש ותׄ[חזק]נׄ[י]בׄבריתכה ולשוני כלמודיך
14 ואין פׄהׄ לרׄוׄח הוות ולא מענה לשון לכול בׄני אשמה כי תאלמנה שפתי
15 שפתי שקר כי כול גדי למשפט תרשיע להׄבדיל בי בין צדיק לרשע
16 כי אתה ידעתה כול יצר מעשה וכול מענה לשון הכרתה ותכן לבי
17 כׄ[ל]מודיכה וכאמתכה לישר פעמי לנתיבות צדקה להתהלך לפניך בגבול
18 [חי]יׄםׄ לׄשבולׄ כבוד {וׄחיים} ושלום לאין הׄ[סר ו]לׄ[ו]אׄ להשבת לנצח
19 ואתה ידעתה יצר עבדכה כי לא צׄ[ ]◦ מׄשׄענתו להרים לבׄ[ו]
20 וׄלהעיז בכוח ומחסי בשר אין לי[ ] אין צדקות להנצל מפ[ ]
21 בׄלׄוא סליחה ואני נשענתי ברׄוׄבׄ[רחמיכה ולהמון] חסדכה אוחיל להציץ
22 כׄמׄטׄע ולגדל נצר להעיז בכוח ולׄ[כי ב]צׄדקתכה העמדתניׄ
23 לבריתכה ואתמוכה בׄאמתכה ואת[ ] ותשימני אב לבני חסד
24 וכאומן לאנשי מופת ויפצו פה כיונ[ק]וׄכשעשע עוליל בח'ק
25 אומניו ותרם קרני על כול מנאצי ויתפׄ[רדו כול ש]אׄרית אנשי מלחמתי ובעלי
26 רבי כמוץ לפני רוח וממשלתיׄ על בוׄזיׄ כיׄ[אתה]אׄלי עזרתה נפשי ותרם קרני
27 למעלה והופעתי באוׄרׄ שבעתים ב◦[ה]כׄינותה לכבודכה
28 כי אתה לי למאור עׄוׄלם ותכן רגלי במׄיׄ[שור] *vacat*
29 *vacat* אׄוׄדׄכׄ[ה אדו]נׄיׄ כי השכלתני באמתכה
30 וברזי פלאׄכׄהׄ הודעתני ובחסדיכה לאיש [פשע] וׄברוב רחמיכה לנעוי לב

Column XV

1. [...]
2. [...]
3. [...]
4. [...] °*m* And as for me, I am speechless on account of their destructive[ness ...]°° °°°°*q* these. And they have reviled me
5. [... (my) ar]m is broken from its joint, and my foot has sunk into the mud. My eyes have sealed shut from seeing
6. evil and my ears from hearing of bloodshed. My mind was appalled by an evil plan. For Belial (is present) when their destructive intention manifests itself.
7. All the foundations of my frame groan, and my bones are dislocated. My bowels are to me like a ship in a raging
8. storm, and my heart beats wildly to the point of destruction. A spirit of confusion engulfs me because of the devastation caused by their sin. *vacat*
9. *vacat* I thank you, O Lord, that you have sustained me by your strength and that
10. you have spread your holy spirit upon me, so that I am not shaken. You have made me strong before the wars of wickedness, and in all their threats of destruction
11. you have not *hḥt*°°*h* from your covenant. You set me like a tower of strength, like a high rampart, and you placed my edifice upon the cliffs
12. and eternal foundations for my base. All my walls are a tested wall that does not sway.
13. And you, O my God, have given me to the weary for holy counsel. You have [strengthened m]e in your covenant, and my tongue has become like (the tongues of) those taught by you.
14. But the spirit of destruction has no speech, and all the children of guilt have no ready answer, for lying lips are rendered speechless.
15. Truly in judgment you declare guilty all who attack me, in order to distinguish through me between the righteous and the wicked,
16. for you yourself know the intention of every deed and scrutinize every reply. You make my heart firm
17. according to your [te]achings and your truth, directing my steps toward the paths of righteousness, so that I may walk before you in the domain of
18. [lif]e on tracks of glory and peace, without tu[rning aside o]r ceasing forever.
19. And you yourself know the intention of your servant, that not *ṣ*[...]° is his support, so as to exalt [his] heart
20. and seek security in strength. There is no refuge in flesh for *y*[...] no righteous deeds that it could be delivered from *p*[...]
21. except by forgiveness. But as for me, I rely upon [your] great [compassion, and upon] your [overflowing] kindness I wait, in order to bloom
22. like a plant, and in order to make a shoot grow, to find security in (your) strength, and to[... for by] your righteousness you have stationed me
23. in your covenant, and I have held fast to your truth, and I *t*[...] and you have made me a father to the children of kindness
24. and like a foster father to the people of good omen. They opened the mouth like a nurs[ing child ...] and like the playing of an infant in the bosom of
25. its foster father. And you have raised my horn above all who despise me, and [all the re]mnant of the people at war with me are sc[attered], and those who
26. have a cause against me are like chaff before the wind. But my dominion (extends) over those who scorn me. For [you,]O my God, have given aid to my soul and have raised my horn
27. on high, and I shine forth with sevenfold light *b*°[...] you have established (me) for your glory.
28. Truly you are an eternal light to me, and you set my feet upon level [ground]. *vacat*
29. *vacat* I thank yo[u, O Lor]d, that you have instructed me in your truth,
30. and made known to me your wondrous mysteries, and (made known) both your kindness toward a [sinful] person and your abundant compassion for the one whose heart is perverted.

31   כֹּי מֹי כֹמֹוֹכה באלים אדוני ומי כאמתכה ומי יצֹדֹק לפניכה בהשפטו ואין

32   להשיב על תוכחתכה כול צֹבֹ^{עֹ}יֹ רֹוח ולא יוכל כול להתיצב לֹפֹנֹיֹ חֹ{כֹ}מתדה וכול בני

33   אמתכה ^{תֹבֹיֹא} בסליחות לפניכה לֹטֹהֹרֹם מפשעיהֹם ברוב טובכה ובהמון רֹחֹמֹיֹכֹה

34   להעמידם לפניכה לעולמי עד   כי אל עולם אתה וכול דֹרֹכֹיֹכֹה יכונו לנצח

35   נֹצחֹיֹם ואין זולתכה ומה הוא איש תהו וֹבֹעֹל הבל להתבונֹן במעשי פלאֹך

36   *vacat*   הֹגֹדֹוֹלֹיֹם

37   אֹוֹדֹכֹה אדונֹי כֹי לוא ^{הֹפֹלֹתֹה} גֹוֹרֹלֹי בֹ{יֹ}^{עֹ}דת שו ובסוד נֹעֹלֹמֹיֹם לֹא שמתה חוקֹי

38   וֹתֹקֹרֹאֹנֹי לחסדיכה ולסליחוֹ[תיכה ה]בֹיֹאֹ[ות]נֹי וֹבֹהֹמֹוֹ֝ן רחמיכה לכול משפטי

39   [צדק ואני אי]ש טֹמֹ]א ומרחם הֹוֹרֹיֹתֹי בֹאֹשֹמת מעל ומשדי אמי]בֹעֹולה ובחיק

40   [אומנתי לרוב נדה ומֹנֹעֹוֹרֹי בֹדֹמֹים ועד שיבה בעוון בשר   ואת]הֹ אֹלֹיֹ

41   [כוננתה רגלי בדרֹך לבכה ולשמועֹות פלאכה גליתה אֹוֹזֹנֹי ולבי להבין ב]אֹמֹתֹךֹ

COLUMN XVI

Parallels: 1QH^b 1 14 (dotted underline; line 1)
           4QH^b 10 7–12 (underline; lines 1–5)
           4QpapH^f 13 1–2 (broken underline; lines 9–10)
           1QH^b 2 1–2 (dotted underline; lines 13–14)

1   [אֹטֹומֹם אוזן בלמודיכה עד אשר   ורוח נעוה[

2   [בלוא דעת הכאתה מתכמי וכבוד לב   ]°°°°[   ]°[ואין לֹי עֹוד]

3   [למכשול עוון כי תגלה ישועתכה] וֹצֹדֹקתכה תכין לֹעֹד כי לֹא לֹא[דם דרכו]

4   [כֹול אלה לכבודכה עֹ]שֹיתה   *vacat*

5   אוד[כה אדֹ]וֹנֹי כֹי נֹתתני במקור נוזלים ביבֹשֹה ומבוע מים בארץ ציה ומשקי

6   גן וֹאֹגֹם °°°° הֹשֹדֹה מטע ברוש ותדהר עֹם תאשור יחד לכבודכה   עצי

7   חיֹים במעין רז מחובאים בתוך כול עצי מים והיו להפריח נצר למטעת עולם

8   להשריש טרם יפריחו ושורשיהם ליוֹבֹ[ל י]שלחו ויפתח למים חיים יגזעו

9   ויהי למקור עולם ובנצר עליו ירעו כול חֹ[יו]ֹת יער ומרמס גזעו לכל עוברֹיֹ

10   דרך ודליתו לכל עוף כנף וירמו עליו כול עֹ[צי] מַיֹם כֹיֹ במטעתם יתשגשגו

11   ואל יובל לא ישלחו שורש ומפֹריח נצר קֹ[ו]דֹש למטעת אמת סותר בלוא

12   נחשב ובלא נודע חותם רזו   ואתֹ[ה א]ֹל שכתה בעד פריו ברז גבורי כוח

13   ורוחות קודש ולהט אש מתהפכת בל יֹ[בוא ז]ֹרֹ בֹמֹעֹין חיים ועם עצֹי עֹוֹלֹם

14   לא ישתֹה מי קודש בל ינובב פריו עם מֹטע שחקים כי ראה בלא הכיר

15   ויחשוב בלא האמין למקור חיים ויתן יבֹ[ו]ֹל פרח עולם ואני הייתי לֹ[ב]ֹזֹאי לֹ{נֹ}יֹהרות

31. Indeed, who is like you among the gods, O Lord? Who has truth like yours? Who can be righteous before you when he is judged? There is no
32. utterance of the breath to offer in reply to your rebuke, and none is able to stand before your wrath. But all the children of
33. your truth you bring before you in forgiveness to cleanse them from their transgressions through your great goodness, and through your overflowing compassion
34. to station them before you for ever and ever. For you are the eternal God, and all your ways are established from age to
35. age, and there is none apart from you. And so, what is a person of nothingness and a possessor of vanity that he should contemplate your wondrous
36. great works? *vacat*
37. I thank you, O Lord, that you have not cast my lot in the assembly of fraud or put my portion in the council of the hypocrites.
38. But you have summoned me to your kindness, and to [your] forgiveness you have broug[ht] me and into your overflowing compassion for all [righteous] judgments.
39. [But I am] an uncl[ean per]son [and from the womb of the one who conceived me (I have lived) in faithless guilt, and from the breasts of my mother]in iniquity, and in the bosom
40. [of my nurse (attached) to great impurity, and from my childhood in blood guilt, and unto old age in the iniquity of flesh. But yo]u, O my God,
41. [have set my feet in the way of your heart. And you have opened my ear to reports of your wonders, and my heart contemplates] your truth.

Column XVI

1. [... I close (my) ear to your teachings until ... and an erring spirit]
2. [without knowledge you expelled from my innermost being and hardness of heart ...]°[...]°°°°[... and not for me any more]
3. [as a stumbling block of iniquity. Truly, you reveal your salvation,] and your righteousness you establish forever. Truly, [the way of] a hu[man] is not in his control.
4. [All these things for your own glory] you have [d]one. *vacat*
5. I thank [you, O Lo]rd, that you have placed me by the source of streams in a dry land, (by) a spring of water in a thirsty land, and (by) a watered
6. garden, and a pool °°°° the field, a planting of juniper and elm with cedar all together for your glory, trees of
7. life at a secret spring, hidden in the midst of all the trees by the water. And they were there so that a shoot might be made to sprout into an eternal planting.
8. Taking root before they caused (it) to sprout, they sent out their roots to the water cou[rse]. But it exposed its rootstock to the living waters,
9. which served as an eternal spring. All the an[ima]ls of the forest pastured upon its leafy shoot. Its rootstock was a grazing place for all who passed by on
10. the way, and its foliage was for every winged bird. And all the tr[ees] by the water towered over it, for in their plantation they grow tall,
11. but they do not send out roots to the watercourse. That which made the h[o]ly shoot sprout up into a planting of truth conceals itself, without
12. being much regarded and without being recognized, sealing up its mystery. And you, [O G]od, have hedged in its fruit by means of the mystery of strong warriors
13. and spirits of holiness, and the whirling flame of fire, so that no [stran]ger might [come] to the fountain of life, nor with the eternal trees
14. drink the waters of holiness, nor bear its fruit with the plantation of heaven. For he sees without recognizing,
15. and he considers without believing in the fount of life, and so he gives away the yi[el]d of the eternal bloom. But I became as things [wa]shed up by rivers

16 שוטפים כי גרשו עלי רפשם *vacat*

17 ואתה אלי שמתה בפי כיורה גשם לכול °[ ]° ומבוע מים חיים ולא יכזב לפתוח

18 ה֯שמ֯ים לא ימישו ויהיו לנחל שוטף ע֯[ל כול עצי] מים ולימים לאין חק֯ר֯[ ]

19 פיתאום יביעו מחובאים בסתר °[ ]° ויהיו למי מ֯ר֯[יבה לכול עץ]

20 לח֯ ו֯י֯בש ו֯מצולה לכול חיה ועצ֯[י]כ֯עופרת במים אדיר֯[ם]

21 ב֯ש֯ב֯י֯ב֯י֯ אש י֯בשו ומטע פרי °[מ]ק֯ור עולם לעדן כבוד ופא֯[רת עד]

22 ובידי פתחתה מקורם עם מפלגי[ ]ד֯ם לפנות על קו נכון ומטע

23 עציהם על משקלת השמש לא°[ ]°ו לפארת כבוד בהניפי יד ל֯עזוק

24 פלגיו יכו שרשיו בצור חלמיש ו[ ]°ו בארץ גזעם ובעת חום יעצור

25 מעוז ואם אשיב יד יהיה כערע֯ר֯[במדבר]ו֯גזעו כחרלים במלחה ופלגיו

26 יעל קוץ ודרדר לשמיר ושית ו°°[ ]שפתו יהפכו כעצי באושים לפני

27 חום יבול עליו ולא נפתח עם מט֯ר֯ °°[ ]° מגור עם חוליים ומ[ ]ע לב֯

28 בנגיעים ואהיה כאיש נעזב ביג֯ו֯ן֯ [ ]°° אין מעוז לי כי פר֯ח֯ נג֯[י]ע֯י

29 למרורים וכאוב אנוש לאין עצור כ֯ו֯ח֯[ותהי מה]ו֯מה עלי כיורדי שאול ועם

30 מתים יחפש ר֯וחי כי הגיעו לשחת חי֯[י]ת֯תעטף נפשי יומ֯ם ולילה

31 לאין מנוח ויפרח כאש בוער עצור בע֯צ֯מ֯י֯ ע֯ד ימימה תואכל שלב֯תה

32 להתם כוח לקצים ולבלות בשר עד מ֯ועדים ויתעופפו ע֯ל֯י֯ מ֯שברים

33 ונפשי עלי תשתוחח לכלה כי נשבת מעוז֯י מגויתי וינגר כמים לבי וימ֯ס

34 כדונג בשרי ומעוז מותני היה לבהלה ותשבר זרועי מ֯ק֯ניה ו֯[א]י֯ן להניף יד

35 ו֯ר֯ג֯לי נ֯לכד֯ה֯ בכבל וילכו כמים ברכי ואין לשלוח פעם ו֯לא מצעד לקול רגלי

36 ו֯ח֯זוק ז֯ר֯ועי֯ ר֯ו֯תקו בזקי מכשול ולשון ה֯גברתה בפי֯ ב֯לא נאספה ואין לה֯ר֯ים

37 ק֯ו֯ל ו֯ל֯ה֯א֯ז֯ין למודימ֯ לחיות רוח כושלים ולעות לעאף דבר נאלם מ֯זל שפתי

38 מפ֯ל֯צ֯ו֯ת֯ ב֯קו משפט לו֯ח לבי °ות°° °°°[ ]או במרורימ֯[ ]° לבב °°°כ֯רים ממשלת֯

39 ב֯יצ֯[רי]°לים וא[ני]ל֯[נ]פ֯ש התבלע֯ה

40 תכ֯[מיהם]° נאלמו כאין

41 °[ ] אנוש לאי[ן]

Column XVII

1 [ ] אפל֯ה֯ °°[ ]

2 [הופ]י֯ע ל֯מ֯ד֯נ֯ים בלילה ו֯ב֯°°°°[ ]

3 [ ]°°°[ ] ל֯אי֯ן רחמים באף יעור֯ר קנאה֯ ולכ֯לה °°°[ ]

4 משברי מות ושאול על יצועי ערשי בקינה תשא ו֯מ֯[טתי] ב֯קול אנחה֯

16. in flood, for they cast up their mud upon me. *vacat*
17. But you, O my God, have put in my mouth (words) like early rain for all °[…]° and a spring of living water that does not fail. When the
18. heavens open they do not cease but become a flowing river o[ver all the trees of] the waters, and to the limitless seas […]
19. Quickly the hidden things bubble forth in secret °[…]°, and they become waters of con[tention for every tree,]
20. green and dry, the deeps of the sea for every living thing, and the tre[es …] like lead in mighty waters […]
21. in flames of fire they wither. But the plantation of fruit trees °[…] eternal [fo]unt becomes a glorious Eden and [an everlasting] splen[dor].
22. And by my hand you opened their fount together with channels […]*dm* to face according to a true measuring line, and the plantation of
23. their trees according to the plumb line of the sun *l*’° […]°*w* for a glorious bough. When I stretch out a hand to hoe
24. its furrows, its roots strike into the flinty rock and[…]°*w* their rootstock in the earth, and at the time of heat it retains
25. strength. When I withdraw (my) hand, it becomes like a juniper[in the wilderness,]and its rootstock like nettles in salty ground. (In) its furrows
26. thorn and thistle grow up into a bramble thicket and a weed patch, and °°[…]its bank they change like rotted trees. Before the
27. heat comes its foliage dries up and does not open with the rain °°[…]° a dwelling with sickness and *m*[…]‘ heart
28. with afflictions. And I am like a man abandoned in agony […]°° without strength, for my af[fl]iction breaks out
29. into bitterness and an incurable pain so that it is not possible to keep (my) strength. [And dis]may [has come] upon me like those who go down to Sheol, and among
30. the dead my spirit searches, for [my] life has reached the pit […] my soul faints day and night
31. without rest. And it (i.e., my affliction) breaks forth like burning fire, enclosed in my bones. For many days flame devours,
32. putting an end to strength for ages and wearing out flesh until the appointed times. And breakers fly against me,
33. and my soul collapses within me to the point of extinction, for my strength has disappeared from my body, and my heart is poured out like water.
34. My flesh melts like wax, and the strength of my loins has turned to terror. My arm is broken from its joint so that the hand [can]not move.
35. My foot is held in a fetter, and my knees have become like water. It is not possible to take a step, nor is there any forward stride in the sound of my footfall.
36. And the strength of my arm they have bound with shackles that make one stumble. Though you made the tongue strong in my mouth, unrestrained, yet it is not possible to lift up
37. (my) voice or to make (my) disciples hear, in order to revive the spirit of those who stumble and to support the weary with a word. The utterance of my lips is silenced
38. by horror. They have laid waste the just claim of the tablet of my heart ᵕ*wt*°° °°°[…]’*w* with bitterness[…]° heart °°°*krym* dominion
39. with incli[nations of …]°*lym* And as for [me …]*l*[… s]oul engulfed
40. [their] inner[most parts …]° silenced as one without
41. °[…] humankind witho[ut]

Column XVII

1. […] darkness °°[…]
2. [… to shine] forth for discord at night and *b*°°°°[…]
3. […]°°°[…] without compassion. In anger he stirs up (his) fury, and for destruction °°°[…]
4. breakers of death, and Sheol (comes) upon my couch. My bed cries out in lamentation, [and my] pa[llet] with the sound of sighing.

5 עיני כעש בכבשן ודמעתי כנחלי מים כלו למנוח עיני ו֯[מעוז]י֯ עמד לי
6 מרחוק וחיי מצד ואני משאה א֯למשואה וממכאוב ל֯נ֯גע ומחבלים
7 למשברים תשוחח נפשי בנפלאותיכה ולא הזנחתני בחסדיכה֯ מ֯קץ
8 לקץ תשת˙ שע נפשי בהמון רחמיכה ואשיבה למבלעי דבר
9 ולמ֯שתוחיחי בי תוכחת וארשיעה דינו ומשפטכה אצדיק כי ידעתי
10 באמתכה ואבחרה במשפטי ובנגיעי רציתי כי יחלתי לחסדיכה ות֯ת֯ן
11 תחנה בפי עבדכה ולא גערתה חיי ושלומי לא הזנחתה ולא עזב֯תה
12 תקותי ולפני נגע העמדתה רוחי כי אתה יסדתה רוחי ו֯תדע מזמתי
13 ובצוק֯ו֯תי נחמתני ובסליח֯ו֯ת֯ אשתעשע ואנחמה על פשע ראשון
14 ואד֯עה֯ כ֯[י] יש מקוה ב֯ח֯סדיכה ותוחלה ברוב כוחכה כי לא יצדק
15 כול במ֯ש֯פ֯טכה ולא יזכ֯[ה]ב֯ר֯'בכה אנוש מאנוש יצדק וגב֯ר מ֯ר֯ע֯ה֯ו֯
16 ישכיל ובשר מיצר °[ ]° יכבד ורוח מרוח תגבר וכגב֯ו֯ר֯ת֯כ֯ה֯ אין
17 בכוח ולכבודכה אי֯ן֯[ו]לחכמתכה אין מדה ו֯לאמ֯ת֯[כה]°°°ם֯
18 ולכול הנעזב ממנה °[ ] ואני בכה הצ֯[בתי ידי ובחסדכה]
19 עמדי ולא המ֯°[ ]ב֯א֯נ֯שי ר֯י֯ב֯י֯ °°[ ]
20 וכזומם לי ת°[ ]° ואם לבושת פנים כו֯ל֯[ ]°°ב֯ו֯
21 לי ואתה֯ בר[ ]י֯תגבר צרי עלי למכשול למ֯°[לכ]ו֯ל֯
22 אנשי מלחמ[תי ולבעלי ריבי בו]שת פנים וכלמה לנרגני בי *vacat*
23 כי אתה אלי ˡמוע֯[ד] תריב ריבי כי ברז חכמתכה הוכחתה בי
24 ותחבא א֯מת לק֯ץ֯[ ] מועדו ותהי תוכחתכה לי לשמחה ו֯ש֯שון
25 ונגיעי למרפא ע[ולם ושלום]נ֯צח ובוז צרי לי לכליל כבוד וכשלוני לגבורת
26 עולם כי בשכ֯ל֯כ֯[ה הודעתני]ובכבודכה הופיע אורי כי מאור מחושך
27 האירותה ל°°°°°°[למח]ץ֯ מכתי ולמכשולי גבורת פלא ור֯ח֯וב
28 ע֯ולם בצרת נפ֯ש֯י֯ כ֯י֯[אתה מפלטי]מ֯נ֯וסי משגבי סלע֯ עו֯ז֯י ומצודתי֯ בכה
29 אחסיה מכול מכ֯א֯ו֯ב֯ [נפשי הושעתה] לי לפלט עד עולם כי אתה מאבי
30 ידעתני ומרחם [הקדשתני ומבטן] אמי גמלתה עלי ומשדי ה'ריתי רחמיך
31 {}לי ובחיק אומנתי֯ ר֯ו֯ב[חסד]י֯כ֯ה֯ ומנעורי הופעתה לי בשכל משפטכה֯

5. My eyes are as a moth in a kiln, and my tears are like streams of water. My eyes fail for (want of) rest, and my [strength] stands
6. far off from me, and my life is on the edge. But as for me, from disaster to desolation, and from pain to affliction, and from travails
7. to breakers my soul meditates on your wonderful deeds. In your kindness you have not rejected me. From season
8. to season my soul delights in your overflowing compassion. I will respond with an answer to those who would confound me
9. and with a reproach to those who are despondent on account of me. And his judgment I will declare wrong, but your decision I will declare right. For I know
10. your truth, and I choose my judgment and accept my afflictions, because I wait expectantly for your kindness. You put
11. a prayer of supplication in the mouth of your servant. And you have not reproached my life, nor rejected my well-being, nor forsaken
12. my hope. But in the face of affliction you have made my spirit stand firm. Truly, you yourself have established my spirit, and you know my thoughts.
13. In my distress you have comforted me, and in (your) forgiveness I take delight; so I am comforted concerning previous sin.
14. And I know th[at] there is hope in your kindness and expectation in the abundance of your strength. Truly, no one can be justified
15. in your judgment, and no one can be acqui[tted] in your proceedings. One person may be more in the right than another, and one man may be wiser than his fellow,
16. and a being of flesh may be more honored than a vessel of °[...]°, and one spirit may prove stronger than another spirit. But compared with your st[ren]gth there is none (equal)
17. in power, and your glory has no [..., and] your wisdom has no measure, and [your] truth [...]°°°*m*
18. and for anyone who is left far from it °[...] But as for me, in you [I have placed my hand, and in your kindness is]
19. my station, and not *hm*°[...] with the men who contend against me °°[...]
20. and when they plot against me *t*°[...]° and if for loss of face all[...]°°*bw*
21. to me, and you *br*[...] my adversary will [not] prevail against me as an obstacle *lm*°[... to a]ll
22. people who are at war [with me, and for my opponents lo]ss of face, and disgrace for those who complain against me. *vacat*
23. Truly, you, my God, at the appointed t[ime ...] you defend my cause. Indeed, in the mystery of your wisdom you reprove me,
24. and you conceal truth until (its) time[...] its appointed time. Your reproof will become a matter for joy and rejoicing to me,
25. and my afflictions a matter of et[ernal] healing [and] everlasting [well-being], and the contempt of my foes will become a crown of glory for me, and my stumbling, eternal strength.
26. Truly, by yo[ur] insight [you have instructed me,]and by your glory my light shines forth, for light from darkness
27. you cause to shine for °°°°°°[... for the inflic]ting of my wound, and for my stumbling wondrous strength, and an
28. eternal expanse in the constriction of my soul. Truly, [you are my place of refuge], my shelter, my stronghold, my strong crag, and my fortress. With you
29. I seek refuge from all the suffering [of my soul. You have come to] my [aid] as an everlasting deliverance. Truly, it is you who from (the time of) my father
30. have known me, and from the womb [you have sanctified me, and from the belly of] my mother you have nurtured me, and from the breasts of the one who conceived me your compassion
31. has been present for me, and in the bosom of my nurse was your great [kindness], and from my youth you have appeared to me in your wise judgment.

32 ובאמת נכון סמכתני וׄבׄרוח קׄודשכה תשעשעׄנׄי ועד היוםׄ [א]תׄהׄ תׄנׄהלׄנׄי
33 ותוכחת צדקכה עם נׄ[ע]וׄיתי ומשמר שלומכה לפלט נׄפׄשי ועם מצעדי
34 רוב סליחות והמון רׄחׄמׄים בהשפטכה בי ועד שיבה אתה תכלכלני כיא
35 אבי לא ידעני ואמי עליכה עזבתני כי אתה אב לכׄוׄל בׄנׄי אׄמתכה ותגל
36 עליהם כמרחמת עׄל עוׄלהׄ וכאומן בחיק תכלכל לכול מעשׄיכה *vacat*
37 *vacat*
38 בׄ[רו]ךׄ אׄתׄ[ה אדוני]לׄ[ ]°°°[ ]רׄ הגברתה עׄדׄ אין מספׄרׄ
39 [ולהל]לׄ שמכה בהפלא מאׄדׄ[ה]
40 [לא]יׄן השבת לׄ[ ]
41 [ולפי] שׄכלו יהלל[שמכה]

Column XVIII

Parallel: 4QH^{b} 11 1–2 (underline; lines 4–5)

1 [ ]
2 [ ]
3 [ב]מחׄשבׄתׄכׄה נהׄיׄהׄ כׄ[ול ו]בׄמׄזמת לבכה תׄוׄ[כ]ןׄ[ומבלעדיכה לא]
4 [יעשה]כׄוׄל ובלוא רצונכה לא יהיה ולא יתבונן כול בחוכׄ[מתכה]
5 וׄבׄ[סוד] רׄזיכה לא יביט כול ומה אפהו אדם ואדמה הוא חׄ[מר]
6 קורץ ולעפר תשובתו כי תשכילנו בנפלאות כאלה ובסוד אמׄ[תכה]
7 תודיענו ואני עפר ואפר מה אזום בלוא חפצתה ומה אׄתׄחשב
8 באין רצונכה מה אתחזק בלא העמדתני ואיכה אכׄשיל[3] בלא יצרתה
9 לי ומה אדבר בלא פתחתה פי ואיכה אשיב בלוא השכלתני
10 הנה אתה שר אלים ומלך נכבדים ואדון לכול רוח ומושל בכל מעשה
11 ומבלעדיכה לא יעשה כול ולא יודע בלוא רצונכה ואין זולתך
12 ואין עמכה בכוח ואין לנגד כבודכה וׄלגבורתכה אין מחיר ומי
13 בכול מעשי פלאכה הגדולים יעצור כוח להתיצב לפני כבודכה
14 ומה אפהוא שבלעפרו כי יעצור כׄוׄחׄ רק לכבודכה עשיתה כול אלה
15 *vacat*
16 ברוך אתה אדוני אל הרחמיםׄ וׄ[רב ה]חסד כי הודעתׄנׄי אלה לסׄפׄרׄ
17 נפלאותכה ולא להס יומם ולׄיׄלׄהׄ[ ]אׄ לךׄ כׄוׄלׄ הׄחיל °בׄ°רׄבׄ[ ]°°
18 לחסדכה בגדול טובכה ורוׄ[ב רחמיכה]אׄשתעשעה בׄסׄ[ליחותיכה]
19 כי נשענתי באמתכה [ו]°°כׄהׄ [ו]אׄיׄן °°°°°[בלא]
20 מצב°°כה ובלא ידׄכׄ[ה אין משפט ובלוא]מׄגערתכה אין מכשוׄלׄ[ואין]

3. Scribal error for אשכיל.

32. With sure truth you have supported me, and in your holy spirit you have made me rejoice, and until this day [y]ou continue to guide me.
33. Your just rebuke has been present when I was w[ay]ward, and your peaceful protection for the deliverance of my soul.
34. Abundant forgiveness and overflowing compassion accompany my steps when you judge me. Until old age you yourself sustain me. Truly,
35. my father did not acknowledge me, and my mother abandoned me to you, but you are a father to all the children of your truth, and you rejoice
36. over them as a woman who loves her nursing child, and like a foster-father you sustain all your creatures in (your) bosom. *vacat*
37. *vacat*
38. B[less]ed are yo[u, O Lord ...]*l* [...]°°°[...]*r* you have increased without number
39. [... and to prai]se your name when you act exceedi[ng] wondrously
40. [... with]out ceasing *l*[...]
41. [... and according to] his insight he will praise[your name ...]

Column XVIII

1. [...]
2. [...]
3. [... by] your plan eve[rything] comes to be, [and] in the intent of your mind it is de[ter]mined. [Apart from you no]thing
4. [is done,] and without your will nothing comes to pass. No one can contemplate [your] wis[dom],
5. and on your [secret] mysteries no one can gaze. What, then, is a mortal being—he is only dirt,
6. pinched-off c[lay], whose return is to dust—that you have given him insight into wonders such as these and that the secret counsel of [your] tru[th]
7. you have made known to him? As for me, dust and ashes, what can I devise unless you desire it, and what can I plan for myself
8. without your will? How can I take courage unless you cause me to stand firm? And how can I have insight unless you have formed it
9. for me? What can I say unless you open my mouth? And how shall I answer unless you give me insight?
10. Behold, you are the prince of gods, the king of the glorious ones, lord of every spirit, and ruler of every creature.
11. Apart from you nothing is done; nothing is known without your will; and except for you, there is nothing.
12. There is none beside you in strength, none comparable to your glory, and for your strength there is no price. Who
13. among all your wondrous great creatures can retain the strength to stand before your glory?
14. And what, then, is he who returns to his dust that he could summon such strength? For your glory alone you have done all these things.
15. *vacat*
16. Blessed are you, O Lord, God of compassion and [abundant] kindness, for you have made known to me these things so that (I may) recount
17. your wonders and not keep silent by day or night[...]' to you belongs all the strength °*b*°*rb*[...]°°
18. for your kindness in your great goodness and the abun[dance of your compassion ...]I take delight in [your] for[giveness],
19. for I have depended upon your truth. [And ...]°° your [and] there is no °°° °°[... without]
20. your *mṣb*°°, and without you[r] hand [there is no judgment, and without]your rebuke there is no stumbling, [and no]

21 נגע בלוא ידעתה ול[א יעשה כול בלוא רצו]נכה *vacat*
22 ואני לפי דעתי באמת[כה אזמרה בחסדכה] ובהביטי בכבודכה אספרה
23 נפלאותיכה ובהביני בס[וד פלאכה אוחיל]ל[ה]מון רחמיכה ולסליחותיכה
24 אקוה כי אתה יצרתה רו[ח עבדכה וכרצ]ונכה הכינותני ולא נתתה
25 משעני על בצע ובהון [חמס לא ל]בי ויצר בשר לא שמתה לי מעוז
26 חיל גבורים על רוב עדנים [וישתעשעו ב]רוב דגן תירוש ויצהר
27 ויתרוממו במקנה וקנין [ויפרחו כעץ ר]ענן על פלגי מים לשת עלה
28 ולהרבות ענף כי בחרתה[בם מכול בני]אדם ולהדשן כול מארץ
29 ולבני אמתכה נתתה שכל °°°[ ]°ת עד ולפי דעתם יכבדו
30 איש מרעהו וכן לבן אדם °[בא]יש הרביתה נחלתו
31 בדעת אמתכה ולפי דעתו י°ב°[כ]י נפש עבדכה תעבה הון
32 ובצע וברום עדנים לא °°°°° כי שש לבי בבריתכה ואמתכה
33 תשעשע נפשי ואפרחה כשושנה ולבי נפתח למקור עולם
34 ומשענתי במעוז מרום ו°°°° °°° °°° עמל ויבול כנץ לפני רוח
35 ויתהולל לבי בחלחלה ומותני ברעדה ונהמתי עד תהום תבוא
36 ובחדרי שאול תחפש יחד ואפחדה בשומעי משפטיכה עם גבורי
37 כוח וריבכה עם צבא קדושיכה בשמים ו[ ]שה
38 ומשפט בכול מעשיכה וצדק י°°[ ]ל
39]]°°°°°[[
40]]°תי
41]]°עוני

Column XIX

Parallels: 4QH[a] 1 1–7 (underline; lines 20–29)
4QH[b] 12 i 1–5 (dotted underline; lines 28–31)

1] [
2] [
3] [
4 בפחד מדהוב [ ]° עמל מעיני ויגון °[ ] מגויתי ובו°°°ן °°°[[
5 בהגי לבי *vacat* [ ] *vacat*
6 אודכה אלי כי הפלתה עם עפר וביצר חמר הגברתה מודה ואני מה כיא
7 [ה]בינותני בסוד אמתכה ותשכילני במעשי פלאכה ותתן בפי הודות ובלשוני
8 ת[ה]לה ומזל שפתי במכון רנה ואזמרה בחסדיכה ובגבורתכה אשוחחה כול
9 היום תמיד אברכה שמכה ואספרה כבודכה בתוך בני אדם וברוב טובכה

21. affliction without your knowing, and n[othing is done without] your [wil]l *vacat*
22. And as for me, according to my knowledge of [your] truth [I will sing of your kindness] and when I gaze upon your glory, I recount
23. your wonders, and when I understand [your wondrous] sec[ret counsel, I will wait expectantly] for your [ov]erflowing compassion. For your forgiveness
24. I wait hopefully, for you yourself have formed the spi[rit of your servant, and according to] your [wil]l you have determined me. You have not put
25. my support upon unjust gain nor in wealth [acquired by violence, nor …] my [hea]rt, and a vessel of flesh you have not set up as my refuge.
26. The strength of the mighty rests upon an abundance of luxuries, [and they delight in] abundance of grain, wine, and oil.
27. They pride themselves on property and acquisitions, [and they sprout like] a [fl]ourishing [tree] beside channels of water, putting forth foliage
28. and producing abundant branches. Truly, you have chosen[them from all human]kind so that all might fatten themselves from the land.
29. But to the children of your truth you have given insight °°°[…]°*t* everlasting, and according to their knowledge they are honored,
30. one more than the other. And thus for the mortal being °[… in a m]an you have made his inheritance great
31. through the knowledge of your truth. According to his knowledge *y*°*b*°[… f]or the soul of your servant abhors wealth
32. and unjust gain and does not °°°°° in the abundance of luxuries. Truly, my heart rejoices in your covenant, and your truth
33. delights my soul. I bloom like a lily, and my heart is opened to the eternal fount.
34. My support is in the stronghold on high, and °°°° °°° °°° trouble. And as a flower withers before the wind,
35. so my heart reels in anguish and my loins in trembling. My groaning reaches to the deep
36. and searches thoroughly through the chambers of Sheol. And I tremble when I hear of your judgments upon the strong warriors
37. and your case against the host of your holy ones in the heavens and […]*šh*
38. and the judgment upon all of your creatures, and righteousness *y*°°[…]*l*
39. […]°°°°°[…]
40. […]°*ty*
41. […]°*'wny*

Column XIX

1. […]
2. […]
3. […]
4. in terror, disaster […]° trouble from my eyes and grief °[…] from my body and *b*°°°*n* °°°[…]
5. in the meditation of my heart. *vacat* […] *vacat*
6. I thank you, O my God, that you have acted wonderfully with dust, and with a vessel of clay you have worked so very powerfully. What am I that
7. you have [inst]ructed me in the secret counsel of your truth and that you have given me insight into your wondrous deeds, that you have put thanksgiving into my mouth, pr[ai]se upon my tongue,
8. and (made) the utterance of my lips as the foundation of jubilation, so that I might sing of your kindness and reflect on your strength all
9. the day? Continually I bless your name, and I will recount your glory in the midst of humankind. In your great goodness

10 תשתעשע נפשי ואני ידעתי כי אמת פיכה ובידכה צדקה ובמחשבתכה

11 כול דעה ובכוחכה כול גבורה וכול כבוד אתכה הוא באפכה כול משפטי נגע

12 ובטובכה רוב סליחות ורחמיכה לכול בני רצונכה כי הודעתם בסוד אמתכה

13 וברזי פלאכה השכלתם ולמׄען כבודכה טהרתה אנוש מפשע להתקדש

14 לכה מכול תועבות נדה ואשמת מעל להוחד ע֯ם֯ בני אמתך ובגורל ע֯ם֯

15 קדושיכה להרים מעפר תולעת מתים לסוד א֯[מתכה] ומרוח נעוה לבינת֯כ֯ה֯

16 ולהתיצב֯ במעמד לפניכה עם צבא עד ורוחו[ת עולם] ו֯להתחדש עם כול ה֯[ווה]

17 ו֯נ֯היה ועם ידעים ביחד רנה *vacat* [ ]

18 [ואנ]י֯ אודכה אלי ארוממכה צורי ובהפלא֯[ ]

19 [ ] כ֯י ה֯ודעתני סוד אמת ו֯ב֯ר֯ז֯[י פלא השכלתני והבינותני בנפלאותיכה]

20 [ונס]ת֯ר֯ותי֯כ֯ה֯ גליתה לי ואביט ב֯[ ]◦◦י חסד ואדעה

21 [כ]י֯ לכה הצדק ובחסדיכה ישפ֯ט֯[ו]ה֯ וכלה בלוא רחמיך

22 ו֯אני נפתח לי מקור לאבל מרורים [ ]ו֯לא נסתר עמל מעיני

23 בדעתי יצרי גבר ותשובת אנוש א֯ת֯[בוננה ואכירה א]ב֯ל חטאה ויגון

24 אשמה ויבואו בלבבי ויגעו בעצמי֯ ל֯◦[ ]◦ים ולהגות הגי

ואנחה בכנור קינה לכול אבל יג֯[ו]ן֯[ ]

25 יגון ומספד מרורים עד כלות עולה וא֯[ין מכאוב]ואין נגע להחלות ואז

26 אזמרה בכנור ישועות ונבל שמח֯[ה ותוף גי]לה וחליל תהלה לאין

27 השבת ומי בכול מעשיכה יוכל לספר כ֯ו֯[ל נפלאותי]כ֯ה בפ֯י כולם יהולל

28 שמכה לעולמי עד יברכוכה כפי שכ֯ל֯[ם ובכול קצ]ים ישמיעו יחד

29 בקול רנה ואין יגון ואנחה ועולה ל֯א֯[תמצא עוד] ואמתכה תופיע

30 לכבוד עד ושלום עולום ברוך אתה֯[אדוני א]שר נתתה לע֯ב֯ד֯כ֯ה֯

31 שכל דעה להבין בנפלאותיכה ו֯[מ]ע[נה לשון ל]ספר ברוב חסדיכה

32 ברוך אתה אל הרחמים וה͏ח͏נינה כגדו[ל]כ֯[ו]ח֯כה ורוב אמתכה והמו[ן]

33 חסדיכה בכול מעשיכה שמח נפש עבדכה באמתכה וטהרני

34 בצדקתכה כאשר יחלתי לטובכה ולחסדיכה אקוה ולסליחות[י]כ֯ה֯

35 פתחתה משב֯רי וביגוני נחמתני כיא נשנתי ברחמיכה ברוך את֯[ה]

36 אדוני כי אתה פעלתה אלה ותשם בפי עבד֯כ֯ה֯ ה֯ו֯ד֯ו֯ת֯ ת֯[ה]ל֯[ה]

37 ותחנה ומענה לשון והכינותה לי פ֯ע֯ול[ת]

38 ואעצו[ר כוח]ל֯[ ]ב[ ]ל֯[ ]◦[ ]

39 ואתה֯[ ]

40 אמת֯[כה]

41 וא[ ]

42]◦◦◦ [ ]◦

10. my soul delights. I know that your command is truth, that in your hand is righteousness, in your thoughts
11. all knowledge, in your strength all power, and that all glory is with you. In your anger are all punishing judgments,
12. but in your goodness is abundant forgiveness, and your compassion is for all the children of your good favor. Truly, you have made known to them the secret counsel of your truth
13. and given them insight into your wonderful mysteries. For the sake of your glory you have purified a mortal from sin, so that he may sanctify himself
14. for you from all impure abominations and from faithless guilt, so that he might be united with the children of your truth and in the lot with
15. your holy ones, so that a corpse-infesting maggot might be raised up from the dust to the council of [your] t[ruth], and from a spirit of perversion to the understanding that comes from you,
16. and so that he may take (his) place before you with the everlasting host and the [eternal] spirit[s], and so that he may be renewed together with all that i[s]
17. and will be and with those who have knowledge in a common rejoicing. *vacat* [...]
18. [And, as for me,] I thank you, O my God, I exalt you, O my rock. And when you act wondrously[...]
19. [...] that you have made known to me the secret counsel of truth and [you have given me insight] into [wonderful] myster[ies, and you have let me understand your wonders,]
20. [and] your [hid]den things you have revealed to me, so that I have gazed upon [...]°°*y* kindness. And I know
21. [th]at righteousness belongs to you, and by your kindness [they] are judged [...]*h* and destruction without your compassion.
22. As for me, a fount of bitter mourning was opened to me [...]and trouble was not hidden from my eyes
23. when I knew the inclinations of humans, and I un[derstood] to what mortals return, [and I recognized the mour]nfulness of sin, and the anguish of
24. guilt. They entered my heart and they penetrated my bones *l*°[...]°*ym* and to utter an agonized moan
25a. and a groan to the lyre of lamentation for all gr[iev]ous mourning[...]
25. and bitter lament until the destruction of iniquity, when there is n[o more pain]and no more affliction to make one weak. And then
26. I will sing upon the lyre of salvation, and the harp of jo[y, and the timbrel of rejoi]cing, and the flute of praise, without
27. ceasing. Who among all your creatures will be able to recount al[l] your [wonders]? With every mouth your name will be praised.
28. For ever and ever they will bless you according to [their] insight, [and at all tim]es they will proclaim together
29. with a joyous voice. There will be no sorrow or sighing, and iniquity [will be found] no [more]. Your truth will shine forth
30. for everlasting glory and eternal peace. Blessed are you,[O Lord, w]ho have given to your servant
31. insightful knowledge to understand your wondrous works and [a ready an]sw[er in order to] tell of the abundance of your kindness.
32. Blessed are you, God of compassion and grace, according to the great[ness of] your st[ren]gth and the magnitude of your truth, and the abundan[ce]
33. of your kindness with all your creatures. Gladden the soul of your servant through your truth, and purify me
34. by your righteousness. Even as I waited for your goodness, so for your kindness I hope. By your forgiveness[s]
35. you relieve my pains, and in my troubles you comfort me, for I depend on your compassion. Blessed are yo[u,]
36. O Lord, for you have done these things, and you have put into the mouth of your servant hymns of pr[a]is[e]
37. and a prayer of supplication, and a ready answer. You have established for me the wor[k of ...]
38. And I reta[in strength] *l*[...]*b*[...]*l*[...]°[...]
39. And you[...]
40. [your] truth[...]
41. and ’[...]
42. °°°[...]°

Column XX

Parallels: 4QHª 3 1–3 (underline; lines 4–6)
4QHᵇ 12 ii 1–3 (dotted underline; lines 5–7)
4QHª 8 ii 10–21 (underline; lines 7–19)
4QHª 9 1–2 (underline; lines 32–33)

1]   [
2]   [
3]   [
4]   [° °]   °תרחבׄ נפשׄי[°ר ל   ]°[   ]°[   ]°[
ש]לום
5]   ה]בׄשמחה ו[ששון ואשב]הׄ לבטח במעון•קוׄ[דש•ב]שׄ{ו}קט ושלוה
6 [בשלו]םׄ וברכה בׄאהלי כבׄוׄדׄ וישועה ואהללה שמכה בתוך יראיכה
7 [למשכי]לׄ[ה]וׄדותׄ ותפלה ל^התנ^פל והתחנן תמיד מקץ לקץ עם מבוא אור
8 לׄממשׁ[לתו]בתקופות יום לתכונו לחוקות מאור גדול בפנות ערב ומוצא
9 אור ברשית ממשלת חושך למועד לילה בתקופתו ל^פנות בוקר ובקץ
10 הׄאספו ^אלמ^עונתו מפני{תׄ} אור למוצא לילה ומבוא יומם תמיד בכול
11 מולדי עת יסודי קץ ותקופת מועדים בתכונם באותותם לכול
12 ממשלתם בתכון נאמנה מפי אל ותעודת הווה והיאה תהיה
13 ואין אפס וזולתה לוא היה ולוא יהיה עוד כי אל ה{וׄ}ד{י}עות
14 הכינה ואין אחר עמו   ואני משׂכיל ידעתיכה אלי ברוח
15 אׄשר נתתה בי ונאמנה שמעתי לסוד פלאכה ברוח ק^ודשכה
16 [פ]תחתה לתוכׄי דעת ברז שכלכה ומעין גבורתׄ[כה   ]הׄ בׄתׄוך
17 [יראיכ]הׄ לרוב חסד וקנאת כלה והשבתׄ[   ]
18 [   ]לׄ[ ]בׄהדר כבודכה לאור עׄוׄלׄ[ם   ]
19 [מ]פׄחד רשעה ואין רמיה וׄ[ול   ]
20 [   ]מׄוׄעדי שממה כיא אין ע[וד   ]
21 [ו]אׄין עוד מדהבה כיא לפני אפכׄ[ה   ]
22 [   ]בׄ° יׄחפזו ואין צדיק עמכה[   ]כׄה
23 וׄ[ל]השכיל בכול רזיכה ולשיב דברׄ[על משפטיכה   ]
24 בׄתוכחתכה ולטובכה יצפו כי^א בחסׄדׄ[כה   כו]לׄ
25 יודעיכה ובקץ כבודכה יגילו ולפי °[כי]אׄ כשכלם
26 הגשתם ולפי ממשלתם ישרתוכה למפלג[יהם   לא ל]שׁוׄב ממכׄה
27 וׄלוא לעבור על דברכה ואני מעפר לקח[תני ומחמר ק]וׄרׄצתׄי
28 למקור נדה וערות קלון מקוי עפר ומגבלׄ[במים סוד רמ]ה ומדור
29 חושך ותשובת עפר ליצר חמר בקץ אׄפׄ[כה   י]שׁוׄב עפרׄ
30 אל אשר לקח משם ומה ישיב עפר ואׄפׄרׄ[על משפטכה ומ]הׄ יבין
31 [במ]עׄשיו ומה יתיצב לפני מוכיח בו וׄ°°°[   ]קׄוׄדש

Column XX

1. […]
2. […]
3. […]
4. […]° °[…]° my soul expands [… °*r l* …]°[…]°[…]°
5. [… *h*]with rejoicing and [joy. And I will dwel]l securely in a ho[ly] dwelling in a {pea[ceful]} dwelling [in] quiet and ease,
6. [in peac]e and blessing in the tents of glory and deliverance. I will praise your name in the midst of those who fear you.
7. [For the Instruc]tor, [th]anksgiving and prayer for prostrating oneself and supplicating continually at all times: with the coming of light
8. for [its] domin[ion]; at the midpoints of the day with respect to its arrangement according to the rules for the great light; when it turns to evening and light goes forth
9. at the beginning of the dominion of darkness at the time appointed for night; at its midpoint, when it turns toward morning; and at the time that
10. it is gathered in to its dwelling place before (the approach of) light, at the departure of night and the coming of day, continually, at all the
11. birthings of time, the foundations of the seasons, and the cycle of the festivals in the order fixed by their signs, for all
12. their dominion in proper order, reliably, at the command of God. It is a testimony of that which exists. This is what shall be,
13. and there shall be no end. Apart from it nothing has existed nor shall yet be. Truly, the God of knowledge
14. has established it, and there is none other with him. And I, the Instructor, I know you, my God, by the spirit
15. that you have placed in me. Faithfully have I heeded your wondrous secret counsel. By your holy spirit
16. you have [o]pened up knowledge within me through the mystery of your wisdom and the fountainhead of [your] pow[er …]*h* in the midst
17. [of those who fear yo]u, for abundant kindness, but also a zeal for destruction, and you have made an end[…]
18. […]*l*[…] with the splendor of your glory for an etern[al] light[…]
19. [… from] dread of wickedness, and there is no deception and [… *wl*]
20. […] appointed times of destruction, for there is no mo[re …]
21. [… and] there is no more oppression, for before yo[ur] anger[…]
22. […]*b*° they make haste. No one is righteous beside you[…]*kh*
23. and [to] have insight into all your mysteries, and to answer [concerning your judgments …]
24. with your reproach, and they will watch for your goodness, for in [your] kindness [… al]l
25. who know you. In the time of your glory they will rejoice, and according to °[… fo]r according to their insight
26. you bring them near, and according to their dominion they serve you in [their] division[s, neither]turning from you
27. nor transgressing your word. As for me, from dust [you] took [me, and from clay] I was [sh]aped
28. as a source of pollution and shameful dishonor, a heap of dust and a thing kneaded [with water, a council of magg]ots, a dwelling of
29. darkness. And there is a return to dust for the vessel of clay at the time of [your] anger […]dust returns
30. to that from which it was taken. What can dust and ashes reply [concerning your judgment? And ho]w can it understand
31. its [d]eeds? How can it stand before the one who reproves it? And °°°[…]holiness

32 [ ]° עולם ומקוי כבוד ומקור דעת וגבור֯ת֯[פל]א ו֯המה ל֯ו֯א

33 [יוכ]ל֯ו֯ לספר כול כבודכה ול˹ה˺תיצב֯ לפני אפכ֯ה֯ ואין להשיב ד֯ב֯ר֯

34 על בוכחתכה[4] כיא צדקתה ואין לנג֯ד֯כה ומ֯ה אפהו שב אל עפרו

35 ואני נאלמתי ומה א֯דבר על זות כדעתי˹דברתי˺מצורוק יצר חמר ומה

36 אדבר כיא אם פתחתה פי ואיכה אבין כיא אם השכלתני ומה אד[בר]

37 בלוא גליתה לבי ואיכה֯ אישר דרך כיא אם הכ֯י֯נ֯ו֯ת֯[ה פ]ע֯מ֯[י ומה]

38 תעמוד פ֯ע֯מ֯[י אין מת]חזק ב֯כ֯וח ואיכה֯ אתקומ֯ם֯[כיא אם]

39 וכול °°[ ]° פ֯ע֯מי בא֯[ין]

40 ה[ ]

41 כ°[ ]

42 ו°[ ]

Column XXI

Parallels: 4QH[a] 10 1–5 (underline; lines 11–16)
4QH[b] 13 1–2 (dotted underline; lines 18–25)
4QH[a] 11 1–5 (underline; lines 23–27)
4QH[a] 12 1 (underline; line 36)

1 [ ]

2 [פ]ש֯ע ילוד א֯[שה]

3 [ ]יכה וצדקתכה

4 [ו]א֯[י]כ֯[ה] א֯כ֯י֯[ר]ב֯[ל]וא ראיתי זות

5 [ואבין באלה בלוא השכלתני ואיכ]ה֯ אביט בלוא גליתה֯ עיני ואשמעה

6 [בלוא]°°°° השם [ל]ב֯בי כיא לערל אוזן נפתח דבר ולב

7 [האבן יתבונן בנ]פ֯ל֯א֯ו֯ת֯ ואדעה כיא לכה עשיתה אלה אלי ומה בשר

8 [כיא כ]ה֯ ל֯ה֯פליא ו֯במחשבתכה להגביר ולהכין כול לכבודכה

9 [ ]° ב֯צבא דעת לספר לש˹ב˺ר גבור˹ו˺ת וחוקי נכונות לילוד

10 [אשה ו]ה֯ב֯י֯אותה בברית עמכה ותגלה֯ לב עפר להשמר

11 [מן ול] מפחי משפט לעומת רחמיכה ואני יצר

12 [חמר ומגבל מים מבנה ע]פ֯ר ולב האבן למי נחשבתי עד זות כיא

13 [ת]ק֯נתה באוזן עפר ונהיות עולם חקותה בלב

14 [האבן ו]° השבתה להביא בברית עמכה ולעמוד

15 [במשפטי עדים]ב֯מכון עולם לאור אורתים עד נצח ונ֯ס֯ חושך

16 [ות°°ל לאי]ן֯ סוף וקצי שלום לאין ח֯[קר]°

17 [ ]ואני יצר העפר °°°[ ]

18 [ולבר]ך֯ ש֯מ֯כ֯ה אפתח פ֯[י א֯]

4. Scribal error for תוכחתכה.

32. […]° eternal and a pool of glory and a fountain of knowledge and [wond]rous power. They are not
33. [abl]e to recount all your glory or to stand fast before your anger. There is none who can reply
34. to your rebuke. Truly, you are just, and there is none corresponding to you. What, then, is he who returns to his dust?
35. As for me, I remain silent. What could I say concerning this? According to my knowledge I have spoken, a thing kneaded together, a vessel of clay. What
36. can I say unless you open my mouth? How can I understand unless you give me insight? What can I s[peak]
37. unless you reveal it to my mind? How should I walk the straight way unless you establ[ish my st]ep? [How shall]
38. [my] step stand [without (your) making it] firm in strength? How shall I raise myself up [unless …]
39. and all °°[…]° my step with[out …]
40. *h*[…]
41. *k*°[…]
42. and°[…]

Column XXI

1. […]
2. [… trans]gression, one born of wo[man]
3. […]your […] your righteousness
4. [… and] h[o]w can I dis[cern] un[l]ess I see this
5. [or understand these things unless you give me insight; and ho]w can I see unless you have opened my eyes, or hear
6. [unless …]°°°° my [m]ind was appalled, for to the uncircumcised ear the matter was opened, and the heart
7. [of stone perceives wo]nders. And I know that for yourself you have done these things, O my God. What is flesh
8. [that yo]ur […] to act wondrously, and by means of your plan to act mightily and to establish everything for your glory.
9. […]° with the heavenly host of knowledge in order to recount to flesh the mighty acts and the established statutes to one born of
10. [woman. And …]you have brought into covenant with you, and you have uncovered the heart of dust that it might guard itself
11. [from … and *l* …] from the snares of judgment corresponding to your compassion. And as for me, a vessel
12. [of clay and a thing mixed with water, a structure of d]ust and a heart of stone, with whom shall I be reckoned until this? Truly,
13. [… you] have set straight in the ear of dust, and that which will be forever you have engraved on the heart
14. [of stone. And …]° you have refrained from bringing into covenant with you, or to stand
15. [… in the judgments of witnesses]in the eternal dwelling for the light of dawn forever. And the darkness will flee
16. [… *wt*°°*l* witho]ut end and times of peace without li[mit …]°
17. […] and as for me, a vessel of dust °°°[…]
18. [… and to ble]ss your name I will open [my] mouth[…']

19 [ ]יׄצרׄ[ד אל°°]
20 [עפר תחה נה מלכודת נסתרה]
21 [ה נפ]רׄשה רׄשׄתׄ שׄ[וחה ובדרכיה צמי אבדון]
22 °°[ ]°°הׄ ואׄ[ ]°°ה נפתחה דרך ל°[ים להתהלך]
23 בׄנתׄיבות שלום ועם בשר להפליאׄ[כאלה כיא פן]
24 תׄהׄלׄכׄו פעמי על מטוני פחיה ומפרשי רׄ[שת וערמת איכה]
25 אשמר ביצר עפר מהתפרד ומת{ו}ך דונג בׄהׄ[מס לפני אש]
26 וׄמקוי אפרׄ איכה אעמוד לפני רוח סוערׄ[ה ואני יכינני ב]
27 וישמורהו לרזי חפצו כיא הוא ידע למ°[ל]
28 [ ]ר כלה ופח לפח יטמונו צמי רשעׄה °°[ ]
29 [ ]°ו בעול יתמו כול יצר רמיה כיא לאףׄ [ ]
30 [מגב]לׄ און ואפס יצר עולה ומעשי רמיה [ ]
31 [ ]°ע *vacat* ואני ׳צר ה°[ ]
32 [ ]°מה יתחזק לכה אתה אׄלׄ הׄדׄעׄוׄתׄ כׄוׄ[ל]
33 [ ] עשיתם ומבלעדיכה לוא פׄ°°°° [ ]
34 [ואני י]צׄרׄ העפר ידעתי ברוח אשר נתתה בי כׄיׄאׄ[ ]
35 [ ]°מה כׄ[ו]ל עולה ורמיה יגורו יחד לזדוׄןׄ[ ]
36 [כול מ]עׄשי נדה לתחלויים ומשפטי נגע וכלתׄ [עולם]
37 [ ]°°חׄ°°°°° ש°°°° לכה חמה וקנאה נוׄקׄ[מת]
38 [ ] יצר החׄמׄרׄ °[ ]
39 [ ]
40 [ ]
41 [ ]
42 [ ]

Column XXII

1 [ ]
2 [ ]
3 [ ]°י
4 [ ]°°°°
5 [ק]וׄדש אשר בשמים
6 [ ]גׄדולׄ והוא הפלׄא וׄהם לוא יוכלו
7 לׄ[הבין באלה ולספר נפלא]וׄתיכה ולוא יעצורו לדעת בכול
8 [ש]ב אל עפרו ואני איש פשע ומגולל
9 [ ]אׄשמת רשעה ואני בקצי חרון
10 [לה]תׄקומם לפני נגע ולׄהׄשמר
11 מׄ[תוד]יׄעני אלי כיא יש מקוה לאיש

19. [...]vessel [... *d 'l*°°]
20. [... dust ... *tḥh nh* ... a trap is concealed ...]
21. [... *h*] a net of the p[it is spr]ead out [and in its paths are the snares of Abaddon ...]
22. °°[...]°° *h w'*[...]°°*h* opened a way *l*°[...*ym* to walk ...]
23. in the paths of peace and with flesh to do wonders [like these, for ... lest]
24. my steps tread on the hiding places of its snares, and the places where n[ets] are spread out, [and the heap of ... How]
25. can I, as a vessel of dust, be preserved from being divided and from dissolving (like) wax when it m[elts before the fire ...]
26. and a heap of ashes. How can I stand before the stormy win[d ... And as for me, he will establish me in ...]
27. And he preserves it for the mysteries of his desire. Truly, he knows *lm*°[... *l* ...]
28. [...]*r* destruction and trap upon trap they hide snares of wickedness °°[...]
29. [...]°*w* with injustice, every deceitful inclination will be at an end, for to the anger [...]
30. [knead]ed with nought and nothingness, a vessel of iniquity and the works of deceit[...]
31. [...]°' *vacat* And as for me, a vessel, *h*°[...]
32. [...]° How shall he strengthen himself before you? You are God of knowledge, al[l ...]
33. [...] you do them. And apart from you no *p*°°°° [...]
34. [And as for me, a ve]ssel of dust, I know by the spirit that you have placed in me that[...]
35. [...]°*mh* ev[er]y iniquity and deceit they attack together presumptuously[...]
36. [all] unclean [de]eds for sicknesses and judgments of affliction and [eternal] destruction[...]
37. [...]°°*ḥ*°°°°° *ś*°°°° to you rage and aven[ging] jealousy [...]
38. [...] vessel of clay °[...]
39. [...]
40. [...]
41. [...]
42. [...]

Column XXII

1. [...]
2. [...]
3. [...]°*y*
4. [...]°°°°
5. [... ho]liness that is in heaven
6. [...]great and it is wonderful. But as for them, they are not able
7. to [understand these things or to recount] your [wonder]s or have the ability to know all
8. [... re]turn to his dust. I am a sinful man and one who has wallowed
9. [...]wicked guilt. And as for me, in the times of wrath
10. [... to] rise up in the face of affliction and to guard myself
11. from[... you te]ach me, O my God, for there is hope for a person

12 [ ]מׄעל ואני יצר החמר נשענתי

13 עׄלׄ זרׄ[ועכה החזקה ו]רׄגׄלי ואדעה כיא אמת

14 פיכה [וכול דברכה לוא ישוב]אחור ואני בקצי אתמוכה

15 בבריׄתׄ[כה]°מה במעמד העמדתני כיא

16 [ ]איש ותשיבהו ובמה יתׄ°°[ ]

17 [ ] הׄשׄ°°°תה עצמתה °°פׄ°[ ]

18 [ ]°ב יש° ללוא מקו[ה]

19 [ ] ואני יצרׄ[ ]

20 [פ]לׄגתהׄ[ ]

21 [ ]אׄ אשר °[ ]

22 [ע]רׄב ובׄוׄקר עם מׄ[בוא]

23 [נג]יׄעי גבר וממכאׄ[וב אנוש]

24 [תוצ]יׄאׄ בׄשמחהׄ[כיא לסלי]חׄות יצפו ועל משמרתםׄ יׄ[תיצבו]

25 וׄנדיבים לוא כׄ[לו]כׄיׄאׄ תׄגׄעׄרׄ בכול שטן משחית ומרצׄ[ ]

26 לי מאז כוננתי לׄ°[ ]°בה ואתה גליתה אוזני כ°[ ]

27 לוא יבוא כי °[ ]°אׄו אנושי ברית פותו בם ויבוא[ ]

28 במבניתי ותכמ[י בתו]כׄחות לפניכה ואני פחדתי ממשפטכהׄ[ ]

29 [לפ]נׄיכה ומי יזכה במשפטכה ומה אפה[וא]

30 [ ]°אנו במשפט ושב אל עפרו מה יׄבׄיׄ[ן]

31 [ב כיא אתה א]לׄיׄ פתחתה לבבי לבינתכה ותגל אׄוזׄ[ני]

32 [ ]וׄלהשען על טובכה ויהם לביׄ כׄ°°°[ ]

33 [ ]° ולבבי כדונג ימס על פשע וחטׄאהׄ

34 [עד]תומה ברוך אתה אל הדעות אשר הכינותׄ[ה]

35 [ ] ותפגע בעבדכה זות למענכה כיא ידעתי

36 [ולחסד]כׄה אׄחׄל בכול היותי ושמכה אברכה תמיד

37 [ ]מׄקׄוׄהׄ לׄעׄבׄדׄכהׄ וׄאׄל תעזובנו בקצי

38 [כ]הׄ וכבודכה וטוׄ[בכה]

39 [ ] על ב[ ]

40 [ ]

41 [ ]

42 [ ]

Column XXIII

Parallel: 4QH[b] 14 1–6 (underline; lines 12–17)

1 [ ]

2 אׄורכה ותעמד מא[ז]

12. […]disloyalty. And I, a vessel of clay, depend
13. upon [your strong] ar[m and …] my feet. And I know that your command
14. is true, [and no word of yours turns] back. And as for me, in the time allotted to me I hold
15. to [your] covenant […]°*mh* in the station in which you have installed me, for
16. […]a person, and you bring him back and in what *yt*°°[…]
17. […] *hš*°°°*th* you are powerful °°*p*°[…]
18. […]°*b yš*° without hop[e …]
19. […] And I, a vessel […]
20. […] you [di]vided[…]
21. […]' which °[…]
22. [… ev]ening and morning with the co[ming of …]
23. [… the afflic]tions of a man and from the suffer[ing of a person]
24. [you bring] forth with joy,[for] they look expectantly [for forgive]ness, and upon their lookout they [take their stand],
25. and the volunteers do not fa[il], for you rebuke every destructive adversary and *mrṣ*[…]
26. to me, from that time I was established *l*°[…]°*bh*, and you yourself have opened my ear *k*°[…]
27. it will not enter, for °[…]°'*w*, and the men of the covenant were deceived by them, and entered[…]
28. into my frame and [my] bowels [in re]proof before you. And I myself was terrified by your judgment[…]
29. [… befo]re you. And who can be cleared of guilt in your judgment? And what, then, is h[e]
30. […]°'*nw* in judgment, and who returns to his dust. What can he understa[nd]
31. [… for you,] O my [Go]d have opened my mind to your understanding, and you have opened [my] ea[r]
32. […]and to rely upon your goodness. But my heart moans *k*°°°[…]
33. […]° and my heart is like wax that melts because of transgression and sin
34. [… until]its end. Blessed are you, God of knowledge, because you have established
35. […] and this happened to your servant for your sake, for I know
36. [… and for] your [kindness] I wait with all of my being, and I bless your name continually
37. […]hope for your servant, and do not forsake him in times of
38. […]yo[ur …] and your glory and [your] goo[dness]
39. […] concerning *b*[…]
40. […]
41. […]
42. […]

Column XXIII

1. […]
2. your light, and you have set up from of [old …]

אורכה לאין השבׄ[ת]
כיא אתכה אור לׄ[ ]
ותגל אוזן עפרׄ[ ]תׄ ול[ ]
מזמה אשר הו°[ ]אׄ°°עׄ°° ותאמנה בׄאׄוׄ[ז]נׄ
עבדכה עד עולם °[ש]מׄועות פלאכה להופׄיׄע
לעיני כול שׄומעי[ ]בימין עוזכה לנהל כׄוׄלׄםׄ
בכוח גבורתכהׄ [יהל]ל שמכה ויתגבר בכבוׄדׄכׄהׄ
אל תשב ידכה מׄ[ל]הׄיות לו מתחזק בבריתכה
ועומד לפניכה בׄ[תמים כיא מק]ור פתחתה בפי עבדכה ובלשוני
חקקתה על קו מׄ[שפט למ]שמיע ליצר מבינתו ולמליץ באלה
לעפר כמוני ותפתׄחׄ מׄק[ור]להוכיח ליצר חמר דרכו ואשמ{ו}ת ילוד
אשה כמעשיו ולפתח מׄ[קו]רׄ אמתכה ליצר אשר סמכתה בעוזכה
לׄ[הרי]םׄ כׄאׄמתכה מׄבשר [ולספ]רׄ טובכה לבשר ענוים לרוב רחמיכה
[ולה]שׄבׄיׄע ממקור דׄ[עת כול נ]כׄאׄי רוח ואבלים לשמחת עולם
[ותפתח פי עבדכה]°תים ל[ ]לׄ[ ]לׄ[ ]
[ ]
[ ]
[ ]
[ ] יׄשׄמׄיׄעׄוׄ [ ]
[ ]° עׄוׄלׄם וׄשׄכׄלׄכׄהׄ [ ]
[ ]°בהׄ וׄבׄארצכה ובבני אלים יׄכבדׄ °[ ]קׄ[ ]אׄשר יעמׄ[ודו]
[לעד]לׄהׄללכה ולספר כולׄ כבודכה ואׄנׄי מה כיא מעפר לוקחתי ואׄ[תה]
[אלי] לׄכׄבׄודכה עשיתה כול אלה כרוב חסדיכה תן משמר צדקכה
[לפניכ]ה תמיד עד פלט ומלׄיׄצי דעתׄ עם כול צעודי ומוכיחי אמת
[בכול]פׄעׄמׄיׄ וׄמה עפר בכׄפׄיׄהׄםׄ[ומ]עׄשה אפר בידם לוא הנה ואתה
[תכנתה יצ]רׄ הׄחׄמׄר וׄמצורׄוׄקׄ עשיתה]לׄרצונכה ׄעל הבנים תבחנני
[ ] כׄגׄודׄלׄכה [שב א]לׄ עׄפרו ועל עפר הניפותה רוח
[קודשכה] בׄטיטׄ[ ]°° אלים להחיד עם בני שמים
[ ]°°[ ]עׄוׄלם ואין תשׄבת חושך כיא
[ ]וׄמאור גליתה ולוא להשיב
[רוח ק]וׄדשכה הניפותה לכפ{°}ר אשמה
[מ]שׄרתים עם צבאכה ומתהלכים
[ ]°בות מלפניכה כיא נכונו באמתכה
[ ]הׄפׄלתה אלה לכבודכה ומצורוק
[ ]לׄגׄוׄרׄל עול יצרׄ נׄתעב
[ ]°°[י]צׄרׄ נתעב
[ ]

3. your light without ceas[ing …]
4. Truly, with you is light *l*[…]
5. and you open the ear of dust[…]*t* and *l*[…]
6. plan that *hw*°[…]’°°‘°° and you entrusted it to the e[a]r
7. of your servant forever °[…] your wonderful [me]ssages to shine forth
8. to the eyes of all who hear[…]with your strong right hand to guide all of them
9. by your mighty power [… he will prai]se your name and magnify himself in your glory.
10. Do not remove your hand from[… so that] he may become one who holds fast to your covenant
11. and one who stands before you in [perfection. Truly,] you open [a foun]tain in the mouth of your servant, and upon my tongue
12. you have engraved ju[dgment] according to the measuring line [for the one who pro]claims to a (human) vessel from his understanding, and for one who interprets these things
13. to a being of dust like me. You open a foun[tain]in order to reprove a vessel of clay with respect to his way and the guilt of the one born
14. of woman according to his deeds, and (you) open the f[oun]tain of your truth to the (human) vessel whom you have sustained by your strength
15. in order to [rai]se up the herald of good news according to your truth, [and to tel]l of your goodness, to proclaim good news to the poor according to the abundance of your compassion,
16. [and to s]atisfy from the fountain of kn[owledge all the contr]ite in spirit and those who mourn (that they may have) eternal joy.
17. [And you open the mouth of your servant …]°*tym l*[…]*l*[…]*l*[…]
18. […]
19. […]
20. […]
21. […] they proclaim […]
22. […]° forever and your insight […]
23. […]°*bh* your land and among the divine beings he is glorious °[…]*q*[…] which shall sta[nd]
24. [forever]to praise you and to recount all your glory. But, as for me, what am I? Truly from dust I was taken. And y[ou,]
25. [O my God,] for your own glory you have done all these things. According to the abundance of your kindness set the guard of your righteousness
26. [before yourse]lf continually until there is deliverance. Truthful interpreters are with my every stride and reliable reprovers
27. [with all]my steps. What is dust in their palms[and a w]ork of ashes in their hand? They are nothing. But you
28. [have set right a ves]sel of clay, and a thing kneaded together [you have made] for your good pleasure. More than precious stones you have tested me.
29. […] according to your greatness [… one who returns t]o his dust. And over the dust you have spread [your holy] spirit
30. […] in the mud[…]°° gods to unite with the children of heaven
31. […]°°[…]forever, and there is no return of darkness, for
32. […]and the light you have revealed and not to return
33. […] your [h]oly [spirit] you have spread forth in order to atone for guilt
34. [… who s]erve with your host and walk
35. […]°*bwt* from before you, for they are established in your truth
36. […]you have wonderfully done these things for your glory, and a thing kneaded together
37. […]to the lot of iniquity, an abhorrent vessel
38. […]°°[…] an abhorrent [ve]ssel
39. […]

40 [ ]
41 [ ]
42 [ ]

Column XXIV

Parallels: 4QH^b 15 1–8 (underline; lines 10–15)
4QH^b 16 1–2 (underline; lines 36–37)

1 [ ]
2 [ ]
3 [ ]
4 [ ]°
5 [ ]°°[ ]°°
6 °°°שׂמֹ[ ]יצר בשר
7 עֹד קצֹ[ו]מֹי יועדכה
8 במשפטי[ ]ה למלאכי
9 עֹדֹ במשפֹ[ט] ורזי פשע להשנות
10 בשר באֹ[שמתם כיא]צ ויעופפו בה כול
11 מלאכי שמֹ[ים מקו]רֹם בעבותי רוח ותכנע
12 אלים ממכון [קודשכה והמה לוא ישר]תֹוכה במעון כבודכה ואתה
13 אדם על הכֹרֹ[כעוף] אסור עד קץ רצונכה
14 בֹל שלחֹ[ידו]רמות כוח ורוב בשר להרשיע
15 בקצֹ[י חרונכה °כה להפ]לֹאֹ להכין בסוד עמכה
16 [ ]°° הֹממזרים כי לֹ[וא]
17 [ ]° פֹגרים לֹלֹ[וא]
18 [ ]
19 [ ]
20 [ ]
21 [ ] צדקה וע°[ ]
22 [ ]°ב ^ש^לחת בעת עוונוֹתֹ[ ]
23 [ ]°ם כול שטן ומשחית [ ]
24 [ ]בֹרֹשתם ולשלחם גוי °[ ]°יכֹהֹ רשע
25 [ ]איש זידן בֹמרבי מעל ו°[ ]° בֹנֹגֹיֹעֹים ובמשפטים
26 לֹ[ ]°בים בבסר[5] כי כול רוחותֹ ממזרים להרשיע בבשר
27 ומֹ[ ]הרשיעו בחייהם וכ[ ]לֹ° כן רוחם להרשיע

5. בבסר = בבשר, as written elsewhere in the scroll.

40. […]
41. […]
42. […]

Column XXIV

1. […]
2. […]
3. […]
4. […]°
5. […]°°[…]°°
6. °°°*šm*[…]vessel of flesh
7. until the time[… and] who could summon you
8. in the judgments of[…]*h* for the everlasting angels
9. in the judgme[nt …] and the mysteries of transgression in order that humankind be changed
10. through [their] gu[ilt, for …]ṣ and in it fly all
11. the angels of heav[en …]their [sour]ce with clouds on the wind. You cast down
12. the heavenly beings from [your holy] place, [and they could no longer ser]ve you in your glorious dwelling. And you,
13. a man upon *hkr*[… like a bird] imprisoned until the time of your favor.
14. Not stretching out[his hand …]the strong heights and the multitude of flesh to declare guilty
15. in the time[s of your wrath … your ° … to do won]drously to determine in council with you
16. […]°° the bastards for n[ot]
17. […]° corpses n[ot] to
18. […]
19. […]
20. […]
21. […] righteousness and ʿ°[…]
22. […]°*b* to destroy at the time of punishments for sin[…]
23. […]°*m* every adversary and destroyer […]
24. […]in dispossessing them and sending them away, a nation °[…]° your […] wicked
25. […]insolent man with an abundance of treachery and °[…]° with blows and with judgments
26. *l*[…]°*bym* with flesh, for all the spirits of the bastards to act wickedly with flesh
27. and *m*[…]they acted wickedly during their lives and *k*[…]*l*° thus their spirit to act wickedly

28 עׄל[ ]°°°[ ]לׄ[ול]פׄלׄא רזיכה גליתה
29 לביׄ[ ]°אׄני לבשר ידעתי
30 כיאׄ[ ]םׄ עולה בקצ
31 כל[ות רשעה]יׄה ולכול מביט
32 [ ] ולואיכחד
33 מׄלׄפׄנׄיׄ[כ]וׄבדתה מבני
34 אל שוׄ[מעי ג]בׄולות עמים
35 לחזקם [ל]הׄרבות אשמה
36 בנחלתו °[ ]עׄזבתם ביד
37 כול מב°[ם]אׄ°°ד
38 תבאׄ°[ ]
39 עׄל[ ]
40 [ ]
41 [ ]
42 [ ]

Column XXV

Parallels: 4QH[b] 17 1–3 (underline; lines 7–9)
4QH[b] 18 1–5 (underline; lines 12–15)
4QH[b] 19 1–7 (underline; lines 22–26)
4QH[b] 20 1–4 (underline; lines 30–33)
4QH[a] 3 4 (dotted underline; line 34)

1 [ ]
2 [ ]
3 [מש]פׄט צדק בׄ[ ]
4 [ ]°° וׄלהפרידם ממעמד קׄדׄ[ושים]
5 [ ]ות עם עדׄת קדושיכה בהפלא[ ]
6 עׄדׄ עׄולם ורוחות רשעה תבית מא[מעשי]
7 רׄעׄ לוא יהיו עוד ותשם מקום רשׁ[עה להפיל גורלות] כול
8 רׄוחות עולה אשר יושדו לאבל [ ]הׄ
9 יעגׄן לדורי נצח וברום רשעה למ[ ]
10 יׄרבה אנינם לכלה ונגד כול מעשׂכׄ[ה]°°
11 חסדיכה ולדעת כול בכבודכה ולפיׄ[מ]וׄעד הׄ[ו]דׄעתה
12 משפט אמתכה ואוזן בשר גליתה ו[הבינותה] לאנׄוש במזמת
13 לבכה וקצ תעודה השכלתה לבשׂ[ר בצ]בׄא המׄרׄוׄם תשׁפוט במרום
14 וביושבי האדמה על האדמה וגם[בשאו]לׄ תחתיה תׄשׄפׄ[ו]טׄ וׄביושבי
15 חושך תריב להצדׄ[י]קׄ צׄדיק ולהר[שיע רשע]כׄיא אין מבׄ[לעדי]כׄהׄ

28. *‘l*[...]°°°[...]*l*[... and as] a wonder you revealed your mysteries
29. to my mind[...]°*’ny* to flesh. I know
30. that[...]*m* iniquity in the time of
31. the utter destruc[tion of wickedness ...]*yh* and to every one who looks upon
32. [...] and it will not be concealed
33. from the presence of[...]you are [ho]nored more than the sons of
34. God who he[ar ... the bo]undaries of the peoples
35. to strengthen them [... to] increase guilt
36. in his inheritance °[...]you abandoned them into the power of
37. all *mb*°[... *m* ...]*’*°°*d*
38. *tb’*°[...]
39. *‘l*[...]
40. [...]
41. [...]
42. [...]

Column XXV

1. [...]
2. [...]
3. [...] right [judg]ment *b*[...]
4. [...]°° and to scatter them from the station of the ho[ly ones ...]
5. [...]*wt* with the congregation of your holy ones in doing wondrously[...]
6. forever. And wicked spirits you will cause to dwell away from ’[... works of]
7. evil will exist no longer. And you will destroy the place of wick[edness, casting lots ...] all
8. the spirits of iniquity who will be devastated by sorrow [...]*h*
9. he will be confined for everlasting generations. And when wickedness rises up to *m*[...]
10. their lamentation will grow great to utter destruction. But before all yo[ur] works [...]°°
11. your kindness and to know everything by means of your glory and according to[... the ap]pointed time. You ma[de] known
12. your true judgment. And you opened the ear of flesh and [... you gave] to humanity [insight] into the plan of
13. your mind, and you caused fles[h] to understand the appointed time. [The h]ost of heaven you will judge in heaven
14. and the inhabitants of the earth upon the earth. And also [in Sheo]l below you will judge. Against the inhabitants
15. of darkness you will bring suit, to declare inno[ce]nt the righteous and declare gu[ilty the wicked], for there is none ap[art from] you.

16 ולוא להפרד מ[   ]דברכה [   ]תֿ אֿ[[

17 לֿ]   [

18   ]   [

19   ]   [

20   ]   [

21   ]   [

22   ]   לבני °°   [°

23 [וגם רוחות   מחושך]

24 [וי°   ס ונמארים   [

25 לבֿלֿ]תי   רשעתם בחכמת כבדכ]הֿ ולוֿאֿ יכֿיֿרוֿ]כול]

26 מֿעֿשֿיֿ] צדקכה לעוון   בעדת בני ש]מֿים ובסוד קד]ושים]

27 יתרוממֿ]ו   [°°°°°°]   [

28 עצה ו]°   [

29 משרתים]   [וֿ

30 והכירום]   ס ירננו [לֿ]זֿ[מֿֿ]ֿרֿ

31 ולהלל לֿ]   לאין השבת ואני יצר החמ]רֿ כדעתי

32 ספרתי בֿעֿד]ת קדושיכה בהגדל והפלא לאל   כיא את]הֿ אל

33 הדעות בֿפֿיֿ [עוז מֿנשף לערב אברכה שמכה   vacat   [

34 למשכיל מזֿמֿ]ור שֿיֿר לֿ   [°°°כֿה

35 כיֿא]   ]° מלכי קדם

36]°   [נֿהֿמתי

37]   א]תֿרוממֿהֿ

38   ]   [

39   ]   [

40   ]   [

41   ]   [

42   ]   [

Column XXVI

Parallels: 4QH^e 1 1–9 (dotted underline; lines 2–9)

         4QH^a 7 i 6–23 (underline; lines 3–19)

         4QH^a 7 ii 3–23 (underline; lines 21–42)

         4QH^e 2 1–9 (dotted underline; lines 20–29)

         4QH^b 21 1–5 (broken underline; lines 38–42)

1   ]   [

2   ]   קוֿדש °   נבזה כמוני   [

3   [כמוני וחדל הרע ידמה בי   תדמה]

16. And not to be scattered from [...] your word [...]° *t* '[...]
17. *l*[...]
18. [...]
19. [...]
20. [...]
21. [...]
22. [... to the children of °° ... °]
23. [and also spirits of ... from darkness]
24. [and *y*° ... *m* and the malignant ones ...]
25. with[out ... their wickedness in yo]ur [glorious] wisdom, and they will not recognize [all]
26. [your righteous] deeds [for iniquity ... In the congregation of the children of he]aven, and in the council of the ho[ly ones]
27. [they] will be exalted [...]°°°°°°[...]
28. council and °[...]
29. those who serve [...]*n*
30. and they recognize them [... *m* they jubilate,] s[in]ging
31. and praising *l*[... without ceasing. And as for me, a vessel of cla]y, according to my knowledge
32. I have spoken in the congregat[ion of your holy ones, ascribing greatness and wonder to God, for yo]u are a God
33. of knowledge. With a [strong] voice [from dawn to evening I will bless your name. *vacat*]
34. For the Instructor, a melo[dy, a song for ...]°°°*kh*
35. for [...]° kings of the east
36. °[...] I shout
37. [... I] exalt myself
38. [...]
39. [...]
40. [...]
41. [...]
42. [...]

Column XXVI

1. [...]
2. [... holiness ° ... despised like me ...]
3. [like me and evil ceases. It will be like me ... will be like]

4 [בהוריתי ומי ישוה ל   מי כמוני]

5 [באלים ל   מזל שפתי מי יכיל מי בלשון]

6 יו[ע]דני   ידיד המלך רע לקדושים ולוא]

7 יבוא [ולכבודי לוא ידמה כיא אני עם אלים מעמדי]

8 וכבוד [ר לוא בפז אכ°° לי וכתם או ביורים לוא   ]

9 בי וה°[לוא יחשב בי זמרו ידידים שירו למלך הכבוד]

10 שמח[ו בעדת אל הרנינו באהלי ישועה הללו במעון קודש]

11 רוממו [יחד בצבא עולם הבו גדול לאלנו וכבוד למלכנו הקדישו]

12 ש[מו בשפתי עוז ולשון נצח הרימו לבד קולכם בכול קצים]

13 השמ[יעו הגי רנה הביעו בשמחות עולמים ואין השבת השתחוו]

14 ביחד [קהל   ברכו המפליא גאות ומודיע עוז ידו לחתום]

15 רזים ולגלות נסתרות לה[רים כושלים ונופליהם לשב לכת קוי דעות]

16 [ולהש]פיל נועדת רום גאים[עולם להתם רזי הוד ולהקים פלאות כבוד]

17 [השופט באף כ]ל[ה]ל° [בחסד צדקה וברוב]

18 [רחמים תחנה   רחמים למפרי טוב גודלו]

19 [ומקור   ]

20 [ותמה רשעה]

21 [ושבתה מדהבה שבת נוגש]

22 [בזעם   כלתה רמיה ואין נעוות בלוא דעת]

23 [הופיע אור ושמחה תביע אבד אבל ונס יגון הופיע שלום]

24 [שבת פחד נפתח מקור לברכת עד ומרפא בכול קצי עולם כלה]

25 [עוון שבת נגע לאין מחלה נאספה עולה ואשמה לוא תהיה]

26 עוד [הש]מ[יעו] ואמר[ו גדול אל עושה פלא כיא השפיל גבהות]

27 רום לאין שרית וירו[ם מעפר אביון לרום עולם ועד שחקים]

28 יגביה בקומה ועם [אלים בעדת יחד ורפ°   אף לכלת]

29 עולם וכישלי ארץ יר[ים לאין מחיר וגבורת עד עם מצעדם]

30 ושמחת עולם במכוניהם[כבוד נצח ואין השבת לעולמי עד]

31a [יומרו ברוך אל המפלי פלאות גאות ומגדיל]

31 להודיע גבורה ומצדי[ק בדעת לכול מעשיו וטוב על פניהם]

32 בדעתם ברוב חסדיו[והמון רחמיו לכול בני אמתו ידענוכה]

33 אל הצדק והשכלנו בא[מתכה מלך הכבוד כיא ראינו קנאתכה]

34 בכוח גבורה והכר[נו משפטיכה בהמון רחמים והפלא סליחות]

35 מה בשר לאלה ומ[ה יחשב עפר ואפר לספר אלה מקץ לקץ]

36 ולהתיצב במעמד[לפניכה ולבוא ביחד עם בני שמים ואין מליץ]

37 להשיב דבר כפיכה ו[לכה כיא העמדתנו]

38 לרצ[ונכ]ה ב°°[ונעצור כוח לשמוע]

39 [נפלאות כאלה   דברנו לכה ולוא]

4. [my teaching. And who can compare to … Who is like me]
5. [among the divine beings? *l* … the utterance of my lips who can sustain? Who in speech]
6. is com[pa]rable [to me? … beloved of the king, companion to the holy ones. And it will not]
7. come [… and to my glory it will not compare. For, as for me, my station is with the divine beings]
8. and glory [… *r* not with fine gold I will *k*°° for myself, and gold or precious stone not …]
9. with me. And *h*°[… will not be reckoned with me. Sing praise, O beloved ones! Sing to the king of glory!]
10. Rejoic[e in the congregation of God! Cry gladly in the tents of salvation! Give praise in the holy dwelling!]
11. Exalt [together with the eternal host! Ascribe greatness to our God and glory to our king! Sanctify]
12. [his] na[me with strong lips and a mighty tongue! Lift up your voices by themselves at all times!]
13. Sound al[oud a joyful noise! Exult with eternal joy and without ceasing! Worship]
14. in common [assembly! … Bless the one who wondrously does majestic deeds and who makes known the strength of his hand, sealing up]
15. mysteries and revealing hidden things, rai[sing up those who stumble and those among them who fall, restoring the steps of those who wait for knowledge]
16. [but bringing] low the lofty assemblies of the [eternally] proud,[bringing to completion splendid mysteries and raising up glorious wonders.]
17. [(Bless) the one who judges with des]tr[uctive wrath] *l*° [… with kindness, righteousness, and with an abundance of]
18. [compassion, supplication … compassion for those who frustrate his great goodness]
19. [and a source of …]
20. [… and wickedness comes to an end]
21. [… and disaster ceases; the oppressor ceases]
22. [with indignation … deceit ends, and there are no senseless perversities]
23. [Light appears, and joy pours forth. Sorrow perishes, and grief flees. Peace appears,]
24. [terror ceases, and a source of everlasting blessing is opened and healing in all the times of eternity. Iniquity]
25. [ends; affliction ceases, so that there is no more sickness. Injustice is taken away, and guilt will exist no]
26. longer. [Pro]c[laim] and declar[e: Great is God who does wonders, for he brings low the haughtiness of]
27. pride, so that there is no remainder. But he lif[ts up the poor one from the dust to the eternal height, and to the clouds]
28. he makes him tall in stature, and (he is) with [the divine beings in the congregation of the community. And *rp*° … wrath for] eternal
29. [destruction.] And those who stumble to the ground he rai[ses up without price, and everlasting power is with their step]
30. and eternal joy in their dwellings,[everlasting glory without ceasing for ever and ever.]
31a. [Let them say, Blessed is God who works exalted wonders, acting mightily]
31. <to make known (his) power> and acting righteou[sly in the knowledge of all his creatures and (with) goodness toward them,]
32. so that they might know the magnitude of his kindness[and the abundance of his compassion for all the children of his truth. We know you]
33. God of righteousness, and we understand [your] tr[uth, O king of glory, for we see your zeal]
34. with (your) powerful strength. And[we] recognize [your judgments in the overflowing of compassion and wonderful forgiveness.]
35. What is flesh in relation to these things? And h[ow is dust and ashes to be reckoned that it should recount these things continually]
36. or take (its) station[before you or come into community with the children of heaven? There is no mediator]
37. to answer at your command or[… to you, for you have established us]
38. at [you]r good fav[or] *b*°°[… and we possess strength to hear]
39. [wonders such as these … We speak to you and not]

40 [לאיש בינים   והטיתה אוזן למוצא]
41 [שפתינו השמיעו ואמורו ברוך אל עליון הנוטה שמים בכוחו]
42 [וכול מחשביהם מכין בעוזו ארץ בגבורתו עושה   ]

Column XXVII

12 [ ]°יםׄ לׄ]
13 רציתה ב°]
14 בלוא °°]

Column XXVIII

11 ע]פׄר כמוני °]
12 [כׄבודכׄהׄ °]
13 [מכה בהפלא ואׄ°]
14 ק]וׄדש על ידי גבורתׄ[כה
15 [בפיׄ]   [לׄ]

Fragment A1

1 [מ]שפטכ[ה
2 [°]

Fragment A2

1 [ךׄ אתחנן]
2 [מענׄהׄ [לשון
3 [°° °]

Fragment A3

1 [°°°° °°°
2 [° נהיה בתבל
3 [°° לאנׄשיׄ בׄרׄיתׄךׄ

Fragment A4

1 [עׄוון ואׄשׄ[מה
2 [אׄ כי אין פ[ה
3 [°°° ותודיעׄ[ני

40. [to an intermediary ... And you inclined an ear to the utterance]
41. [of our lips. Declare and say: Blessed be God Most High who stretches out the heavens by his might]
42. [and establishes all their structures by his strength, who makes the earth through his power ...]

Column XXVII

12. [...]°*ym l*[...]
13. you were pleased with °[...]
14. without °°[...]

Column XXVIII

11. [... d]ust like me °[...]
12. [...]your glory °[...]
13. [...]your [...]*m* in working wonders and ’°[...]
14. [... ho]liness on account of [your] mighty hands[...]
15. [...] at the command of[...]*l*[...]

Fragment A1

1. ...] yo[ur ju]dgment [...
2. ...]°[...

Fragment A2

1. ...]*k* I appeal for mercy [...
2. ...] a [ready] reply [...
3. ...]°° °[...

Fragment A3

1. ...]°°°° °°°
2. ...]° will occur in the world
3. ...]°° to the men of your covenant

Fragment A4

1. ...] iniquity and gui[lt ...
2. ...]’ for there is no sp[eech ...
3. ...]°°° and you caused [me] to understand [...

Fragment A5

קד]ושיכה ובפק[וד 1
]לׄ[ ]כה בני אׄ[2

Fragment A6

]קׄדׄושׄים [1
]יברכו שמכׄהׄ בׄ[2

Fragment A7

]בׄיׄנׄה בׄלׄ[ב 1
] כׄבודׄ ולספר גׄבׄוׄ[רותיך 2

Fragment A8

ל]סׄפר °°[1
כ]וׄל אלה ואדׄעׄה כׄיׄ בׄ[2
]°°°°°°°°°° בש[3
]לׄ° °לׄ[ ]לׄ[4

Fragment C1

]°°[1
גד]וׄל רׄחמיׄ[כה 2
הו]דׄעתה א[לה 3
ת]עׄות מרמׄ[ה 4
]° מׄעׄנׄה[5

Fragment C2

]°שלׄ°[1
י]אׄירו כשמשׄ[2
מ]עׄוׄן הקודׄ[ש 3

Fragment C3

] אבׄ°[1
]להב[2
]°°°°[3
]°° ולהבי[ן 4

Fragment A5

1. ...]your [hol]y ones and in vis[iting ...
3. ...]*l*[...]your [...] sons of ’[...

Fragment A6

1. ...] holy ones [...
2. ...] they will bless your name *b*[...

Fragment A7

1. ...] understanding with a mi[nd ...
2. ...] your glory and to recite [your] migh[ty acts ...

Fragment A8

1. ... to] recite °°[...
2. ... a]ll these things, and I know that *b*[...
3. ...]°°°°°°°°°° *bš*[...
4. ...]*l*° °*l*[...]*l*[...

Fragment C1

1. ...]°°[...
2. ... gre]at, [your] mercy compassion[...
3. ...] you [made k]nown the[se things...
4. ... er]ror, dece[it...
5. ...]° reply[...

Fragment C2

1. ...]°*šl*°[...
2. ... th]ey shine like the sun [...
3. ...] hol[y dw]elling ...

Fragment C3

1. ...] ’*b*°[...
2. ...]*lhb*[...
3. ...]°°°°[...
4. ...]°° and to underst[and ...

5 ע]דׄ קץ משפטכהׄ[
6]לרוות ב°°°°[

FRAGMENT C4

1 להב]יׄןׄ בׄתׄשׄוׄבׄתׄ[
2 מע]מׄדׄיׄ בׄלׄוׄא תוׄ[
3]עׄד קץ תשובׄ[ה
4]יׄרׄים למׄ°[
5]°לׄקׄצׄ[

FRAGMENT C5

1]°°° [
2]°°מ[
3]שׄל ע°[
4] °°מׄ°°[
5]°°°עׄ°[

FRAGMENT C6

1 [ ] °°°°°[
2 כׄיׄאׄ מאו[ר
3 וׄלטהר נׄמׄהׄ[רי
4 ברצונכהׄ[

FRAGMENT C7

1]°°°°°°°[
2 ת]פתח לוחות °[
3]° מע°[

FRAGMENT C8

1]°י °[
2] *vacat* [
3]°תה בלו[א
4]°°[

5. … un]til the time of your judgment […
6. …] to saturate *b*°°°°[…

Fragment C4

1. …] to under]stand the return of[…
2. …] my st[anding] without *tw*[…
3. …] until the time of return[ing …
4. …] *yrym lm*°[…
5. …]°to the time of[…

Fragment C5

1. …]°°°[…
2. …]°°*m*[…
3. …]*šl* ʿ°[…
4. …] °°*m*°°[…
5. …]°°°ʿ°[…

Fragment C6

1. […]°°°°°[…
2. For a lumina[ry …
3. and to purify those who are qui[ck of …
4. in your good favor[…

Fragment C7

1. …]°°°°°°°[…
2. … you] open the tablets °[…
3. …]° *m*ʿ°[…

Fragment C8

1. …]°*y* °[…
2. …] *vacat* […
3. …]°*th* witho[ut …
4. …]°°[…

Word List

אב father, ancestor (n)
12:35; 15:23; 17:29, 35

אבד to be lost, perish, destroy (v)
12:10

אבדון place of destruction, Abaddon (n)
11:17, 20, 33; [21:21] = 4QH[b] frg. 13 4

אביון needy, oppressed, distressed (adj)
2:27; 10:34; 11:26; 13:18, 20, 24; [26:27] = 4QH[a] frg. 7 2:8 = 4QH[e] frg. 2 7

אבל in mourning, mourner (adj)
3:17; 23:16

אבל sorrow, mourning, mourning ritual (n)
10:7 = 4QpapH[f] frg. 3 4; 19:22, 23 = 4QH[a] frg. 1 3; 19:25a = 4QH[a] frg. 1 4; 25:8 = 4QH[b] frg. 17 2; [26:23] = 4QH[a] frg. 7 2:5 = 4QH[e] frg. 2 3

אבן stone (n)
14:29; 21:12; 23:28

אגם pool (n)
14:29

אגף river bank (n)
11:30 = 4QH[b] frg. 5 4

אדון lord, master (n)
18:10

אדיר noble, mighty, majestic (adj)
10:37; 13:9; 16:20

אדם human, man (n)
4:39 = 4QH[b] frg. 1 1; 7:19 = 4QH[a] frg. 8 1:11; 7:25; 9:17, 29, 36; 10:27; 12:31, 33, 39; 13:13, 17; 14:14; 16:3 = 4QH[b] frg. 10 10; 18:5, 28, 30; 19:9; 24:13

אדם Adam (n)
4:27

אדמה ground, earth, land (n)
18:5; 25:14 (2x)

אדני Lord (n)
5:15; 6:19, 34; 8:26; [10:5] = 4QpapH[f] frg. 3 1; 10:22, 33; 11:20, 38; 12:6; 13:7, 22; 15:9, 29, 31, 37; 16:5 = 4QH[b] frg. 10 11; 18:16; [19:30] = 4QH[b] frg. 12 1:4; 19:36

אהב to love (v)
4:36, 40; 6:14, 21, 30, 32, 37; 7:22, 23; 8:25, 31, 35, 10:16

אהל tent, dwelling (n)
20:6; [26:10] = 4QH[a] frg. 7 1:14

או or (conj.)
[26:8] = 4QH[a] frg. 7 1:12

אולת folly (n)
5:20, 21

און iniquity, injustice, deception (n)
21:30

אוצר treasure, storehouse (n)
9:14

אור to be light, shine (v)
11:4; 12:6, 28; 17:27; C2 2

אור light (n)
8:14; 14:20; 15:27; 17:26; 20:7 = 4QH[a] frg. 8 2:11; 20:9 = 4QH[a] frg. 8 2:12; 20:10 = 4QH[a] frg. 8 2:13; 20:18; 21:15; 23:2, 3, 4; [26:23] = 4QH[a] frg. 7 2:4 = 4QH[e] frg. 2 3

אורתים early light (n)
12:7, 24; 21:15

אוש foundation (n)
11:14, 31 = 4QpapH[f] frg. 6 6; 11:36; 15:7, 12

אות sign (n)
7:33; 20:11

אז then (part)
14:32, 25; 22:26; 23:2

אזן to hear (v)
8:17; 12:18; 16:37

אזן ear (n)
6:13; 9:23; 14:7; 15:6; [15:41] = 4QH[b] frg. 10 6; [16:1] = 4QH[b] frg. 10 7; 21:6, 13; 22:26, 31; 23:5, 6; 25:12 = 4QH[b] frg. 18 1; [26:40] = 4QH[a] frg. 7 2:22

אזר to gird (v)
14:20

אחור back, behind (n)
5:35, 36; 22:14

אחז to hold, seize (v)
12:34; 13:32 = 4QH[c] frg. 3 3

אחר other, another (adj)
10:21; 12:17; 20:14

איך how? (part)
7:34

איכה how? (part)
7:27; 18:8, 9; 20:36, 37, 38; 21:4, 5; [21:24] = 4QH[b] frg. 13 8; 21:26

אין nothing, is not, without (part)
2:12; 7:16, 29, 36; 9:7; 10:28; 11:21, 28 (2x), 29; 12:21, 28; 13:22, 23, 30 = 4QH[c] frg. 2 10; 13:31, 36, 39; [13:39] = 4QH[c] frg. 3 12; 13:40, 41; 14:6 (2x), 10, 15, 16, 20 = 4QH[b] frg. 8 5; 14:21, 26, 30, 34, 35 (3x), 36; 15:14, 18, 20 (2x), 31, 35; 16:18, 28, 29, 31, 34, 35, 36, 40, 41; 17:3, 16, 17 (2x), 38, 40; 18:8, 11, 12 (4x), 19, 20; 19:25 (2x), 26, 29 = 4QH[b] frg. 12 1:2; 20:13, 14, 19, 20, 21, 22, 33, 34, 39; 21:16 (2x); 23:3, 31; 25:15; [26:13] = 4QH[a] frg. 7 1:17; [26:22] = 4QH[a] frg. 7 2:4; [26:25] = 4QH[a] frg. 7 2:6 = 4QH[e] frg. 2 5; 26:27 = 4QH[a] frg. 7 2:8 = 4QH[e] frg. 2 7; [26:29] = 4QH[a] frg. 7 2:10; [26:30] = 4QH[a]

frg. 7 2:11; [26:36] = 4QH^{a} frg. 7 2:18; A4 2

איש man, husband, human (n)
3:26; 5:34; 6:13, 18, 24, 25, 29, 31; 7:19 = 4QH^{a} frg. 8 1:11; 8:22, 29; 10:16, 18; 11:23; 12:21; 13:26; 14:14, 16, 21; 15:24, 25, 30, 35, 39; 16:28; 17:19, 22; 18:30 (2x); 22:8, 11, 16, 27; 24:25; [26:40] = 4QH^{a} frg. 7 2:21 = 4QH^{b} frg. 21 3; A3 3

אכל to eat, devour (v)
4:15; 10:28; 11:30 = 4QH^{b} frg. 5 4 = 4QpapH^{f} frg. 6 4; 11:31, 32; 13:25, 35; 16:31

אל no, not (part)
8:33 (2x), 36 (2x); 9:39; 22:37; 23:10

אל God, god, divine being (n)
3:19, 30; 5:12; [7:18] = 4QH^{a} frg. 8 1:10; 7:38; 9:28; 10:36; 11:4, 35; 12:13, 19, 32 (2x), 38; 13:13, 16, 20 = 4QH^{c} frg. 1 2:5; 13:34, 38; 14:23, 28, 32, 36; 15:13, 26, 31, 34 = 1QH^{b} frg. 1 5; 15:40 = 4QH^{b} frg. 10 5; 16:12, 17; 17:23; 18:10, 16; 19:6, 18, 32; 20:12, 13, 14; 21:7, 32; 22:11, 31, 34; 23:23, 30; 24:12, 34; [25:32] = 4QH^{b} frg. 20 3; 25:32; [26:5] = 4QH^{a} frg. 7 1:8 = 4QH^{e} frg. 1 4; [26:7] = 4QH^{a} frg. 7 1:11; [26:10] = 4QH^{a} frg. 7 1:14; [26:11] = 4QH^{a} frg. 7 1:15; [26:26] = 4QH^{a} frg. 7 2:7 = 4QH^{e} frg. 2 6; [26:28] = 4QH^{a} frg. 7 2:9 = 4QH^{e} frg. 2 8; [26:31a] = 4QH^{a} frg. 7 2:12; 26:33 = 4QH^{a} frg. 7 2:14

אל to, toward, into (prep)
4:39; 8:35; 12:12; 13:17; 16:11; 20:10 = 4QH^{a} frg. 8 2:13; 20:30, 34; 22:8, 30; 23:29

אלה these (adj)
3:27; 5:24, 30, 31; 6:20; 8:24, 27; 9:23, 40; 13:5; 15:4; 18:6, 14, 16; 19:36; 21:7; [21:23] = 4QH^{b} frg. 13 6; 23:12 = 4QH^{b} frg. 14 1; 23:25, 36; 26:35 = 4QH^{a} frg. 7 2:16; [26:35] = 4QH^{a} frg. 7 2:17; A8 2; C1 3

אלם to be dumb, speechless (v)
15:4, 14; 16:37, 40; 20:35

אם if, whether (part)
5:33; 6:31; 12:32; 16:25; 17:20; 20:36 (2x), 37

אם mother (n)
17:30, 35

אמה female servant (n)
8:36

אמונה faithfulness (n)
4:26; 8:35

אמן to be reliable, to trust (v)
16:15; 20:12, 15; 23:6

אמן to guard, nurse (v)
15:24, 25; 17:31, 36

אמץ to be strong, courageous (v)
10:8 = 4QpapH^{f} frg. 3 5; 13:11 = 4QH^{c} frg. 1 1:3

אמץ strength (n)
10:10

אמר to say (v)
10:27; 12:18 = 4QH^{d} frg. 1 6; 12:36 = 4QpapH^{f} frg. 10 1; 26:26 = 4QH^{a} frg. 7 2:7 = 4QH^{e} frg. 2 6; [26:31a] = 4QH^{a} frg. 7 2:12

אמת truth (n)
5:20, 21; 6:13, 26, 31, 32, 36; 7:23, 36, 38; 8:22, 25 (2x), 34; 9:29, 32; [10:6] = 4QpapH^{f} frg. 3 2; 10:6 [deleted], 12, 16; 11:6, 35; 12:15, 26, 41; 13:5, 11 = 4QH^{c} frg. 1 1:3; 13:28; 14:12, 13, 15, 28, 29, 32, 41; 15:17, 23, 29, 31, 33, 41 = 4QH^{b} frg. 10 6; 16:11; 17:10, 17, 24, 32, 35; 18:6, 19, 22, 29, 31, 32; 19:7, 10, 12, 14, 15, 19, 29, 32, 33, 40; 22:13; 23:14 = 4QH^{b} frg. 14 3; 23:15, 26, 35; 25:12; [26:32] = 4QH^{a} frg. 7 2:14; 26:33

אנוש incurable, sick (adj)
13:30 = 4QH^{c} frg. 2 11; 16:29

אנוש man, humanity (n)
4:39; 5:14; 6:22; 7:26; 8:20; 9:27, 34, 36; 12:31, 32, 38; 16:41; 17:15 (2x); 19:13, 23 = 4QH^{a} frg. 1 3; 25:12

אנחה sighing, groaning (n)
13:15, 35 = 4QH^{c} frg. 3 7 = 4QpapH^{f} frg. 11 1; 13:36 = 4QH^{c} frg. 3 8; 14:27; 17:4; 19:25a = 4QH^{a} frg. 1 4; 19:29

אנחנו we (pron)
7:17

אני I, myself (pron)
4:33; 5:35; 6:23, 28, 36; 7:22, 25, 35, 38; 8:28, 37; 9:23; 10:13, 27, 30; 11:24, 25; 12:2 = 4QpapH^{f} frg. 7 4; 12:23, 31, 34, 36; 13:24; 15:4, 21; 16:15, 39; 17:6, 18; 18:7, 22; 19:6, 10, 18, 22 = 4QH^{a} frg. 1 2; 20:14 = 4QH^{a} frg. 8 2:17; 20:27, 35; 21:11, 17; [21:26] = 4QH^{a} frg. 11 4; 21:31; 22:8, 9, 12, 14, 19, 28; 23:24; [25:31] = 4QH^{b} frg. 20 2; [26:7] = 4QH^{a} frg. 7 1:11 = 4QH^{e} frg. 1 7

אניה ship (n)
11:7, 14; 14:25; 15:7

אנין lamentation (n)
25:10

אסף to gather (v)
13:16, 35 = 4QH^{c} frg. 3 6; 14:10; 16:36; 20:10; [26:25] = 4QH^{e} frg. 2 5

אסר to bind, confine, halt (v)
13:38; 24:13 = 4QH^{b} frg. 15 5

אף also, indeed (part)
7:34; 18:5, 14; 20:34; 22:29

אף nose, anger (n)
4:29; 8:34; 9:8, 39; 11:28 = 4QH^{b} frg. 5 2; 13:25; 17:3; 19:11; 20:21, 29, 33 = 4QH^{a} frg. 9 2; 21:29; [26:17] = 4QH^{a} frg. 7 1:21; [26:28] = 4QH^{a} frg. 7 2:10

אפלה darkness (n)
13:34 = 4QH^{c} frg. 3 5; 17:1

אפס end, nothing (n)
10:35; 11:31, 37; 14:20; 20:13; 21:30

אפעה wickedness, serpent(?) (n)
10:30; 11:13, 18, 19

אפף to surround (v)
11:29; 13:41

אפק to hold out, persevere (v)
6:15, 20

אפר dust, ashes (n)
18:7; 20:30; 21:26; 23:27

ארב to ambush (v)
13:12 = 4QH^{c} frg. 2 10; 13:29

ארי lion (n)
13:9, 15, 21
ארך to be long (v)
9:38
ארך long (adj)
4:29; 8:34; 9:8
ארך length (n)
5:35
ארץ land, earth (n)
5:26; 8:10, 21; 9:15; 11:33; 12:9, 27; 16:5 = 4QH[b] frg. 10 12; 16:24; 18:28; 23:23; 26:29 = 4QH[a] frg. 7 2:10 = 4QH[e] frg. 2 9; [26:42] = 4QH[a] frg. 7 2:23
אש fire, flame (n)
4:25; 10:28; 11:30 = 4QpapH[f] frg. 6 4; 12:34; 13:18; 14:21; 16:13, 21, 31; [21:25] = 4QH[a] frg. 11 3
אשה woman, wife (n)
5:31; 11:8; 21:2; 23:14
אשמה guilt, sin, offense (n)
5:32; 8:13; 12:31, 35, 38; 13:7, 9, 28, 38; 14:8, 11, 22, 25 = 4QH[c] frg. 4 1:12; 14:33, 35; 15:14; [15:39] = 1QH[b] frg. 1 11 = 4QH[b] frg. 10 3; 19:14, 24; 22:9; 23:13 = 4QH[b] frg. 14 2; 23:33; 24:10, 35; [26:25] = 4QH[a] frg. 7 2:7; A4 1
אשר which (part)
3:31; 4:21, 29, 33, 36 (2x); 5:24, 28 (2x), 36; 6:21 (2x); 7:24, 31, 32; 8:23, 26, 29, 30, 31; 9:16, 17, 36 = 4QpapH[f] frg. 2 1; 10:19, 34, 38; 11:21, 34, 39; 12:5, 11, 20, 22, 39; 13:11, 15; 14:10; [16:1] = 4QH[b] frg. 10 7; 19:30 = 4QH[b] frg. 12 1:4; 19:34; 20:15, 30; 21:34; 22:5, 21, 34; 23:6, 14, 23; 25:8
את (direct object marker, part)
4:25, 33; 5:25, 28; 6:21, 32, 40; 7:22, 27, 33 (2x); 8:25, 27
את with (prep)
7:35; 10:24, 25 (2x), 35; 19:11; 23:4
את, אתה you (m. sing) (pron)
3:17, 30; 4:32; 5:15, 18, 20, 27, 29 (2x); 6:13, 16, 26; 7:27, 35, 38; 8:26, 27 (2x), 28; 9:10, 11, 15, 28, 29, 33; 10:36; 12:13, 19, 39, 41; 13:13, 16, 20, 22, 34; 14:23, 28; 15:13, 16, 19, 28, 34, 40; 16:12, 17; 17:12, 21, 23, 29, 32, 34, 35, 38; 18:10, 16, 24; 19:30, 32, 35, 36, 39; 21:32; 22:26, 34; 23:24, 27; 24:12; 25:32
באש worthless thing, wild grapes (n)
16:26
בגד to act treacherously, betray (v)
10:12
בד separation, alone (n)
[26:12] = 4QH[a] frg. 7 1:16
בדל to be separate, exclude, distinguish (v)
13:31; 15:15
בהלה calamity (n)
16:34
בוא to come, enter (v)
3:32; 6:32; 8:9, 33; 11:9, 23, 40; 12:16; 13:18, 25, 37; 14:8, 15, 22, 28, 30 (2x), 31, 38; 15:33, 38; 16:13 = 1QH[b] frg. 2 1; 18:35; 19:24; 21:10, 14; 22:27 (2x); 26:7 = 4QH[a] frg. 7 1:10
בוז contempt, shame (n)
10:35 = 4QH[b] frg. 3 2; 16:15; 17:25
בזא to wash away (v)
16:15
בזה to despise (v)
12:23; 13:22; 15:26; [26:2] = 4QH[e] frg. 1 1
בחיר chosen (n)
6:13, 26; 10:15
בחן to try, test, prove (v)
10:15; 23:28
בחן testing (n)
14:29; 15:12
בחר to choose (v)
4:33; 6:21; 7:32, 36; 8:28, 31; 12:5, 18; 17:10; 18:28
בטח security (n)
20:5 = 4QH[a] frg. 3 2 = 4QH[b] frg. 12 2:1
ביורים precious stone (n)
[26:8] = 4QH[a] frg. 7 1:12
בין to understand, consider (v)
4:33; 5:13, 14, 30, 38; 6:20; 8:13; 9:39; 10:20; 15:35 = 4QpapH[f] frg. 12 3; [15:41] = 4QH[b] frg. 10 6; 18:4, 23; 19:7, 23 = 4QH[a] frg. 1 3; 19:31; 20:30, 36; 22:30; C3 4; C4 1
בין between, among (prep)
6:22; 9:4; 15:15
בינה understanding (n)
5:17, 19; 6:14, 19, 23, 24; 7:25; 8:24; 9:23, 25; 10:12, 19, 21; 12:8; 13:28; 19:15; 22:31; 23:12; A7 1
בית to dwell (v)
25:6
בכי weeping, mourning (n)
11:2
בכר to bear the first child (v)
11:8
בל no, never, without (part)
8:13; 11:40; 14:24, 30, 31, 38; 15:10; 16:13, 14; 24:14
בלה to wear out (v)
16:32
בליעל devilry, worthlessness, Belial (n)
10:18, 24; 11:29, 30 = 4QpapH[f] frg. 6 4; 11:33; 12:11, 14 (2x); 13:28 = 4QH[c] frg. 2 8; 13:41; 14:24 = 4QH[c] frg. 4 1:11; 15:6
בלע to swallow, destroy (v)
15:8; 16:39; 17:8
בלע to confuse (v)
11:15 = 4QpapH[f] frg. 5 2
בלעדי without (part)
8:14, 29; 9:22; 18:11; 21:33; 25:15
בלתי except, no, not (part)
6:28, 29; 7:24 (2x); 8:23, 31 = 4QH[c] frg. 3 1; 25:25
בן son, descendant, child (n)
7:19 = 4QH[a] frg. 8 1:11; [7:19] = 4QH[a] frg. 8 1:11; 8:36; 9:29, 36 (2x); 10:26; 11:9, 23; 12:31, 33 (2x); 13:9, 10, 13, 17, 27; 14:14, 21 = 4QH[c] frg. 4 1:5; 14:32, 33; 15:14, 23, 32; 17:35; 18:29, 30; 19:9, 12, 14; 23:23, 30; 24:33; [25:22] = 4QH[b] frg. 19 1; [26:32] = 4QH[a] frg. 7 2:14; [26:36] = 4QH[a] frg. 7 2:18; A5 2
בניה building (n)
14:29 = 4QH[c] frg. 4 2:9
בנים space between (n)
14:16; [26:40] = 4QH[a] frg. 7 2:21 = 4QH[b] frg. 21 3

בעבור because of, for (prep, part)
5:19, 27; 8:27; 10:26; 12:29; 13:27

בעד behind, through, around, for (prep)
4:24; 10:23; 11:19 = 4QpapH^f frg. 5 6; 11:19 = 4QpapH^f frg. 5 7; 13:16, 35; 16:12

בעל owner, husband, partner (n)
10:16; 13:37 = 4QH^c frg. 3 9; 15:25, 35 = 4QpapH^f frg. 12 3

בער to burn, ignite (v)
14:21 (2x); 16:31

בעת to terrify (v)
9:25; 11:15 = 4QpapH^f frg. 5 1

בץ mire (n)
15:5

בצע unjust gain, wealth (n)
18:25, 32

בקע to split, burst forth (v)
4:25; 10:29; 11:33

בקר morning (n)
20:9; 22:22

בקשׁ to seek, attempt, request (v)
6:14; 8:24; 10:23

ברא to create (v)
5:25, 28; 7:27 (2x), 30; 9:9, 15, 29; 12:39

ברושׁ juniper (n)
16:6

ברזל iron (n)
11:40; 13:39

בריח bar (n)
11:19, 40; 13:39; 14:31 = 4QH^c frg. 4 2:11

ברית covenant (n)
4:17, 39; 6:33; 7:28, 31; 8:25, 33; 10:24, 30; 11:4; 12:2, 6, 20, 25, 35, 36, 40; 13:11, 25; 15:11, 13, 23; 18:32; 21:10, 14; 22:15, 27; 23:10; A3 3

ברך knee (n)
12:34; 16:35

ברך to bless (v)
6:20; [7:16] = 4QH^a frg. 8 1:8; 7:21; 8:26; 9:33; 10:32; 13:22; 17:38; 18:16; 19:9, 28, 30, 32, 35; 21:18; 22:34, 36; [26:14] = 4QH^a frg. 7 1:18; [26:31a] = 4QH^a frg. 7 2:12; A6 2

ברכה blessing (n)
3:18; 4:32; 20:6 = 4QH^a frg. 3 2; [26:24] = 4QH^a frg. 7 2:5 = 4QH^e frg. 2 4

ברק lightning, flash (n)
9:14

ברר to purify, purge (v)
6:15; 7:23; 8:28

בשׂר to bear news (v)
[10:8] = 4QpapH^f frg. 3 4; 23:15 (2x) = 4QH^b frg. 14 4 (1x)

בשׂר flesh, meat, kin, human (n)
4:15, 20, 37; 5:14, 15, 30, 33; 7:25, 30, 34; 10:40 = 4QH^b frg. 3 7; 12:30; 15:20; 16:32, 34; 17:16; 18:25; 21:7, 9, 23 = 4QH^a frg. 11 1 = 4QH^b frg. 13 6; 24:6, 10, 14 = 4QH^b frg. 15 7; 24:26 (2x), 29; 25:12 = 4QH^b frg. 18 1; 25:13; 26:35 = 4QH^a frg. 7 2:16

בשת shame (n)
12:24; 13:37; 17:20, 22

גאה proud (adj)
26:16 = 4QH^a frg. 7 1:20; [26:31a] = 4QH^a frg. 7 2:12

גאות majesty, pride, rising
[26:14] = 4QH^a frg. 7 1:18

גבה to be high (v)
26:28 = 4QH^a frg. 7 2:9 [יגבירהו] = 4QH^e frg. 2 8

גבהות pride, loftiness (n)
[26:26] = 4QH^a frg. 7 2:8

גבול boundary, restriction, realm (n)
10:10; 11:25; 15:17

גבולה boundary (n)
24:34

גבור mighty, warrior (adj)
7:18; 8:16; 10:27; 11:36; [11:40] = 4QpapH^f frg. 7 1; 11:41 = 4QpapH^f frg. 7 2; 13:9 = 4QH^c frg. 1 1:1;13:23; 14:33, 36; 16:12; 18:26, 36

גבורה mighty deed, strength (n)
2:29, 32; 5:15; 7:12; 9:7; 11:11; [12:1] (2x) = 4QH^b frg. 6 1 (2x) = 4QpapH^f frg. 7 3 (1x); 12:20, 30, 33; 13:22; 14:14; 17:16, 25, 27; 18:12; 19:8, 11; 20:16, 32; 21:9; 23:9; [26:29] = 4QH^a frg. 7 2:10; 26:31 [deleted] = 4QH^a frg. 7 2:12; 26:34 = 4QH^a frg. 7 2:15; [26:42] = 4QH^a frg. 7 2:23; 28:14; A7 2

גבר to be strong, prevail, strengthen, confirm (v)
9:36 = 4QpapH^f frg. 2 1; 10:26; 12:9, 24, 28, 29; 13:17, 27; 16:36; 17:16, 21, 38; 19:6; 21:8; 23:9

גבר man (n)
10:19; 11:10, 11; 17:15; 19:23 = 4QH^a frg. 1 3; 22:23

גדוד band, troop (n)
11:40; 14:31

גדול great (adj)
5:31 (2x); 6:34; 7:32, 34; 8:26; 9:7; 11:35; 15:36 = 1QH^b frg. 1 7; 18:13; 20:8; 22:6; [26:26] = 4QH^a frg. 7 2:7 = 4QH^e frg. 2 6; C1 2

גדול greatness (n)
[26:11] = 4QH^a frg. 7 1:15

גדופה reviling, slander (n)
10:37 = 4QH^b frg. 3 4

גדל to grow up, become great, increase (v)
12:30; 13:26; 14:13, 18; 15:22; [25:32] = 4QH^b frg. 20 3; [26:31a] = 4QH^a frg. 7 2:12

גדל greatness, exultation (n)
6:34; 8:30; 9:34; 18:18; 19:32; 23:29; [26:18] = 4QH^a frg. 7 1:23

גדף to blaspheme (v)
15:4

גוי nation, people, heathen (n)
14:15; 24:24

גויה body (n)
16:33; 19:4

גור to sojourn, dwell (v)
11:26; 13:7

גור to attack (v)
10:25; 15:15; 21:35

גורל lot, membership (n)
6:22; 11:23, 26, 28 = 4QH^b frg. 5 2; 14:16, 17; 15:37; 19:14; 23:37

גזע stem, trunk (n)
16:8, 9, 24, 25

גיח to burst forth (v)
11:10

גיל to rejoice (v)
17:35; 20:25

גילה rejoicing (n)
19:26
גל wave (n)
10:14, 30; 11:16; 14:26
גלה to uncover, remove, reveal (v)
4:14; 5:20; 6:27; 9:23; 13:14; 14:7; [16:3] = 4QH^{b} frg. 10 9; 19:20 = 4QH^{a} frg. 1 1; 20:37; 21:5, 10; 22:26, 31; 23:5, 32; 24:28; 25:12 = 4QH^{b} frg. 18 1; 26:15 = 4QH^{a} frg. 7 1:19
גלול idol, impurity (n)
12:16, 20
גלל to wallow, pollute (v)
4:31; 14:25 = 4QH^{c} frg. 4 1:12; 22:8
גם also (part)
13:25; 25:14; [25:23] = 4QH^{b} frg. 19 2
גמול recompense (n)
[12:1] = 4QpapH^{f} frg. 7 3
גמל to reward, produce (v)
7:13; 17:30
גן garden (n)
16:6
גער to rebuke, drive off (v)
17:11; 22:25
גערה rebuke, threat (n)
18:20
גרם strong bone (n)
12:34
גרש to drive out, divorce (v)
10:15; 11:33; 16:16
גשם rain (n)
16:17
דבה bad report, defamation (n)
10:13
דבק to cling (v)
8:25; 13:33 = 4QH^{c} frg. 3 4
דבר to speak (v)
4:24; 9:25; 12:17; 18:9; 20:35 (2x), 36 (2x); [26:39] = 4QH^{a} frg. 7 2:21 = 4QH^{b} frg. 21 2
דבר word, thing, matter, speech (n)
4:35; 5:35, 36; 6:26; 7:27; 8:23, 25, 37; 9:30 (2x); 12:8, 18, 36; 13:28 = 4QH^{c} frg. 2 8; 16:37; 17:8; 20:23, 27, 33; 21:6; 25:16; 26:37
דגן grain (n)
18:26
דונג wax (n)
12:34; 16:34; 21:25 = 4QH^{a} frg. 11 3; 22:33
דור generation (n)
5:33; 6:17; 9:18 (2x), 19 (2x), 20; 14:14; 25:9
דיג fisherman (n)
13:10
דין to judge (v)
13:24
דין judgment (n)
17:9
דכא to crush (v)
9:38; 13:19
דלית branch (n)
14:18, 19 = 4QH^{b} frg. 8 5; 16:10
דלת door, gate (n)
11:19, 40; 13:39; 14:30
דם blood (n)
10:34; 13:9; 15:6; [15:40] = 1QH^{b} frg. 1 12 = 4QH^{b} frg. 10 4
דמה to be like, intend (v)
[26:3] = 4QH^{e} frg. 1 2; [26:3] = 4QH^{e} frg. 1 3; [26:7] = 4QH^{a} frg. 7 1:11 = 4QH^{e} frg. 1 7
דממה silence, quiet (n)
8:16; 13:20; 14:26
דמעה tears (n)
13:36 = 4QH^{c} frg. 3 7; 17:5
דעה knowledge (n)
6:36; 9:28; 19:11, 31; 20:13 = 4QH^{a} frg. 8 2:16; 21:32; 22:34; 25:33; [26:15] = 4QH^{a} frg. 7 1:20
דעת knowledge (n)
7:15 = 4QH^{a} frg. 8 1:7; 7:18 = 4QH^{a} frg. 8 1:10 [בעדת]; 9:6, 21, 37 = 4QpapH^{f} frg. 2 2; 10:15, 20; 11:24; 12:12, 19 = 4QH^{d} frg. 1 6; [16:2] = 4QH^{b} frg. 10 8; 18:22, 29, 31 (2x); 20:16, 32, 35; 21:9; 23:16, 26; 25:31; [26:22] = 4QH^{a} frg. 7 2:4 = 4QH^{e} frg. 2 3; [26:31] = 4QH^{a} frg. 7 2:13
דרדר thistle (n)
16:26
דרך to tread, travel, bend the bow (v)
14:33
דרך way, path (n)
4:33; 5:20; 6:37; 7:26, 31, 35, 39; 9:19, 37, 38; 10:12; 12:4, 5, 18, 19, 22, 25, 32 (2x), 33; 14:10, 23 (2x) = 4QH^{c} frg. 4 1:8 (1x); 14:24 = 4QH^{c} frg. 4 1:10; 14:27; 15:34 = 4QpapH^{f} frg. 12 2; [15:41] = 1QH^{b} frg. 1 13 = 4QH^{b} frg. 10 5; [16:3] = 4QH^{b} frg. 10 10; 16:10; 20:37; [21:21] = 4QH^{b} frg. 13 4; 21:22 = 4QH^{b} frg. 13 5; 23:13 = 4QH^{b} frg. 14 2
דרש to seek, examine, interpret (v)
4:18; 6:13; 10:17, 34, 36; 12:7, 15 = 4QH^{d} frg. 1 1; 12:16, 17, 25; 13:11
דשן to become fat, savor (v)
8:32; 18:28
הבל vanity, futility, breath (n)
15:35
הגה to meditate, speak, moan, mutter (v)
19:24 = 4QH^{a} frg. 1 4
הגי meditation (n)
19:5, 24 = 4QH^{a} frg. 1 4; [26:13] = 4QH^{a} frg. 7 1:17
הדר majesty, honor (n)
5:34; 20:18
הוא he, it (pron)
5:31; 6:40; 7:34; 12:30; 15:35 = 1QH^{b} frg. 1 6; 18:5 (2x), 14; 19:11; 20:34; 21:27; 22:6, 29
הוד splendor (n)
13:34 = 4QH^{c} frg. 3 5; 14:18 = 4QH^{b} frg. 8 2; [26:16] = 4QH^{a} frg. 7 1:21
הודות praise; thanksgiving (n)
19:7, 36; 20:7 = 4QH^{a} frg. 8 2:10
הוה to be, exist (v)
20:12 = 4QH^{a} frg. 8 2:15
הוה destruction, threat (n)
10:8, 38; 11:26, 34, 35, 39; 13:27, 28, 33 = 4QH^{c} frg. 3 4; 14:6, 24; 15:4, 7, 8, 10, 14; 19:16
הולל delusion, deception (n)
10:38; 12:9, 21
הון wealth, property (n)
6:31; 7:36; 18:25, 31

הוריה teaching (n)
[26:4] = 4QH^a frg. 7 1:7 = 4QH^e frg. 1 3

היא, היאה she, it (pron)
5:30; 12:14, 19; 20:12 = 4QH^a frg. 8 2:15

היה to be (v)
4:26; 5:29 (2x), 33; 6:12, 38; 7:33, 38; 9:13, 22 (2x), 30, 37; 10:10, 12, 13, 16, 17; 11:8, 34, 38; 13:24, 30 = 4QH^c frg. 2 11; 14:17 = 4QH^b frg. 8 1; 14:19 = 4QH^b frg. 8 5; 14:20, 25, 27 = 4QH^c frg. 4 2:5; 14:33; 16:7, 9, 15, 18, 19, 25, 28, 34; 17:24; 18:3, 4 = 4QH^b frg. 11 1; 19:17; 20:12, 13 (2x); 21:13; 22:36; 23:10; 25:7; [26:25] = 4QH^e frg. 2 6; A3 2

הלך to walk, go (v)
3:28; 4:36; 5:14, 21; 7:28, 31; 11:21, 30 = 4QpapH^f frg. 6 4; 12:22, 25, 34; 13:27; 14:9; [14:23] = 4QH^c frg. 4 1:9; 15:17; 16:35; [21:22] = 4QH^b frg. 13 5; 21:24; 23:34; [26:15] = 4QH^a frg. 7 1:20

הלל to praise (v)
3:32; 7:15; 8:15; 9:32; 11:24; 17:39, 41; 19:27 = 4QH^a frg. 1 6; 20:6 = 4QH^a frg. 3 3; 23:9, 24; 25:31 = 4QH^b frg. 20 1; [26:10] = 4QH^a frg. 7 1:14

הלל to be mad, mock (v)
10:38; 11:34; 12:13, 18; 18:35

הם they (m.) (pron)
7:37; 10:24, 25, 31; 12:7, 10, 14, 17 = 4QH^d frg. 1 4; 13:28; 14:17, 22; 20:32; 22:6

המה to roar (v)
10:14, 18; 11:14, 16 = 4QpapH^f frg. 5 2; 11:33, 35; 13:31 = 4QH^c frg. 3 2; 13:33; 14:26, 27 = 4QH^c frg. 4 2:4; 15:8; 22:32

המון multitude, abundance, tumult (n)
2:14; 7:13, 29; 10:18, 29; 11:14, 15 = 4QpapH^f frg. 5 1; 11:17 = 4QpapH^f frg. 5 4; 11:33, 35; 12:37, 38; 13:4; 14:10, 12; 15:33, 38 = 1QH^b frg. 1 10 = 4QH^b frg. 10 2; 17:8, 34; 18:23; 19:32

הנה they (f.) (pron)
23:27

הנה behold (part)
8:26; 18:10

הסה to be silent (v)
18:17

הפך to turn, change, overthrow (v)
10:19 = 4QpapH^f frg. 4 1; 11:8, 12; 13:34, 37; 16:13, 26

הר mountain (n)
4:25; 11:32

הרגה slaughter (n)
7:30

הרה to conceive (v)
11:12; [15:39] = 1QH^b frg. 1 11 = 4QH^b frg. 10 3; 17:30

הריה pregnant woman (n)
11:9, 10, 11 (2x), 13 (2x) = 4QH^b frg. 4 1 (1x) [הריה, deleted by scribal stroke]; 11:19 = 4QpapH^f frg. 5 6

זבל lofty abode (n)
11:35

זד proud (adj)
14:38

זדון pride, arrogance, presumption (n)
21:35

זה, זאת this (pron)
6:38; 12:30; 13:11; 20:35, 21:4, 12; 22:35

זהב gold (n)
13:18

זולה except, only (part)
15:35; 18:11; 20:13

זוע to tremble (v)
14:30; 15:12

זור to turn aside (v)
12:20

זחל to crawl (v)
13:29

זידון insolence (n)
24:25

זכה to be clean (v)
17:15; 22:29

זכר to remember (v)
12:35, 36

זכר male (n)
11:10

זכרון memorial, remembrance (n)
9:26

זלעפה burning (n)
13:32 = 4QH^c frg. 3 3

זמה wickedness, plan (n)
12:14; 13:8

זמם to plot (v)
12:11, 27; 17:20; 18:7

זמר to sing praise (v)
19:8, 26; 25:30 = 4QH^b frg. 20 1; [26:9] = 4QH^a frg. 7 1:13 = 4QH^e frg. 1 9

זנח to reject (v)
8:36; 17:7, 11

זעם indignation (n)
13:3; [26:22] = 4QH^e frg. 2 2

זעף rage, storm (of the sea) (n)
14:25; 15:7

זפת pitch (n)
11:32 = 4QH^b frg. 5 7

זק fetter (n)
13:39 = 4QH^c frg. 3 11; 16:36

זק firebrand, dart, meteor (n)
9:14

זקק to refine (v)
6:14; 13:18; 14:11

זר stranger (adj)
14:22, 30; 16:13 = 1QH^b frg. 2 1

זרוע arm (n)
15:5; 16:34, 36; 22:13

זרם rainstorm (n)
10:29

זרע seed (n)
4:26

חבא to hide (v)
16:7, 19; 17:24

חבה to hide (v)
13:13, 27

חבל labor pain (n)
11:9, 10, 12, 13; 13:32 = 4QH^c frg. 3 3; 17:6

חבל cord, snare (n)
11:10, 29 = 4QH^b frg. 5 3

חבר community, spell (n)
13:30 = 4QH^c frg. 2 11

חד sharp (adj)
13:12

חדל to cease, refrain (v)
[26:3] = 4QH^e frg. 1 2

חדר room (n)
18:36
חדשׁ to renew (v)
19:16
חדשׁ new (adj)
5:29
חוה to bow down (v)
[26:13] = 4QH[a] frg. 7 1:18
חומה wall (n)
11:38; 13:39; 14:28; 15:11, 12
חושׁ to rush, shake (v)
11:11; 14:32
חזה seer (n)
10:17; 12:11, 21
חזון vision (n)
6:18; 12:19 = 4QH[d] frg. 1 6
חזק to be strong, hold fast, support (v)
4:34, 35; 6:16; 7:24; 8:25; 9:34, 38; 10:30, 39; 12:37, 40; 13:31 = 4QH[c] frg. 3 1; 15:10, 13; 18:8; 20:38; 21:32; 23:10; 24:35
חזק strong, severe (adj)
10:8, 37
חזק strength (n)
10:9; 16:36
חטא to miss, sin (v)
4:34, 35; 6:28; 14:11
חטאה sin, sin offering (n)
4:24; 5:32; 9:24, 27; 14:9; 19:23; 22:33
חי living, alive (adj)
7:35, 39; 10:22; 12:30; 16:8, 17
חיה to live (v)
16:37
חיה animal, beast, creature (n)
16:9, 20
חיה desire (n)
3:25
חיים life (n)
10:19; 13:8; 15:18; 16:7, 13 = 1QH[b] frg. 2 1; 16:15, 30; 17:6, 11; 24:27
חיל to writhe, birth, wait (v)
11:9
חיל strength, wealth, army (n)
18:17, 26
חיק bosom, embrace (n)
15:24, 39; 17:31, 36

חך roof of mouth (n)
13:33 = 4QH[c] frg. 3 4
חכם wise (adj)
9:37; 11:15 = 4QpapH[f] frg. 5 1; [12:2] = 4QH[b] frg. 6 2
חכמה wisdom (n)
5:20; 9:8, 9, 16, 21; 11:16 = 4QpapH[f] frg. 5 2; 17:17, 23; 18:4; [25:25] = 4QH[b] frg. 19 5
חלה to entreat, be sick, weak (v)
8:29; 19:25
חלחלה anguish, trembling (n)
18:35
חלי sickness (n)
16:27
חליל flute (n)
19:26
חלכה unfortunate, wretched (adj)
11:26, 27 = 4QpapH[f] frg. 6 1; 12:26, 36
חלמישׁ flint (n)
11:32 = 4QH[b] frg. 5 7; 16:24
חלק to be smooth, flatter (v)
12:8
חלק smooth, slippery (adj)
10:17, 34; 12:11
חם heat (n)
16:24, 27
חמדה desire (n)
5:23
חמה wrath, heat, poison (n)
5:16; 11:29; 13:12, 29 = 4QH[c] frg. 2 9; 15:32; 21:37
חמס violence, wrong (n)
10:6; 14:8
חמץ vinegar (n)
12:12
חמר mortar, clay (n)
3:29; 9:23; 11:25, 31 = 4QH[b] frg. 5 6; 12:30; 18:5; 19:6; 20:29, 35; 21:38; 22:12; 23:13, 28; 25:31 = 4QH[b] frg. 20 2
חנה to camp (v)
10:27
חנון gracious (adj)
8:34
חנינה favor, grace (n)
19:32
חנית spear (n)
10:28; 13:12

חנן to show favor (v)
4:30; 6:36; 8:24, 27; 20:7; A2 1
חסד lovingkindness, mercy, graciousness (n)
5:16, 22; 6:35; 8:27, 30 (2x), 34; 9:34; 10:25, 27; 12:38; 13:24; 14:12; 15:21, 23, 30, 38; 17:7, 10, 14, 31; 18:16, 18; 19:8, 20, 21, 31, 33, 34; 20:17, 24; 23:25; 25:11; [26:17] = 4QH[a] frg. 7 1:22; 26:32 = 4QH[a] frg. 7 2:13
חסה to take refuge, trust (v)
17:29
חפז to hurry, panic (v)
20:22
חפץ to delight (v)
18:7
חפץ delight, pleasure (n)
5:37; 9:15 = 4QpapH[f] frg. 1 3; 21:27
חפשׂ to search (v)
16:30; 18:36
חץ arrow (n)
10:28; 11:17, 28 = 4QH[b] frg. 5 1; 14:31 = 4QH[c] frg. 4 2:12; 14:34
חק statute (n)
6:16; 7:25; 8:33; 9:12; 10:39; 15:37 = 4QH[b] frg. 10 1; 21:9
חקה statute (n)
20:8
חקק to inscribe, decree (v)
9:26; 21:13 = 4QH[a] frg. 10 3; 23:12
חקר searching (n)
5:16; 11:21; 14:6, 20 = 4QH[c] frg. 4 1:2; 16:18; 21:16
חרב sword (n)
13:12, 15, 17; 14:32
חרול nettle (n)
16:25
חרון fury, burning (n)
7:30, 32; 11:29 = 4QpapH[f] frg. 6 3; 13:3; 22:9
חרישׁי sharp, scorching (adj)
15:8
חרפה reproach, shame (n)
10:11, 36 = 4QH[b] frg. 3 2
חרץ to decide, cut, appoint (v)
11:37

חרק to gnash, sting (v)
9:41; 10:13

חרת ink; inscription (?) (n)
9:26

חשׂך to spare, refrain (v)
4:34

חשב to weave, think, account (v)
2:30; 8:12; 10:34; 11:7, 25, 33, 34; 12:9, 10, 15 = 4QH^{d} frg. 1 1; 12:24; 13:28 = 4QH^{c} frg. 2 8; 13:40; 16:12, 15; 18:7; 21:12 = 4QH^{a} frg. 10 2; [26:9] = 4QH^{a} frg. 7 1:13 = 4QH^{e} frg. 1 9; [26:35] = 4QH^{a} frg. 7 2:16

חשבון explanation, reflection, calculation (n)
9:31

חשך to be dark (v)
13:34

חשך dark (n)
17:26; 20:9 = 4QH^{a} frg. 8 2:12; 20:29; 21:15; 23:31; 25:15; [25:23] = 4QH^{b} frg. 19 3

חתם to seal (v)
16:12; [26:14] = 4QH^{a} frg. 7 1:19

חתף to snatch, slaughter (v)
13:29 = 4QH^{c} frg. 2 10

חתף robbery, slaughter (n)
13:12

חתת to be dismayed (v)
10:37

טאטאי sweepings (?), trampling (?) (n)
13:23

טבע to sink (v)
15:5

טהר to be clean, purify (v)
4:38; 8:30; 9:34; 10:5; 11:22; 12:38; 13:18 = 4QH^{c} frg. 1 2:3; 14:11; 15:33; 19:13, 33; C6 3

טוב good, pleasant, fine (adj)
4:36; 6:23; 7:31; 8:36; 9:4

טוב goodness, favor (n)
5:16, 33; 6:28; 15:33; 18:18; 19:9, 12, 34; 20:24; 22:32, 38; 23:15; [26:18] = 4QH^{a} frg. 7 1:23; [26:31] = 4QH^{a} frg. 7 2:13

טוח to plaster, seal, cover (v)
12:24

טיט mud (n)
10:15; 23:30

טמא unclean, defiled (adj)
14:23 = 4QH^{c} frg. 4 1:9; 15:39

טמם to shut (v)
[16:1] = 1QH^{b} frg. 1 14

טמן to hide (v)
10:31; 21:28

טרם before (part)
5:25; 7:27; 9:9, 12, 21, 30; 16:8

טרף to tear (v)
13:16

טרף prey (n)
13:20 = 4QH^{c} frg. 1 2:6

יאל to undertake, be willing (v)
5:18; 8:16, 26

יבול produce (n)
16:15

יבישה dry land (n)
4:16

יבשׁ to be dry, wither (v)
16:21

יבשׁ dry (adj)
11:31 = 4QH^{b} frg. 5 5; 16:20

יבשה dry land (n)
11:32 = 4QH^{b} frg. 5 6; 16:5 = 4QH^{b} frg. 10 12

יגון sorrow, agony (n)
10:7 = 4QpapH^{f} frg. 3 4; 13:15, 36 = 4QH^{c} frg. 3 8; 16:28; 19:4, 23, 25 (2x) = 4QH^{a} frg. 1 4 (1x); 19:29, 35; [26:23] = 4QH^{a} frg. 7 2:5

יד hand, part, power, penis (n)
4:24; 6:16, 38; 7:25, 26; 8:11; 10:37 (2x); 12:23 = 4QpapH^{f} frg. 9 1; 12:26, 36; 13:6; 16:22, 23, 25, 34; 18:20; 19:10; 23:10, 27; 24:36 = 4QH^{b} frg. 16 1; [26:14] = 4QH^{a} frg. 7 1:18; 28:14

ידה to praise, confess (v)
4:30; 10:22, 33; 11:20, 38; 12:6; 13:7, 22 [deleted]; 15:9, 29, 37; 16:5 = 4QH^{b} frg. 10 11; 19:6, 18

ידיד beloved (adj)
[26:6] = 4QH^{e} frg. 1 6; [26:9] = 4QH^{a} frg. 7 1:13

ידע to know (v)
5:19, 30, 35, 37; 6:23, 26, 28; 7:14, 17 = 4QH^{a} frg. 8 1:9; 7:19 = 4QH^{a} frg. 8 1:11; 7:25, 26, 33, 35, 36, 38, 39; 8:22, 24, 28, 29, 34; 9:9, 10, 23, 25, 30, 31, 33; 10:24, 35; 11:21; 12:28, 29, 31, 33; 13:5; 14:9, 15; 15:16, 19, 30; 16:12; 17:9, 12, 14, 30, 35; 18:7, 11, 16, 21; 19:10, 12, 17, 19, 20, 23; 20:14, 25; 21:7, 27, 34; 22:7, 11, 13, 35; 24:29; 25:11 (2x); [26:14] = 4QH^{a} frg. 7 1:18; 26:31[deleted] = 4QH^{a} frg. 7 2:12 [להופיע]; 26:32 = 4QH^{a} frg. 7 2:13; [26:32] = 4QH^{a} frg. 7 2:14; A4 3; A8 2; C1 3

יהב to give (v)
[26:11] = 4QH^{a} frg. 7 1:15

יובל stream (n)
16:8, 11

יום day (n)
4:26, 27; 5:35; 7:22, 30; 9:17; 13:3, 19, 36 = 4QH^{c} frg. 3 8 = 4QpapH^{f} frg. 11 2; 16:31; 17:32; 19:9; 20:8

יומם by day (part)
16:30; 18:17; 20:10

יורה early rain (n)
16:17

יחד to unite (v)
8:15; 19:14; 23:30

יחד together (part)
6:29; 7:17, 18 = 4QH^{a} frg. 8 1:10; 11:23, 24; 12:25; 13:24, 32; 14:16; 16:6; 18:36; 19:17, 28 = 4QH^{b} frg. 12 1:2; 21:35; [26:11] = 4QH^{a} frg. 7 1:15; 26:14 = 4QH^{a} frg. 7 1:18

יחד Yahad, community (n)
[26:28] = 4QH^{a} frg. 7 2:9

יחל to wait, hope (v)
15:21; 17:10; 19:34; 22:36

יכח to decide, reprove (v)
9:27; 10:6 = 4QpapH^{f} frg. 3 2; 14:7; 17:23; 20:31; 23:13, 26

יכל to be able, prevail (v)
7:26, 27, 34; 8:20; 15:32; 19:27; 20:33; 22:6

ילד to bear, beget (v)
5:31; 13:33; 21:2, 9; 23:13

ים sea, west (n)
5:26; 9:16; 10:14; 11:7, 15 =

4QpapH[f] frg. 5 1; 11:16; 14:19 = 4QH[b] frg. 8 5; 14:26; 16:18

ימין right hand, south (n)
4:30; 23:8

ינק to suck (v)
15:24

יסד to lay a foundation, establish (v)
13:11; 17:12

יסוד foundation, principle (n)
11:32; 20:11

יסור lesson, correction by suffering (n)
4:34

יסף to add, do again (v)
9:37

יסר to instruct, warn, rebuke (v)
7:17 = 4QH[a] frg. 8 1:9

יעד to appoint, meet (v)
5:37; 7:17, 24; 12:25; 13:9, 25; 24:7; 26:16 = 4QH[a] frg. 7 1:20

יעל to profit (v)
14:23

יעף tired, exhausted (adj)
15:13

יעץ to counsel, plan (v)
11:11; 14:24 = 4QH[c] frg. 4 1:11

יער forest (n)
16:9

יפע to appear, shine (v)
12:7, 24; 13:34; 15:6, 27; 17:2, 26, 31; 19:29 = 4QH[b] frg. 12 1:3; 23:7; [26:23] = 4QH[a] frg. 7 2:4 = 4QH[e] frg. 2 3; [26:23] = 4QH[a] frg. 7 2:5 = 4QH[e] frg. 2 4

יצא to go out (v)
2:13; 4:31; 9:31; 12:26; 14:34; 22:24

יצב to stand (v)
11:22, 25; 15:32; 18:13; 19:16; 20:31, 33; 22:24; 26:36 = 4QH[a] frg. 7 2:17

יצהר oil (n)
18:26

יצוע couch, bed (n)
17:4

יצר to form, plan, make pottery (v)
7:35; 9:10, 17; 11:22; 12:32; 18:8, 24

יצר inclination, thought, vessel (n)
3:29; 7:26, 30, 34; 8:18; 9:23, 37; 10:11, 38; 11:24; 12:30; 13:8, 33; 14:35; 15:6, 16, 19; 16:39; 17:16; 18:25; 19:6, 23; 20:29, 35; 21:11, 17, 19 = 4QH[b] frg. 13 2; 21:25 = 4QH[b] frg. 13 8; 21:29, 30, 31, 34, 38; 22:12, 19; 23:12, 13, 14 = 4QH[b] frg. 14 3; 23:28, 37, 38; 24:6; [25:31] = 4QH[b] frg. 20 2

ירא to fear (v)
5:31; 20:6 = 4QH[a] frg. 3 3 = 4QH[b] frg. 12 2:2

ירד to go down (v)
11:15 = 4QpapH[f] frg. 5 1; 16:29

ירה to shoot, throw (v)
11:28, 41 = 4QpapH[f] frg. 7 2; 14:35

ירה to teach, show (v)
14:12

ירש to posses, inherit, dispossess (v)
24:24

יש there is (part)
11:21; 14:9; 17:14; 22:11

ישב to sit, dwell, remain, inhabit (v)
11:14; 20:5; 25:14 (2x) = 4QH[b] frg. 18 3 (1x)

ישועה salvation, deliverance (n)
6:16; 7:29; 14:10; 19:26 = 4QH[a] frg. 1 5; 20:6 = 4QH[a] frg. 3 3; [26:10] = 4QH[a] frg. 7 1:14

ישע to deliver, save (v)
10:25; 11:7

ישע salvation (n)
13:14

ישר to be smooth, straight, right (v)
[10:5] = 4QpapH[f] frg. 3 1; 14:27; 15:17; 20:37

ישר straight, correct, upright (adj)
10:12

ישר uprightness, integrity (n)
8:13; 14:13

יתום orphan (n)
13:22

כאוב pain (n)
13:30 = 4QH[c] frg. 2 11; 16:29

כבד to be heavy, honored (v)
3:30; 8:17; 10:26; 17:16; 18:10, 29; 23:23; 24:33

כבוד glory, rank, heaviness (n)
4:27; 5:19, 23, 28, 30; 7:14, 15 = 4QH[a] frg. 8 1:7; 7:30, 33; 8:21, 27; 9:12, 32; 11:5, 36; 12:29; 13:22; 14:13, 15, 17 = 4QH[b] frg. 8 1; 15:18, 27; [16:2] = 4QH[b] frg. 10 8; 16:6, 21, 23; 17:17, 25, 26; 18:12, 13, 14, 22; 19:9, 11, 13, 30 = 4QH[b] frg. 12 1:3; 20:6, 18, 25, 32, 33; 21:8; 22:38; 23:9, 24, 25, 36; 24:12 = 4QH[b] frg. 15 4; 25:11; [26:7] = 4QH[a] frg. 7 1:11; 26:8; [26:11] = 4QH[a] frg. 7 1:15; [26:16] = 4QH[a] frg. 7 1:21; [26:30] = 4QH[a] frg. 7 2:11; [26:33] = 4QH[a] frg. 7 2:15; 28:12; A7 2

כבל fetter (n)
16:35

כבשן furnace (n)
17:5

כוכב star (n)
9:14

כול to provide, contain, remain, endure (v)
17:34, 36; [26:5] = 4QH[e] frg. 1 5

כון to establish, prepare, ordain (v)
4:33; 5:17, 24, 27, 29; 6:23, 40; 7:26, 27, 28, 32, 34, 35; 9:11, 12, 16, 19, 21, 30; 10:19, 39; 12:4, 7, 14, 15, 19, 23, 32; 14:13, 25; 15:11, 16, 27, 28, 34; [15:41] = 4QH[b] frg. 10 5; 16:3, 22; 17:32; 18:3, 24; 19:37; 20:14 = 4QH[a] frg. 8 2:16; 20:37; 21:8, 9; [21:26] = 4QH[a] frg. 11 4; 22:26, 34; 23:35; 24:15; [26:42] = 4QH[a] frg. 7 2:23

כור furnace, womb, crucible (n)
9:24; 11:9, 11, 13 = 4QH[b] frg. 4 1; 13:18

כזב to lie, fail (v)
16:17

כזב lie, falsehood (n)
10:33; 12:11, 17 = 4QH[d] frg. 1 4

כח strength, power (n)
5:15; 6:34; 7:14, 33; 9:15; [10:7] = 4QpapH[f] frg. 3 3; 10:10; 11:25,

35; 12:24, 33, 36; 13:31, 38; 15:20, 22; 16:12, 29, 32; 17:14, 17; 18:12, 13, 14, 37; 19:11, 32; 20:38; 23:9; 24:14; 26:34 = 4QH^{a} frg. 7 2:15; [26:38] = 4QH^{a} frg. 7 2:20 = 4QH^{b} frg. 21 1; [26:41] = 4QH^{a} frg. 7 2:23 = 4QH^{b} frg. 21 5

כחד to be hidden, effaced (v)
24:32

כי, כיא that, because, when (part)
3:17; 4:31, 32, 33, 37; 5:27, 28, 29, 35; 6:22, 24, 25, 26, 31, 38; 7:13, 15 (2x), 20, 25, 26, 31, 32, 34, 35, 36, 37, 39; 8:15, 22, 27, 28, 29, 33; 9:6, 23; [10:5] = 4QpapH^{f} frg. 3 1; 10:22, 23, 24, 25, 27, 33, 35 (2x); 11:8, 9, 10, 15, 20, 21, 25, 35, 38, 39; 12:6, 8, 9 (2x), 13, 18 = 4QH^{d} frg. 1 5; 12:18 = 4QH^{d} frg. 1 6; 12:19, 21, 23, 28, 31, 32, 35, 37, 39, 41; 13:7, 13, 14, 22 (2x), 33 = 4QH^{c} frg. 3 4; 13:36, 38; 14:9, 15, 17, 28, 30 = 4QH^{c} frg. 4 2:10; 14:36; 15:6, 9, 14, 15, 16, 19, 26, 28, 29, 31, 34 = 1QH^{b} frg. 1 5; 15:37; [16:3] = 4QH^{b} frg. 10 9; 16:3 = 4QH^{b} frg. 10 10; 16:5 = 4QH^{b} frg. 10 11; 16:10 = 4QpapH^{f} frg. 13 2; 16:14, 16, 28, 30, 33; 17:9, 10, 12, 14 (2x), 23 (2x), 26 (2x), 28, 29, 34, 35; 18:6, 14, 16, 19, 24, 28, 31, 32; 19:6 (2x), 10, 12, 19, 21, 35, 36; 20:13, 20, 21, 24, 25, 34, 36 (2x), 37; 21:6, 7, 12; [21:23] = 4QH^{b} frg. 13 6; 21:27, 29, 34; 22:11, 13, 15, 25, 27, 35; 23:4, 24, 31, 35; 24:16, 26, 30; 25:15, 35; [26:7] = 4QH^{a} frg. 7 1:11 = 4QH^{e} frg. 1 7; [26:26] = 4QH^{a} frg. 7 2:8; [26:33] = 4QH^{a} frg. 7 2:15; [26:37] = 4QH^{a} frg. 7 2:19; A4 2; A8 2; C6 2

כל all, whole, everyone, everything (n)
3:24, 25, 27, 30; 4:23, 26, 27 (2x), 35, 36 (2x), 39; 5:16, 17, 21, 22 (2x), 25 (2x), 26 (3x), 28, 30, 31 (2x), 36 (2x); 6:17, (2x), 20, 21 (2x), 25 (2x), 26 (3x), 27, 29 (2x), 31, 37 (2x), 38; 7:22, 23 (2x), 24, 25, 26, 27, 28, 29, 31, 33 (2x), 35, 36 (2x), 38, 39; 8:8, 11, 12, 13, 15, 21, 22, 23, 24, 26, 27, 28, 31, 33, 35; 9:4, 8, 9 [deleted], 10, 11 (2x), 12, 16, 17, 18, 20 (2x), 21, 22, 25, 26 (2x), 28, 32, 33, 35, 36, 38; 10:5 = 4QpapH^{f} frg. 3 1; 10:6, 8, 10, 11, 17 (2x), 20, 23, 27, 36, 40 = 4QH^{b} frg. 3 8; 11:5, 11, 12, 13 = 4QH^{b} frg. 4 2; 11:16 = 4QpapH^{f} frg. 5 2; 11:17, 19, 24, 27 (2x), 28, 29 = 4QpapH^{f} frg. 6 3; 11:30 = 4QpapH^{f} frg. 6 4; 11:30 = 4QH^{b} frg. 5 4; 11:30; 11:31 = 4QH^{b} frg. 5 6 = 4QpapH^{f} frg. 6 6; 11:34 (2x), 39; 12:10, 13, 18 = 4QH^{d} frg. 1 5; 12:21 (2x), 23, 25, 27 (2x), 30, 32, 33 (2x), 34, 39, 41; 13:6, 12, 19, 24, 25, 26; 14:11, 15 (2x), 16, 18, 19, 21 (2x), 26 = 4QH^{c} frg. 4 2:2; 14:30, 31 = 4QH^{c} frg. 4 2:12; 14:32, 33, 36; 15:7, 10, 12, 14, 15, 16 (2x), 25, 32 (3x), 34, 38 = 4QH^{b} frg. 10 2; [16:4] = 4QH^{b} frg. 10 10; 16:7, 9 (2x), 10 (2x), 17, 20; 17:15, 18, 20, 21, 29, 35, 36; 18:3, 4 (2x), 5, 10 (2x), 11, 13, 14, 17, 28, 38; 19:8, 11 (4x), 12, 14, 16, 25a = 4QH^{a} frg. 1 4; 19:27 (3x) = 4QH^{a} frg. 1 6 (1x); 19:33; 20:10, 11, 23, 24, 33, 39; 21:8, 29, 32, 35; 22:7, 25; 23:8 (2x), 24, 25, 26; 24:10, 23, 26, 31, 37; 25:7, 10, 11; [26:12] = 4QH^{a} frg. 7 1:17; [26:24] = 4QH^{a} frg. 7 2:6 = 4QH^{e} frg. 2 5; [26:31] = 4QH^{a} frg. 7 2:13; [26:32] = 4QH^{a} frg. 7 2:14; [26:42] = 4QH^{a} frg. 7 2:23 = 4QH^{b} frg. 21 5; A8 2

כלא prison (n)
13:40

כלה to be complete, finished; destroy (v)
13:38; 17:5; 19:25; 22:25; 24:31; [26:22] = 4QH^{a} frg. 7 2:4; [26:24] = 4QH^{a} frg. 7 2:6 = 4QH^{e} frg. 2 5

כלה complete destruction, annihilation, end (n)
11:37; 13:36; 14:6, 22, 35; 15:8; 16:33; 17:3; 19:21 = 4QH^{a} frg. 1 2; 20:17; 21:28, 36 = 4QH^{a} frg. 12 1; 25:10; 26:17 = 4QH^{a} frg. 7 1:21; [26:28] = 4QH^{a} frg. 7 2:10 = 4QH^{e} frg. 2 9

כלי utensil, weapon, vessel, garment (n)
10:28; 12:10; 14:31 = 4QH^{c} frg. 4 2:12; 14:34

כליל crown, ornament (n)
17:25

כלמה disgrace (n)
17:22

כמו like, as (part)
11:8, 37; 14:24 = 4QH^{c} frg. 4 1:11; 15:31; 23:13; [26:2] = 4QH^{e} frg. 1 1; [26:3] = 4QH^{e} frg. 1 2; [26:4] = 4QH^{e} frg. 1 4; 28:11

כן so, thus (part)
6:24, 29, 32; 18:30; 24:27

כנור lyre (n)
13:32 = 4QH^{c} frg. 3 2; 19:25a = 4QH^{a} frg. 1 4; 19:26

כנע to humble, subdue (v)
24:11

כנף wing, flank, hem or skirt of garment (n)
6:41; 16:10

כסף silver, money (n)
13:18

כעס anger (n)
13:36

כף hand, palm of hand (n)
8:28; 23:27

כפיס rafter (n)
14:29, 39

כפיר young lion (n)
13:11

כפר to cover, atone (v)
4:24; 12:38; 23:33

כפר ransom, atonement (n)
7:37

כרת to cut, cut off, exclude (v)
12:21, 27; 13:17; 14:32

כשל to stumble (v)
4:16, 35; 8:23; 13:30 = 4QH^{c} frg. 2 12; 13:38; 14:24 = 4QH^{c} frg. 4

1:11; 16:37; [26:15] = 4QH[a] frg. 7 1:19; 26:29 = 4QH[a] frg. 7 2:10 = 4QH[e] frg. 2 9

כשלון stumbling (n)
17:25

כתם gold (n)
[26:8] = 4QH[a] frg. 7 1:12

לא no, not (part)
4:14, 15, 16, 17, 18, 19, 21, 31; 5:19, 28, 35, 36; 6:25, 26, 30 (2x), 31, 32, 38 (2x); 7:14, 25, 26, 31 (2x), 36, 37 (2x), 38; 8:13, 20, 29; 9:10 (2x), 22, 24, 25 (2x), 27 (2x), 39; 10:21, 24, 37 = 4QH[b] frg. 3 4; 11:37; 12:8, 9, 15, 18 (2x), 19 (2x), 21, 22, 24 (2x), 26, 31 (2x), 32, 39; 13:7, 8, 12, 14, 17, 22 (2x), 31, 39 = 4QH[c] frg. 3 11; 14:30 = 4QH[c] frg. 4 2:9; 14:30 = 4QH[c] frg. 4 2:10; 14:31, 33; 15:11, 12, 14, 18, 19, 21, 32, 37 (2x) = 1QH[b] frg. 1 9 (1x); 16:3 = 4QH[b] frg. 10 10; 16:11 (2x), 12, 14 (2x) = 1QH[b] frg. 2 2 (1x); 16:15, 17, 18, 27, 35, 36; 17:7, 11 (3x), 14, 15, 19, 35; 18:4 (3x) = 4QH[b] frg. 11 1 (1x); 18:5, 7, 8 (2x), 9 (2x), 11 (3x), 17, 20, 21 (2x), 24, 25, 32; 19:21 = 4QH[a] frg. 1 2; 19:22, 29 = 4QH[b] frg. 12 1:2; 20:13 (2x), 27, 32, 37; 21:4, 5, 33; 22:6, 7, 18, 25, 27; 23:27, 32; 24:16, 17, 32; 25:7, 16, 25; [26:6] = 4QH[a] frg. 7 1:10; [26:7] = 4QH[a] frg. 7 1:11 = 4QH[e] frg. 1 7; [26:8] (2x) = 4QH[a] frg. 7 1:12 (2x); [26:9] = 4QH[a] frg. 7 1:13; [26:22] = 4QH[a] frg. 7 2:4 = 4QH[e] frg. 2 3; [26:25] = 4QH[a] frg. 7 2:7; [26:39] = 4QH[a] frg. 7 2:21 = 4QH[b] frg. 21 2; 28:14; C4 2; C8 3

לאם people, nation (n)
14:15

לב heart, mind (n)
3:25; 4:34, 38; 6:19; 7:23; 8:25, 35; 9:39; 10:11, 30; 12:14, 15 (2x), 16, 19, 22 (2x), 25; 13:28, 33 (2x); 14:5, 10, 24 = 4QH[c] frg. 4 1:10; 15:8, 16, 19, 30; [15:41] = 1QH[b] frg. 1 13; [15:41] = 4QH[b] frg. 10 6; 16:27, 33, 38; 18:3, 25, 32, 33, 35; 19:5; 20:37; 21:6, 10, 12, 13 = 4QH[a] frg. 10 3; 22:32; 24:29; 25:13 = 4QH[b] frg. 18 2; A7 1

לבב heart, mind (n)
4:31; 8:13; 10:5 = 4QpapH[f] frg. 3 1; 10:8 = 4QpapH[f] frg. 3 5; 10:20; 12:11, 34; 13:11, 35 = 4QH[c] frg. 3 6; 14:25 = 4QH[c] frg. 4 1:11; 15:6; 16:38; 19:24; 21:6; 22:31, 33

לבט to thrust down, ruin (v)
10:21; 12:8

לביא lion (n)
13:9

לבש to wear, dress (v)
13:33

לדה giving birth (n)
11:8

להט flame (n)
16:13

לוה to join (v)
4:31; [11:41] = 4QpapH[f] frg. 7 1

לוהב flame, blade (n)
10:28; 11:31

לוז to turn aside, pervert (v)
13:26

לוח tablet, plank (n)
16:38; C7 2

לון to grumble (v)
13:27

לועג mocking (n)
12:17 = 4QH[d] frg. 1 4

לח moist, fresh (adj)
11:30 = 4QH[b] frg. 5 5 = 4QpapH[f] frg. 6 5; 16:20

לחלח to moisten, water (v)
14:19 = 4QH[b] frg. 8 4

לחם bread, food (n)
13:25, 35 = 4QH[c] frg. 3 7; 13:37

לילה night (n)
16:30; 17:2; 18:17; 20:9, 10

ליץ to scoff, interpret, speak on behalf of (v)
10:15, 16, 33; 12:8, 10; 14:16, 22; 23:12, 26; [26:36] = 4QH[a] frg. 7 2:18

לכד to capture (v)
10:31; 16:35

למוד disciple; teaching (n)
10:41 = 4QH[b] frg. 3 9; 15:13, 17; [16:1] = 4QH[b] frg. 10 7; 16:37

למען on account of, in order to (part)
12:12, 20, 33; 13:17, 27; 14:13; 19:13; 22:35

לענה wormwood, bitterness (n)
12:15 = 4QH[d] frg. 1 2

לץ scoffer (n)
10:13

לקח to take, marry, learn (v)
7:37; 20:27, 30; 23:24

לשון tongue, speech, language (n)
4:29; 8:24; 9:30; 10:9, 21, 41 = 4QH[b] frg. 3 9; 12:17; 13:15, 16, 29, 33 = 4QH[c] frg. 3 4; 15:13, 14, 16; 16:36; 19:7; [19:31] = 4QH[b] frg. 12 1:5; 19:37; 23:11; [26:5] = 4QH[a] frg. 7 1:9; [26:12] = 4QH[a] frg. 7 1:16

מאד very, exceedingly, strength, property (part)
7:20; 17:39; 19:6 (2x)

מאור light, luminary (n)
9:13; 13:34 = 4QH[c] frg. 3 5; 15:28; 17:26; 20:8; 23:32; C6 2

מאס to reject, despise (v)
4:36; 7:31; 9:39; 12:9

מאר to be painful, malignant (v)
13:30 = 4QH[c] frg. 2 11; [25:24] = 4QH[b] frg. 19 4

מבוא entrance, entering (n)
14:31; 20:7 = 4QH[a] frg. 8 2:11; 20:10; 22:22

מבוע spring (n)
16:5 = 4QH[b] frg. 10 12; 16:17

מבלגה poison (n)
13:29 = 4QH[c] frg. 2 10

מבנה structure (n)
5:32; 9:24

מבנית building, structure (n)
15:7, 12; 22:28

מבע utterance (n)
9:31 (2x)

מבצר fortress (n)
11:8; 14:38

מגבל kneaded, kneading (n)
5:32; 9:23; 11:25; 20:28; 21:30

מגדל tower (n)
15:11
מגור dwelling (n)
13:10 = 4QH[c] frg. 1 1:1; 16:27
מגן shield, armor (n)
14:30
מדה measure, way (n)
4:13; 9:31; 13:23; 14:6; 17:17
מדהבה fury, oppression, disaster (n)
11:26; 20:21; [26:21] = 4QH[a] frg. 7 2:3 = 4QH[e] frg. 2 2
מדהוב disaster (n)
19:4
מדור dwelling (n)
20:28
מדן strife (n)
10:17; 13:25, 37 = 4QH[c] frg. 3 9; 17:2
מה what? (pron)
5:31; 7:13, 34; 8:12; 9:25, 27 (2x), 28; 11:25 (2x); 12:30; 15:35; 18:5, 7 (2x), 8, 9, 14; 19:6; 20:30 (2x), 31, 34, 35 (2x), 36; 21:7; 22:16, 29, 30; 23:24, 27; 26:35 (2x) = 4QH[a] frg. 7 2:16 (2x)
מהומה tumult, turmoil, panic (n)
11:26, 39; 16:29
מהר to hasten, act hastily, be eager (v)
9:37 = 4QpapH[f] frg. 2 2; 10:11; 13:19, 23; C6 3
מוג to melt, waver (v)
11:35, 36
מודע relative (n)
12:10
מוט to totter, stagger (v)
14:24 = 4QH[c] frg. 4 1:10; 14:30 = 4QH[c] frg. 4 2:10; 15:10
מולד birth, origin, offspring (n)
11:12 (2x); 20:11
מוסד foundation, council (n)
4:25
מוסר discipline, instruction (n)
5:17; 10:16; 14:7
מועד festival, appointed place, appointment (n)
7:16 (2x) = 4QH[a] frg. 8 1:8 (2x); 7:28; 9:19, 26; 12:13; 16:32; 17:23, 24; 20:9, 11 = 4QH[a] frg. 8 2:14; 20:20; 25:11
מופת sign, wonder (n)
5:33; 7:33; 8:9; 15:24
מוצא going forth, departure, exit (n)
20:8, 10 = 4QH[a] frg. 8 2:13; [26:40] = 4QH[a] frg. 7 2:22 = 4QH[b] frg. 21 4
מוקש snare (n)
10:23
מור to exchange, change (v)
6:31; 10:20, 38; 12:11 = 4QpapH[f] frg. 8 1
מורא fear (n)
12:27
מורד descent (n)
12:35
מוש to depart, be absent (v)
16:18
מות to die (v)
14:37; 16:30; 19:15
מות death (n)
11:9, 10, 29; 14:27; 17:4
מזל flow, utterance (n)
16:37; 19:8
מזמה plan, plot, prudence (n)
10:18; 12:22; 13:12; 17:12; 18:3; 23:6; 25:12
מזמור psalm (n)
7:21; 25:34
מזרות stars (Mazzaroth) (n)
10:29
מחיה survival, provision (n)
14:11
מחיר price (n)
18:12; [26:29] = 4QH[a] frg. 7 2:10
מחלה sickness (n)
[26:25] = 4QH[a] frg. 7 2:6 = 4QH[e] frg. 2 5
מחסה refuge (n)
15:20
מחסור need, poverty (n)
7:29
מחץ wound (n)
10:7 = 4QpapH[f] frg. 3 3; 17:27
מחשב design, crafted item (n)
9:16; [26:42] = 4QH[a] frg. 7 2:23 = 4QH[b] frg. 21 5
מחשבה thought, plan (n)
4:22; 5:17, 26; 9:15; 10:19; 12:13, 14, 15 = 4QH[d] frg. 1 2; 12:20; 14:25; 15:6; 18:3; 19:10; 21:8
מטה bed (n)
17:4
מטמון hiding place (n)
21:24 = 4QH[b] frg. 13 7
מטע planting, plant (n)
15:22; 16:6, 14, 21, 22
מטעת planting, plant (n)
14:18; 16:7, 10, 11
מטר rain (n)
16:27
מי who? (pron)
2:26, 28, 29, 30, 31; 3:27; 11:25; 12:30; 15:31 (3x); 18:12; 19:27; 21:12 = 4QH[a] frg. 10 2; 22:29; 24:7; [26:4] = 4QH[e] frg. 1 3; [26:4] = 4QH[e] frg. 1 4; [26:5] = 4QH[e] frg. 1 5; [26:5] = 4QH[a] frg. 7 1:9 = 4QH[e] frg. 1 5
מים water (n)
5:32; 9:23; 10:18, 29, 30; 11:14, 15 = 4QpapH[f] frg. 5 1; 11:16 = 4QpapH[f] frg. 5 3; 11:17, 25, 27 = 4QpapH[f] frg. 6 1; 12:35; 13:10 = 4QH[c] frg. 1 1:2; 14:27; 16:5 = 4QH[b] frg. 10 12; 16:7, 8, 10 = 4QpapH[f] frg. 13 2; 16:14, 17, 18, 19, 20, 33, 35; 17:5; 18:27
מישור plain, uprightness, level (n)
10:31; 11:21; 15:28
מישרים evenness, uprightness (n)
12:26
מכאוב pain (n)
17:6, 29; 22:23
מכה wound, blow, defeat (n)
10:7 = 4QpapH[f] frg. 3 3; 17:27
מכון fixed place, foundation (n)
19:8; 21:15; 24:12 = 4QH[b] frg. 15 3; 26:30 = 4QH[a] frg. 7 2:11
מכמרת fishing net (n)
11:27; 13:10
מכשול obstacle (n)
8:33; 12:16 = 4QH[d] frg. 1 3; [16:3] = 4QH[b] frg. 10 9; 16:36; 17:21, 27; 18:20
מלא fullness (n)
8:21 (2x)

מלאך angel, messenger (n)
9:13; 14:16; 24:8, 11

מלח sailor (n)
11:15; 14:25

מלחה barren, salty ground (n)
16:25

מלחמה war, battle (n)
10:28; 11:36; 14:31 = 4QH[c] frg. 4 2:12; 14:32, 34, 36, 38; 15:10, 25; 17:22

מלט to escape, rescue (v)
11:10

מלך king (n)
18:10; 25:35; [26:6] = 4QH[a] frg. 7 1:10 = 4QH[e] frg. 1 6; [26:9] = 4QH[a] frg. 7 1:13; [26:11] = 4QH[a] frg. 7 1:15

מלכדת trap (n)
[21:20] = 4QH[b] frg. 13 3

מלכות kingdom (n)
3:27

ממזר bastard (n)
24:16, 26

ממלכה kingdom (n)
14:10

ממשלה dominion, authority (n)
4:37; 5:28; 9:13, 19; 15:26; 16:38; 20:8 = 4QH[a] frg. 8 2:11; 20:9 = 4QH[a] frg. 8 2:12; 20:12, 26

מנוח rest (n)
16:31; 17:5

מנוס refuge (n)
13:31; 14:36; 17:28

מסס to melt (v)
10:8 = 4QpapH[f] frg. 3 5; 10:30; 12:34; 16:33; 21:25 = 4QH[a] frg. 11 3; 22:33

מספחה restraining cloth (n)
13:31 = 4QH[c] frg. 3 2

מספד wailing, lament (n)
19:25

מספר number (n)
8:9; 9:7, 20, 26; 12:28; 17:38

מעוז refuge, stronghold, strength (n)
16:25, 28, 33, 34; 18:25, 34

מעון dwelling (n)
13:15; 20:5 = 4QH[a] frg. 3 2 = 4QH[b] frg. 12 2:1; 24:12; [26:10] = 4QH[a] frg. 7 1:14; C2 3

מעין spring, source (n)
[5:19] = 4QH[b] frg. 2 1; 7:12; 9:7; 13:28 = 4QH[c] frg. 2 7; 14:20; 16:7, 13 = 1QH[b] frg. 2 1; 20:16

מעל unfaithful act, treachery (n)
4:24; 8:34; 12:31, 35; [15:39] = 4QH[b] frg. 10 3; 19:14; 22:12; 24:25

מעל above, upward (prep)
15:27

מעמד office, station, position, assignment, rank (n)
8:31; 10:24; 11:21; 12:37; 13:31 = 4QH[c] frg. 3 1; 19:16; 22:15; 25:4; [26:7] = 4QH[a] frg. 7 1:11; 26:36 = 4QH[a] frg. 7 2:17; C4 2

מענה response, answer (n)
4:29; 8:24; 10:9; 15:14, 16; 19:31, 37; A2 2; C1 5

מענה dwelling (n)
20:10 = 4QH[a] frg. 8 2:13

מעשׂה work, deed (n)
4:30, 31; 5:12, 20 = 4QH[b] frg. 2 2; 5:21, 23, 25, 27, 36; 6:18, 27; 7:33, 39; 8:15, 17, 23, 26, 29, 32; 9:8, 9, 11, 28, 29, 32, 35; 10:5; 11:13, 18 = 4QpapH[f] frg. 5 6; 11:24; 12:9, 18 = 4QH[d] frg. 1 5; 12:21, 32, 33, 41; 13:18, 38; 14:12; 15:16, 35; 17:36; 18:10, 13, 38; 19:7, 27, 33; 20:31; 21:30, 36; 23:14, 27; 25:10, 26; [26:31] = 4QH[a] frg. 7 2:13

מפלג channel, division (n)
16:22; 20:26

מפץ smashing (n)
12:27

מץ chaff (n)
15:26

מצא to find (v)
4:29, 39; 8:24; 12:21; [19:29] = 4QH[b] frg. 12 1:3

מצודה net, trap (n)
11:27; 12:13

מצודה stronghold (n)
17:28

מצוה commandment (n)
4:19; 8:31, 35

מצולה deep, depth (n)
11:7, 15 = 4QpapH[f] frg. 5 2; 16:20

מצוקה distress, affliction (n)
13:19 = 4QH[c] frg. 1 2:4

מצור fortress (n)
14:28, 33

מצורוק mixture, mixed (n)
20:35; 23:28, 36

מצעד step, path, way (n)
10:25, 35; 11:18 = 4QpapH[f] frg. 5 5; 11:26; 12:5; 16:35; 17:33; [26:29] = 4QH[a] frg. 7 2:11

מצער small, few (n)
14:11

מצר distress, straights (n)
13:31

מצרף crucible, test (n)
4:21; 6:15; 13:18 = 4QH[c] frg. 1 2:2

מקוה hope (n)
11:21; 14:9; 17:14; 22:11, 18, 37

מקוה gathering, reservoir (n)
9:6; 20:28, 32 = 4QH[a] frg. 9 1; 21:26

מקום place (n)
25:7

מקור spring, flow, source (n)
5:32; 8:14; 9:24; 10:20; 14:20 = 4QH[c] frg. 4 1:4; 16:5, 9, 15, 21, 22; 18:33; 19:22; 20:28, 32; 23:11, 13, 14, 16 = 4QH[b] frg. 14 5; 24:11; [26:19] = 4QH[a] frg. 7 1:23; [26:24] = 4QH[a] frg. 7 2:5 = 4QH[e] frg. 2 4

מקנה cattle, property (n)
18:27

מרבה increase, abundance (n)
24:25

מרה to rebel, defy, hold a grudge (v)
6:25

מרום height, deceit (n)
25:13 (2x) = 4QH[b] frg. 18 3 (1x)

מרור bitterness (n)
13:14, 34, 36 = 4QH[c] frg. 3 8 = 4QpapH[f] frg. 11 2; 16:29, 38; 19:22, 25

מרחב open place, width (n)
13:35; 14:34

מריבה strife (n)
16:19

מרמה deceit (n)
12:21; C1 4
מרמס trampling (n)
16:9
מרפא health, healing (n)
10:10, 28; 17:25; [26:24] = 4QH[a] frg. 7 2:6
מרץ to be painful (v)
11:9, 13
מרץ pain (n)
11:12
משׂא burden, task (n)
9:14 = 4QpapH[f] frg. 1 2
משׂגב stronghold (n)
17:28
משׂכיל instructor, sage (n)
5:12; 7:21; 20:7 = 4QH[a] frg. 8 2:10 = 4QH[b] frg. 12 2:3; 20:14 = 4QH[a] frg. 8 2:17; 25:34
משבר womb opening, breaking wave, torment (n)
11:9 (2x), 10, 11, 12, 13 = 4QH[b] frg. 4 2; 11:17; 14:26 = 4QH[c] frg. 4 2:2; 16:32; 17:4, 7; 19:35
משגה error, straying (n)
10:21
משה Moses (n)
4:24
משואה desolation (n)
13:32; 17:6
משחית ruin (n)
13:34
משל to rule (v)
5:32, 34; 6:39; 8:18; 18:10
משמר jail, watch, protection (n)
8:23; 11:40 = 4QpapH[f] frg. 7 1; 17:33; 23:25
משמרת watch, course, obligation (n)
22:24
משען support, supply (n)
18:25
משענה support (n)
15:19; 18:34
משפט judgment, ordinance, justice (n)
4:14, 16, 18, 22, 23, 25; 5:16, 23; 6:15, 17, 31, 38; 8:11, 17; 9:8, 11, 18, 25, 28, 32, 35, 39; 10:26, 41; 11:28 = 4QpapH[f] frg. 6 2; 12:21, 26, 27; 13:6, 10; 14:29, 32; 15:15, 38; 16:38; 17:9, 10, 15, 31; 18:36, 38; 19:11; 21:11 = 4QH[a] frg. 10 1; [21:15] = 4QH[a] frg. 10 4; 21:36; 22:28, 29, 30; 23:12; 24:8, 9, 25; 25:3, 12; [26:34] = 4QH[a] frg. 7 2:15; A1 1; C3 5
משקה drink, juice (n)
12:12; 16:5
משקלת level, plumb line (n)
14:29 = 4QH[c] frg. 4 2:8; 16:23
מתך outpouring (n)
11:29
מתלעה fang (n)
13:12
מתנים loins (n)
4:35; 10:9; 16:34; 18:35
נאץ to despise, reject (v)
12:13, 23; 15:25
נאצה contempt, disgrace (n)
14:5
נבוך spring (n)
11:16 = 4QpapH[f] frg. 5 3
נבט to look (v)
4:39; 12:12; 18:5, 22; 19:20 = 4QH[a] frg. 1 1; 21:5; 24:31
נביא prophet (n)
12:17
נבל to fade, wither, droop (v)
16:27; 18:34
נבל harp (n)
19:26 = 4QH[a] frg. 1 5
נבע to flow, utter, pour out (v)
16:19; [26:13] = 4QH[a] frg. 7 1:17; [26:23] = 4QH[e] frg. 2 3
נגד in front of, opposite (prep)
8:12; 9:35; [10:6] = 4QpapH[f] frg. 3 2; 10:17, 26; 11:24; 12:16 = 4QH[d] frg. 1 3; 12:29; 13:13, 17; 18:12; 20:34; 25:10
נגה brightness, bright light (n)
14:21
נגינה stringed music, mocking song (n)
10:13; 13:32
נגע to touch, strike (v)
16:30; 19:24
נגע blow, skin blemish, plague (n)
3:18; 4:20; 8:33; 9:20, 34, 35; 10:9; 12:37; 13:30 = 4QH[c] frg. 2 11; 16:28 (2x); 17:6, 10, 12, 25; 18:21; 19:11, 25; 21:36 = 4QH[a] frg. 12 1; 22:10, 23; 24:25; [26:25] = 4QH[a] frg. 7 2:6 = 4QH[e] frg. 2 5
נגר to pour (v)
12:35; 16:33
נגשׂ to oppress (v)
[26:21] = 4QH[e] frg. 2 2
נגשׁ to approach, participate (v)
6:24, 29, 30; 7:28; 8:30; 14:27; 20:26
נדבה freewill offering, willingness (n)
6:35, 37; 7:23
נדה impurity, sprinkling (n)
4:31; 5:32; 9:24; [15:40] = 4QH[b] frg. 10 4; 19:14; 20:28; 21:36
נדח to banish, drive away (v)
12:9, 10
נדיב willing, noble (adj)
3:16; 22:25
נהל to guide, lead (v)
17:32; 23:8
נהם to growl, roar (v)
25:36
נהמה roaring, groaning (n)
18:35
נהר river (n)
14:19; 16:15
נוב to bear fruit (v)
16:14
נוס to flee (v)
21:15; [26:23] = 4QH[a] frg. 7 2:5
נוף to wave, extend, spread (v)
4:38; 15:10; 16:23, 34; 23:29, 33
נזל stream (n)
16:5
נחל to inherit, possess (v)
4:27; 6:17
נחל torrent, brook, wadi (n)
11:30 = 4QpapH[f] frg. 6 4; 11:32 = 4QH[b] frg. 5 7; 11:33; 16:18; 17:5
נחלה possession, inheritance, allotment (n)
6:30; 8:22; 14:11; 18:30; 24:36
נחם to comfort, relent (v)
3:17; 8:35; [10:7] = 4QpapH[f] frg. 3 3; 13:5; 14:10; 17:13 (2x); 19:35

נחשול wind, gale (n)
10:14

נטה to stretch out (v)
8:13; 9:11; [26:41] = 4QH[b] frg. 21 4

נכא to scourge (v)
[16:2] = 4QH[b] frg. 10 8

נכא broken (adj)
23:16

נכה to strike, defeat (v)
16:24

נכחה uprightness (n)
10:17

נכר to recognize, disguise, treat as foreign (v)
6:30; 13:15; 15:16; 16:14; [19:23] = 4QH[a] frg. 1 3; 21:4; 25:25, 30; 26:34 = 4QH[a] frg. 7 2:15

נכר foreigner (n)
13:7

נס standard, banner (n)
10:15; 14:37

נסה to test, try (v)
10:16

נסוי testing (n)
4:34

נעויה sin, perverseness (n)
4:31; 17:33; [26:22] = 4QH[a] frg. 7 2:4 = 4QH[e] frg. 2 3

נעורים youth (n)
[15:40] = 1QH[b] frg. 1 12 = 4QH[b] frg. 10 4; 17:31

נפח to breathe, set aflame, smelt (v)
13:18 = 4QH[c] frg. 1 2:3

נפל to fall (v)
4:30; 5:12; 6:22; 8:24; 10:31; 11:23, 28 = 4QpapH[f] frg. 6 2; [12:1] = 4QH[b] frg. 6 1 = 4QpapH[f] frg. 7 3; 15:37 = 4QpapH[f] frg. 12 4; 20:7; [25:7] = 4QH[b] frg. 17 1; [26:15] = 4QH[a] frg. 7 1:19

נפץ storm (n)
10:29

נפש soul, person, self (n)
6:28; 7:23 (2x), 29, 31; 8:28; 9:34; 10:9, 22, 23, 25, 26, 30, 31, 33, 34, 36 = 4QH[b] frg. 3 3; 10:37; 11:7 (2x), 20, 26; 12:22; 13:14 (2x), 15, 16, 17, 19, 20 (2x; deleted 1x) = 4QH[c] frg. 1 2:5 [not in 4QH[C]]; 13:20; 13:36, 41; 14:26; 15:26; 16:30, 33, 39; 17:7, 8, 28, 33; 18:31, 33; 19:10, 33; 20:4

נץ blossom (n)
18:34

נצב to stand, set (v)
17:18

נצח forever, splendor (n)
9:18, 21, 26; 12:14, 23, 26; 15:18, 34, 35; 17:25; 21:15; 25:9; [26:12] = 4QH[a] frg. 7 1:16; [26:30] = 4QH[a] frg. 7 2:11

נצל to take away, deliver (v)
10:33; 11:6; 13:15; 15:20

נצר shoot, sprout (n)
14:18; 15:22; 16:7, 9, 11

נקם to avenge (v)
21:37

נשׂא to lift, carry, take (v)
4:24; 6:30; 8:34; 14:37; 17:4; 18:27

נשׂג to reach, overtake, obtain (v)
4:21; 13:31

נשף twilight (n)
[25:33] = 4QH[b] frg. 20 4

נתיבה path (n)
9:14; 12:5; 14:27; 15:17; 21:23

נתך to melt (v)
21:25

נתן to give, put, set (v)
4:29; 5:36; 6:19; 8:20, 29; 10:9, 39 = 4QH[b] frg. 3 6; 11:36; 12:27; 13:8; 15:13; 16:5, 15; 17:10; 18:24, 29; 19:7, 30 = 4QH[b] frg. 12 1:4; 20:15; 21:34; 23:25

נתק to tear off (v)
13:39 = 4QH[c] frg. 3 11

סבב to go around, surround, turn (v)
10:27; 13:33 = 4QH[c] frg. 3 4; 13:37 = 4QH[c] frg. 3 8

סביב all around, environs, surrounding (part)
11:41 = 4QpapH[f] frg. 7 2; 13:27

סגר to shut, hand over (v)
11:19; 13:11, 16

סדר to order, arrange (v)
5:37

סוג to turn back, change (v)
4:40

סוד secret counsel, council, foundation (n)
4:31; 5:14, 32; 6:17, 29, 32; 9:24, 29; 10:12, 24; 11:22; 12:26, 29; 13:11, 26, 28 = 4QH[c] frg. 2 7; 14:8, 15, 29 = 4QH[c] frg. 4 2:7; 15:12, 37 = 1QH[b] frg. 1 9; 18:6, 23; 19:7, 12, 15, 19; 20:15; 24:15; 25:26 = 4QH[b] frg. 19 7

סוף end (n)
21:16

סור to turn aside, depart, remove (v)
7:24; 12:4; 14:21; 15:18

סלח to forgive (v)
6:35

סליחה forgiveness (n)
13:4; 14:12; 15:21, 33, 38; 17:13, 34; 18:18, 23; 19:12, 34; 22:24; [26:34] = 4QH[a] frg. 7 2:16

סלע rock (n)
12:4; 14:29; 15:11; 17:28

סמך to lean, support, be firm (v)
9:37; 10:9, 11, 38; 15:9; 17:32; 23:14

סער to storm (v)
21:26

סערה storm (n)
9:14; 13:20 = 4QH[c] frg. 1 2:5

ספר to recount, tell (v)
4:29; 5:28; 7:14 = 4QH[a] frg. 8 1:6; 7:18 = 4QH[a] frg. 8 1:10; 9:25, 27, 32, 35 (2x); 11:24; 14:14; 18:16, 22; 19:9, 27, 31; 20:33; 21:9; 23:15, 24; 25:32; [26:35] = 4QH[a] frg. 7 2:17; A7 2; A8 1

סרר to be rebellious, stubborn (v)
13:26

סתר to hide, conceal (v)
4:21; 9:27; 11:39; 13:13, 28; 16:11; 19:20, 22; [21:20] = 4QH[b] frg. 13 3; 26:15 = 4QH[a] frg. 7 1:19

סתר secret (n)
16:19

עב cloud (n)
24:11

עבד to work, serve, honor (v)
4:26; 8:25, 36

עבד servant, slave (n)
4:23, 24, 35, 37, 38; 5:35; 6:19, 22, 36; 8:28, 30, 36; 13:17, 30 = 4QH[c] frg. 2 12; 15:19; 17:11; 18:31; 19:30, 33, 36; 22:35, 37; 23:7, 11; [23:17] = 4QH[b] frg. 14 6

עבד work, deed (n)
8:32

עבודה work, service (n)
9:14, 18, 29; 10:35 = 4QH[b] frg. 3 1; 10:38 = 4QH[b] frg. 3 5; 14:22

עבר to pass, transgress, join (v)
12:28; 14:24, 38; 16:9 = 4QpapH[f] frg. 13 1; 20:27

עבת cord, rope (n)
13:38

עגן to refrain (v)
25:9

עד forever, everlasting (n)
4:40; 5:18, 23, 27, 30; 6:27, 36; 7:29, 37; 9:10; 11:37; 12:22; 15:34; 16:3 = 4QH[b] frg. 10 10; 18:29; 19:16, 28, 30 = 4QH[b] frg. 12 1:3; 24:9; [26:24] = 4QH[e] frg. 2 4

עד until, as far as (prep)
2:30; 6:34; 7:18 = 4QH[a] frg. 8 1:10 [ועם]; 8:14; 11:9, 31, 32, 37; 12:24, 28, 31, 40; 13:13; 14:19 (2x), 20, 22, 27, 28, 34; [15:40] = 1QH[b] frg. 1 12; [16:1] = 4QH[b] frg. 10 7; 16:31, 32; 17:29, 32, 34, 38; 18:35; 19:25; 21:12, 15; 23:7, 26; 24:7, 13; 25:6; [26:27] = 4QH[a] frg. 7 2:9; C3 5; C4 3

עד witness (n)
[21:15] = 4QH[a] frg. 10:4

עדה congregation, nation (n)
3:32; 5:25; 7:19; 10:24, 34; 11:23; 14:8; 15:37; 25:5, 32; [26:10] = 4QH[a] frg. 7 1:14; [26:28] = 4QH[a] frg. 7 2:9 = 4QH[e] frg. 2 8

עדן luxury, delight (n)
5:34; 18:26, 32

עדן Eden (n)
14:19 = 4QH[b] frg. 8 4; 16:21

עדר to be missing (v)
9:27

עוד to help, stand up, hold up (v)
12:23, 37

עוד to be like (v)
26:6 = 4QH[a] frg. 7 1:9

עוד again, still, longer (part)
6:15; 12:21; 14:33; [16:2] = 4QH[b] frg. 10 9; [19:29] = 4QH[b] frg. 12 1:3; 20:13, 20, 21; 25:7; 26:26 = 4QH[a] frg. 7 2:7 = 4QH[e] frg. 2 6

עוה to twist, commit iniquity (v)
5:32; 8:18; 9:24; 11:22; 15:30 = 1QH[b] frg. 1 1 = 4QH[b] frg. 9 2; 19:15

עוז to seek refuge (v)
14:28; 15:20, 22

עול nursing child (n)
17:36

עול iniquity (n)
11:19; 13:26; 14:10; 21:29; 23:37

עול unrighteous one (n)
9:28

עולה evil, malice, injustice (n)
6:26, 36, 37; 7:38; 8:29; 9:38; 10:5; 13:10; [14:21] = 4QH[c] frg. 4 1:5; 15:39; 19:25, 29 = 4QH[a] frg. 1 7 = 4QH[b] frg. 12 1:2; 21:30, 35; 24:30; 25:8

עולל child (n)
15:24

עולם forever, everlasting, age, ancient times (n)
2:13, 30; 3:24; 4:32, 40 = 4QH[b] frg. 1 3; 5:13, 18 (2x), 22, 23, 24, 26, 27, 29, 30, 33, 35; 6:17, 34 (2x); 7:15, 29, 33; 8:14, 16, 30, 32; 9:5, 9, 10, 13, 17, 20, 26, 33 (2x); 11:5; [11:18] = 4QpapH[f] frg. 5 6; 11:19 = 4QpapH[f] frg. 5 7; 11:21, 22, 23, 36; 12:5; 14:14, 18 (2x) = 4QH[b] frg. 8 2 (1x); 14:21 = 4QH[c] frg. 4 1:4; 14:34; 15:12, 28, 34 (2x); 16:7, 9, 13 = 1QH[b] frg. 2 2; 16:15, 21; 17:25, 26, 28, 29; 18:33; 19:28, 30 = 4QH[b] frg. 12 1:3; 20:18 = 4QH[a] frg. 8 2:20; 20:32 = 4QH[a] frg. 9 1; 21:13 = 4QH[a] frg. 10 3; 21:15; 23:7, 16, 22, 31; 25:6; [26:11] = 4QH[a] frg. 7 1:15; [26:13] = 4QH[a] frg. 7 1:17; [26:16] = 4QH[a] frg. 7 1:20; [26:24] = 4QH[a] frg. 7 2:6 = 4QH[e] frg. 2 5; 26:29 = 4QH[a] frg. 7 2:10 = 4QH[e] frg. 2 9; 26:30 = 4QH[a] frg. 7 2:11

עון iniquity, guilt, punishment (n)
4:23, 24, 27; 6:35; 7:23; 9:24, 27, 29, 34; 10:12; 12:16 = 4QH[d] frg. 1 3; 12:30, 38; [16:3] = 4QH[b] frg. 10 9; 24:22; [25:26] = 4QH[b] frg. 19 6; [26:25] = 4QH[a] frg. 7 2:6 = 4QH[e] frg. 2 5; A4 1

עועים distortion (n)
14:26; 15:8

עוף to fly (v)
11:28 = 4QpapH[f] frg. 6 1; 16:32; 24:10 = 4QH[b] frg. 15 1

עוף bird (n)
16:10; [24:13] = 4QH[b] frg. 15 5

עור to arouse, stir up, uncover (v)
14:32; 17:3

עות to be bent, pervert, sustain (v)
16:37

עז might (n)
4:30; 9:12; 11:38; 13:39; 14:30 = 4QH[c] frg. 4 2:9; 14:31 = 4QH[c] frg. 4 2:11; 15:9, 11; 17:28; 23:8, 14; [26:12] = 4QH[a] frg. 7 1:16; [26:14] = 4QH[a] frg. 7 1:18; [26:42] = 4QH[a] frg. 7 2:23

עזב to forsake, leave (v)
7:25; 10:38; 11:29; 12:36; 13:7, 8, 14, 22; 14:9; 16:28; 17:11, 18, 35; 22:37; 24:36

עזק to dig around (v)
16:23

עזר to help (v)
3:16; 10:36; 13:8; 15:26

עטף to be faint, feeble (v)
16:30

עין eye, spring (n)
4:36; 6:27, 29; 7:33; 8:36; 10:33; 13:36; 15:5; 17:5 (2x); 19:4, 22; 21:5; 23:8

עיף weary (adj)
16:37

עיר city (n)
11:8; 14:28

על upon, over, above, against (prep)
2:27; 4:30 (2x), 35, 38; 6:20, 25,

28, 41; 7:24, 28; 8:23, 24, 35, 37; 9:22, 27, 28, 30; 10:12, 14, 18, 26, 27, 33, 35; 11:9, 14, 16, 27, 28 = 4QpapH[f] frg. 6 2; 11:29 (2x) = 4QH[b] frg. 5 2 (1x); 11:30 = 4QpapH[f] frg. 6 4; 11:34 (2x); 12:4, 11, 23 (2x) = 4QpapH[f] frg. 9 1 (1x); 12:27, 33, 35, 36; 13:6, 10 = 4QH[c] frg. 1 1:2; 13:13, 19, 24, 26 (2x), 33, 37; 14:10 (2x), 18, 20 = 4QH[b] frg. 8 5; 14:26, 27, 29 (2x); 15:7, 11, 25, 26, 32; 16:10, 16, 18, 22, 23, 29, 32, 33; 17:4, 13, 21, 30, 35, 36 (2x); 18:25, 26, 27; 20:27, 34, 35; 21:24 = 4QH[b] frg. 13 7; 22:13, 24, 32, 33, 39; 23:12, 28, 29; 24:13, 39; 25:14; [26:31] = 4QH[a] frg. 7 2:13; 28:14

עלה to go up, arise, sacrifice (v)
11:21; 13:24; 16:26

עלה leaf (n)
16:9, 27; 18:27

עליון upper, highest, Most High (adj)
12:32; 14:36

עלילה deed (n)
6:20; 7:37

עליליה deed (n)
8:26

עלם to conceal, deceive (v)
11:29 = 4QpapH[f] frg. 6 3; 12:14; 15:37 = 1QH[b] frg. 1 9

עם people (n)
6:12; 10:21; 12:7, 12, 17, 27 (2x); 13:7, 19 = 4QH[c] frg. 1 2:4; 13:23; 14:10, 11; 24:15, 34

עם with (prep)
5:16, 25 (2x), 26, 34; 6:18; 7:17 = 4QH[a] frg. 8 1:9; 7:18, 19 = 4QH[a] frg. 8 1:11; 8:15, 30; 9:19, 20; 10:40; 11:5, 11, 18 = 4QpapH[f] frg. 5 5; 11:22, 23 (2x), 26 (3x); 12:16, 35, 36; 13:10, 23, 32, 40; 14:7, 16, 25 = 4QH[c] frg. 4 1:11; 14:31 = 4QH[c] frg. 4 2:12 [עד]; 15:6; 16:6, 13, 14, 22, 27 (2x), 29; 17:33 (2x); 18:12, 36, 37; 19:6, 14 (2x), 16 (2x), 17; 20:7, 14, 22; 21:10, 14, 23 = 4QH[b] frg. 13 6; 22:22; 23:26, 30, 34; 25:5; [26:7] = 4QH[a] frg. 7 1:11; 26:28 = 4QH[a] frg. 7 2:9 = 4QH[e] frg. 2 8

עמד to stand, go up (v)
3:24; 4:35; 8:31; 10:10, 27, 31; 12:22; 15:22, 34; 17:5, 12; 18:8; 20:38; 21:14, 26; 22:15; 23:2, 11, 23; [26:37] = 4QH[a] frg. 7 2:19

עמד with (prep)
8:31; 12:29; 17:19

עמה beside, corresponding (prep)
21:11 = 4QH[a] frg. 10 1 [לערמת]

עמל trouble, acquisition, harm (n)
18:34; 19:4, 22

עמק depth (n)
5:19

ענה to answer, testify (v)
12:19 = 4QH[d] frg. 1 7

ענו meek, humble, oppressed (adj)
6:14; 13:23; 23:15

ענוה humility (n)
4:34

עני poor, afflicted (adj)
10:36 = 4QH[b] frg. 3 3; 13:15, 16

עני misery, affliction (n)
6:15; 9:38; [10:6] = 4QpapH[f] frg. 3 2

ענף branch (n)
18:28

עפי foliage (n)
14:18

עפר dust, dirt (n)
3:23; 5:32; 7:34; 8:18, 19; 11:14 = 4QpapH[f] frg. 5 1; 11:22; 13:29 = 4QH[c] frg. 2 10; 14:37; 18:6, 7, 14; 19:6, 15; 20:27, 28, 29 (2x), 30, 34; 21:10, 12, 13, 17; [21:20] = 4QH[b] frg. 13 3; 21:25 = 4QH[b] frg. 13 8; 21:34; 22:8, 30; 23:5, 13 = 4QH[b] frg. 14 1; 23:24, 27, 29 (2x); [26:27] = 4QH[a] frg. 7 2:8 = 4QH[e] frg. 2 7; 28:11

עפרת lead (metal) (n)
16:20

עץ tree, wood (n)
10:28; 11:30; 16:6, 7, 10, 13 = 1QH[b] frg. 2 2; 16:20, 23, 26

עצה counsel, council, congregation (n)
8:14, 26; 9:7; 12:14; 13:26; 14:8, 13, 14, 16; 15:13; 25:28

עצם to be mighty (v)
14:34; 22:17

עצם bone (n)
13:9, 37; 15:7; 16:31; 19:24

עצר to restrain, withhold (v)
7:14; 12:12; 16:24, 29, 31; 18:13, 14; 19:38; 22:7

עקב heel, footprint (n)
13:26

ערב to mix (v)
8:32

ערב evening (n)
20:8; 22:22

ערוה nakedness, impurity, shame (n)
5:32; 9:24; 20:28

ערום crafty, prudent (adj)
2:31

עריץ ruthless (adj)
9:41; 10:13, 23

ערך to arrange, prepare (v)
12:25

ערל uncircumcised (adj)
14:23 = 4QH[c] frg. 4 1:9; 21:6

ערל uncircumcision (n)
10:9, 20

ערמה craftiness, discernment (n)
9:37; 10:11; [12:2] = 4QH[b] frg. 6 2 = 4QpapH[f] frg. 7 4

ערמה heap (n)
[21:24] = 4QH[a] frg. 11 2

ערער juniper (n)
16:25

ערף (back of) neck (n)
8:16

ערשׂ couch (n)
17:4

עשׂה to do, make (v)
3:27; 6:16, 29; 7:32; 8:13, 26, 27, 30; 9:10, 16, 22; 12:39; 14:13, 29; 16:4; 18:11, 14; 21:7, 33; 23:25; [26:26] = 4QH[a] frg. 7 2:7 = 4QH[e] frg. 2 6; [26:42] = 4QH[b] frg. 21 5

עשׁ moth (n)
17:5

עשׁק to oppress (v)
2:26

עשׁשׁ to become weak (v)
13:36 = 4QpapH[f] frg. 11 2

עת time, age, era, occasion (n)
6:15; 16:24; 20:11; 24:22

פאר to beautify, glorify (v)
5:34

פארה branch (n)
16:23

פארה glory (n)
16:21

פגע to meet, encounter, fall upon (v)
4:17; 22:35

פגר corpse (n)
14:35; 24:17

פדה to redeem, release (v)
4:32; 10:34, 37; 11:20

פה mouth (n)
2:12; 3:26; 6:22, 24, 25, 29, 31; 7:15 (2x) = 4QH[a] frg. 8 1:7 (1x); 8:15, 25; 9:22, 33 (2x); 10:19, 36; 11:6; 12:17, 28; 13:6, 11, 13, 20; 14:5, 12, 17; 15:14, 24; 16:17, 36; 17:11; 18:9, 22, 29, 31; 19:7, 10, 27 = 4QH[a] frg. 1 6; 19:28, 36; 20:12, 25, 26, 36; 21:18; 22:14; 23:11; [23:17] = 4QH[b] frg. 14 6; 25:11, 33 = 4QH[b] frg. 20 4; 26:37; 28:15; A4 2

פז refined gold (n)
[26:8] = 4QH[a] frg. 7 1:12 = 4QH[e] frg. 1 8

פח snare (n)
10:10, 31; 11:27; 21:11, 24 = 4QH[b] frg. 13 7; 21:28 (2x)

פחד to fear, dread (v)
18:36; 22:28

פחד dread, awe, fear (n)
10:38; 19:4; 20:19; [26:24] = 4QH[a] frg. 7 2:5 = 4QH[e] frg. 2 4

פלא to be wonderful (v)
2:12; 6:34; 7:13, 14 = 4QH[a] frg. 8 1:6; 7:18 = 4QH[a] frg. 8 1:10; 7:20; 9:32, 35, 36; 11:24; 12:29; 13:17; 14:14; 17:7, 39; 18:6, 17, 23; 19:6, 18, 31; 21:7, 8, 23 = 4QH[b] frg. 13 6; 22:7; 23:36; 24:15; 25:5; [25:32] = 4QH[b] frg. 20 3; [26:14] = 4QH[a] frg. 7 1:18; [26:31a] = 4QH[a] frg. 7 2:12; [26:34] = 4QH[a] frg. 7 2:16; [26:39] = 4QH[a] frg. 7 2:20a; 28:13

פלא wonder (n)
5:19; 7:13; 8:10; 9:23; 10:15; 11:11; 12:29 (2x), 30; 13:23; 15:30, 35 = 1QH[b] frg. 1 7; 17:27; 18:13; 19:7, 13; 20:15, 32; 22:6; 23:7; 24:28; [26:16] = 4QH[a] frg. 7 1:21; [26:31a] = 4QH[a] frg. 7 2:12

פלג to divide, apportion (v)
5:30; 9:18, 20; 22:20

פלג stream, division (n)
11:31 = 4QH[b] frg. 5 5; 16:22, 24, 25; 18:27

פלט to escape, deliver (v)
11:11; 13:20

פלט fugitive, survivor (n)
11:29; 13:8, 41; 14:28, 35; 17:29, 33; 23:26

פלצות horror (n)
11:12, 13; 16:38

פן lest (part)
8:23; 11:41 = 4QpapH[f] frg. 7 2; 13:16

פנה to turn, abandon, prepare (v)
16:22; 20:8, 9, 10 = 4QH[a] frg. 8 2:13

פנה front, face; before (n)
3:29; 4:26; 5:12; 6:30; 7:38; 8:29, 32, 33, 34, 36; 9:8, 26, 27, 34; 10:9; 11:4, 8, 14, 27 = 4QpapH[f] frg. 6 1; 12:6, 16 = 4QH[d] frg. 1 3; 12:22, 24, 28, 34, 37; 13:10, 34 = 4QH[c] frg. 3 5; 13:37; 14:16, 27; 15:10, 17, 26, 31, 32 = 1QH[b] frg. 1 3; 15:33, 34; 16:26; 17:12, 20, 22; 18:13, 34; 19:16; 20:10 = 4QH[a] frg. 8 2:13; 20:21, 31, 33 = 4QH[a] frg. 9 2; [21:25] = 4QH[a] frg. 11 3; 21:26; 22:10, 28, 29; 23:11, 35; 24:33; [26:31] = 4QH[a] frg. 7 2:13

פעל to do, make (v)
6:25; 8:15; 19:36

פעלה work, wage, result (n)
6:23; 7:26, 35; 9:11; 19:37

פעם beat, foot, time, occurrence (n)
4:22; 10:10; 12:4; 15:17; 16:35; 20:37, 38, 39; 21:24 = 4QH[b] frg. 13 7; 23:27

פצה to open, free (v)
13:13; 15:24

פקד to number, appoint, punish, visit (v)
6:35; 8:23; A5 1

פקדה punishment, visitation (n)
5:27; 9:19

פרד to separate (v)
15:7, 25; 21:25 = 4QH[b] frg. 13 8; 25:4, 16

פרה to bear fruit, produce (v)
12:15

פרח to bud, sprout, break out (v)
13:29 = 4QH[c] frg. 2 9; 14:18; 16:7, 8, 11, 28, 31; 18:33

פרח flower (n)
16:15

פרי fruit (n)
9:30; 16:12, 14, 21

פריץ violent (adj)
14:23

פרר to break, destroy, frustrate (v)
5:29; 10:28; [26:18] = 4QH[a] frg. 7 1:23

פרשׂ to spread out (v)
10:31; 11:27; 13:10; 21:21 = 4QH[b] frg. 13 4; 21:24 = 4QH[a] frg. 11 2 = 4QH[b] frg. 13 7

פשׁע to transgress, rebel (v)
10:10, 13

פשׁע transgression, rebellion (n)
4:23, 24, 27, 30; 6:35; 8:24, 34; 10:11; 11:22; 12:20, 36 = 4QpapH[f] frg. 10 1; 13:38 = 4QH[c] frg. 3 10; 14:9, 24; 15:8, 33; 17:13; 19:13; 21:2; 22:8, 33; 24:9

פתאם suddenly (part)
4:17; 16:19

פתה to be foolish, entice, deceive (v)
12:17 = 4QH[d] frg. 1 4; 14:22; 22:27

פתח to open (v)
7:16, 29; 8:14; 10:20; 11:17, 18 = 4QpapH[f] frg. 5 5 [ו]יפתח[ו]; 11:27; 13:28, 35 = 4QH[c] frg. 3 6; [13:40] = 4QH[c] frg. 3 12; 14:33; 16:8, 17, 22, 27; 18:9, 33; 19:22, 35; 20:16, 36; 21:6, 18, 22 = 4QH[b] frg. 13 5; 22:31; 23:11,

13, 14; [23:17] = 4QH[b] frg. 14 6; [26:24] = 4QH[a] frg. 7 2:5 = 4QH[e] frg. 2 4; C7 2

פתי simple, naïve, ignorant (n)
5:13; 10:11

פתן adder (n)
13:29 = 4QH[c] frg. 2 10

פתע suddenly (part)
4:17

צאצא offspring (n)
5:26; 7:19; 9:20; 10:40 = 4QH[b] frg. 3 8

צבא host, army, war, service (n)
5:25, 26; 8:15; 11:23, 36; 18:37; 19:16; 21:9; 23:34; 25:13; [26:11] = 4QH[a] frg. 7 1:15

צבי ?
15:32

צד side (n)
17:6

צדיק righteous, just (adj)
6:26; 7:28; 8:19, 28; 9:38; 12:39; 15:15; 20:22; 25:15

צדק to be just (v)
5:34; 8:29; 9:8; 15:31 = 4QH[b] frg. 9 3; 17:9, 14, 15; 20:34; 25:15; 26:31

צדק righteousness, justice (n)
3:28; 5:20, 36; 6:13, 21, 37; 8:23; 9:25, 28, 32; 10:6 = 4QpapH[f] frg. 3 2; 10:15; 12:41; 13:24; 14:7, 22; 17:33; 18:38; 19:21; 23:25; 25:3; [25:26] = 4QH[b] frg. 19 6; 26:33 = 4QH[a] frg. 7 2:14

צדקה righteousness, justice (n)
4:29, 32 (2x); 6:17, 27; 8:22, 27; 9:28; 12:31, 32, 38; 15:17, 20, 22; 16:3; 19:10, 34; 21:3; 24:21; [26:17] = 4QH[a] frg. 7 1:22

צוה to command (v)
7:24, 32; 14:23 = 4QH[c] frg. 4 1:8

צוץ to flourish, blossom (v)
15:21

צוקה anguish, distress (n)
11:8; 13:35 = 4QH[c] frg. 3 6; 17:13

צור rock (n)
16:24; 19:18

ציד hunter (n)
13:10 = 4QH[c] frg. 1 1:2

ציה dry (adj)
16:5

ציץ flower, rosette (n)
14:18

ציר pain (n)
11:8, 12; 13:32 = 4QH[c] frg. 3 3

צל shadow (n)
14:18

צלל to get dark, shade (v)
14:18

צלמות deep darkness (n)
13:35

צמא thirst (n)
12:12

צמא thirsty (adj)
12:12

צמד join (v)
13:26; 14:22

צמים snare (n)
[21:21] = 4QH[b] frg. 13 4; 21:28

צעד step, walk (n)
7:26, 34; 23:26

צפה to watch, wait (v)
6:16; 20:24; 22:24

צפור bird (n)
12:10; 13:20

צר narrow, distress (adj)
17:21, 25

צרה distress (n)
7:29; 13:14; 17:28

צרור bundle (n)
10:22

צרח to cry, shout (v)
11:34

צרר to bind, restrict, distress (v)
11:10

קבל to receive, take (v)
7:37

קדוש holy (adj)
3:32; 5:18; 9:3; 11:23; 12:26; 18:37; 19:15; 25:4, 5, 26 = 4QH[b] frg. 19 7; [26:6] = 4QH[a] frg. 7 1:10 = 4QH[e] frg. 1 6; A5 1; A6 1

קדם east, ancient times (n)
5:18, 27, 28, 29; 25:35

קדרות blackness (n)
13:33

קדש to consecrate (v)
7:30; 8:13; 19:13; [26:11] = 4QH[a] frg. 7 1:16

קדש holiness, holy object (n)
3:31; 4:38; 5:18, 25; 6:17, 24; 7:36, 40; 8:15, 20, 21, 25, 30; 9:13; 11:35; 14:8, 23; 15:10, 13; 16:11, 13, 14; 17:32; 20:5 = 4QH[a] frg. 3 2 [not in 4QH[a]]; 20:15, 31; 22:5; 23:33; [24:12] = 4QH[b] frg. 15 3; [26:2] = 4QH[e] frg. 1 1; 28:14; C2 3

קהל assembly (n)
10:32; [26:14] = 4QH[a] frg. 7 1:18

קהלה assembly (n)
10:14

קו line, measuring line (n)
9:30, 31; 11:28 = 4QpapH[f] frg. 6 2; 14:29; 16:22, 38; 23:12

קוה to wait for, hope (v)
18:24; 19:34; [26:15] = 4QH[a] frg. 7 1:20

קול voice, sound (n)
7:17; 8:17; 10:18, 29; 11:14, 17 = 4QpapH[f] frg. 5 4; 11:18, 36; 16:35, 37; 17:4; 19:29 = 4QH[b] frg. 12 1:2; [26:12] = 4QH[a] frg. 7 1:16

קום to arise, stand (v)
4:26; 5:29; 6:28; 7:24; 12:14, 23, 35, 37; 20:38; 22:10; [26:16] = 4QH[a] frg. 7 1:21

קומה height (n)
26:28 = 4QH[a] frg. 7 2:9 = 4QH[e] frg. 2 8

קוץ thorn (n)
16:26

קים standing, being (n)
5:29

קינה lament, dirge (n)
17:4; 19:25a = 4QH[e] frg. 1 4

קיר wall (n)
11:14; 15:12

קלון shame (n)
5:32; 20:28

קלס derision (n)
10:12; 11:7

קן nest (n)
12:10

קנאה jealousy, zeal (n)
5:16; 6:25; 9:7; 10:17, 33; 13:25; 17:3; 20:17; 21:37; [26:33] = 4QH[a] frg. 7 2:15

קנה reed, shoulder, branch, shaft (n)
15:5; 16:34

קנין possession (n)
18:27

קץ time, end, era (n)
4:22; 5:22, 26, 37; 7:16 (2x), 32; 9:18, 26; 11:29 = 4QpapH[f] frg. 6 3 [וקו]; 13:13, 22, 29 = 4QH[c] frg. 2 9; 14:32, 34; 16:32; 17:7, 8, 24; 19:28 = 4QH[b] frg. 12 1:1; 20:7 (2x), 9, 11, 25, 29; 21:16; 22:9, 14, 37; 24:7, 13, 15, 30; 25:13 = 4QH[b] frg. 18 2; [26:12] = 4QH[a] frg. 7 1:17; [26:24] = 4QH[a] frg. 7 2:6; [26:35] (2x) = 4QH[a] frg. 7 2:17 (2x); C3 5; C4 3; C4 5

קצה end (n)
14:34 (2x)

קרא to call, read (v)
8:14; 15:38 = 4QH[b] frg. 10 1

קרב to come near, offer (v)
6:25; 8:37

קרב entrails, midst (n)
9:35

קרוב near (adj)
6:25

קרן horn (n)
15:25, 26

קרץ to mold, pinch (v)
18:6; 20:27

קשה hard, difficult (adj)
8:16

קשת bow (n)
14:33

ראה to see (v)
5:28; 15:5; 16:14; 21:4; [26:33] = 4QH[a] frg. 7 2:15

ראש bitter and poisonous herb, venom (n)
12:15 = 4QH[d] frg. 1 2

ראשון first, former (adj)
4:30; 17:13

ראשית beginning, first, best (n)
5:17; 20:9 = 4QH[a] frg. 8 2:12

רב great, many, much (adj)
7:24; 8:26, 34; 10:18, 29 (2x); 11:22, 26, 33; 12:28, 29; 13:10

רב multitude, abundance, greatness (n)
4:27; 5:16, 34 (2x); 6:28, 30, 34; 8:26; 9:34; 12:20, 33; 14:12, 35; 15:21, 30, 33; [15:40] = 4QH[b] frg. 10 4; 17:14, 31, 34; 18:18, 26 (2x); 19:9, 12, 31, 32; 20:17 = 4QH[a] frg. 8 2:19; 23:15, 25; 24:14 = 4QH[b] frg. 15 7; [26:17] = 4QH[a] frg. 7 1:22; 26:32 = 4QH[a] frg. 7 2:13

רבה to increase, be many, great (v)
6:24; 8:22; 18:28, 30; 24:35; 25:10

רגל foot (n)
10:31 (2x); 12:4; 13:23; 15:5, 28; [15:41] = 4QH[b] frg. 10 5; 16:35 (2x); 22:13

רגן to murmur, grumble (v)
17:22

רגן grumbling, backbiting (n)
13:25

רגש to be in tumult (v)
10:14 (2x); 11:16 = 4QpapH[f] frg. 5 3; 11:17

רוה to be saturated, drink (v)
C3 6

רוח spirit, breath, wind (n)
3:26; 4:14, 18, 19, 29, 35, 37, 38; 5:14, 15, 25, 30, 32, 36, 39; 6:14, 22, 24, 36, 41; 7:26, 35; 8:16, 18, 20, 21, 24, 25, 27, 28, 29, 30, 32; 9:11, 12, 13, 17, 24, 30, 31 (2x), 34; 10:8, 17; 11:19, 22, 23; 12:32, 37; 13:30 = 4QH[c] frg. 2 12; 13:38; 14:17, 26; 15:8, 9, 14, 26, 32; 16:13, 30, 37; 17:12 (2x), 16 (2x), 32; 18:10, 24, 34; 19:15, 16; 20:14, 15 = 4QH[a] frg. 8 2:18; 21:26, 34; 23:16, 29; 24:11, 26, 27; 25:6, 8; [25:23] = 4QH[b] frg. 19 2

רום to be high, exalted (v)
7:29; 10:30; 14:11, 37; 15:19, 25, 26; 16:10, 36; 18:27; 19:15, 18; 23:15; 25:9, 27, 37; 26:11 = 4QH[a] frg. 7 1:15; [26:12] = 4QH[a] frg. 7 1:16; 26:15 = 4QH[a] frg. 7 1:19; 26:27 = 4QH[a] frg. 7 2:8 = 4QH[e] frg. 2 7; 26:29 = 4QH[a] frg. 7 2:10

רום height (n)
11:16 = 4QpapH[f] frg. 5 3; 11:21, 30 = 4QH[b] frg. 5 4; 18:32, 34; 26:16 = 4QH[a] frg. 7 1:20; 26:27 = 4QH[a] frg. 7 2:8 [רוח] = 4QH[e] frg. 2 7

רוע to shout, sound (v)
11:13, 34; 15:7

רוש to be poor (v)
10:36; 13:16, 22

רז mystery, secret (n)
5:17, 19, 30; 9:13 = 4QpapH[f] frg. 1 1; 9:15, 23, 31; 10:15; 12:28; 13:27, 38; 15:30; 16:7, 12 (2x); 17:23; 18:5 = 4QH[b] frg. 11 2; 19:13, 19; 20:16, 23; 21:27; 24:9, 28; 26:15 = 4QH[a] frg. 7 1:19; [26:16] = 4QH[a] frg. 7 1:21

רחב to be wide, enlarge (v)
20:4

רחב expanse (n)
17:27

רחום compassionate (adj)
8:34

רחוק far (adj)
5:33; 17:6

רחם to have compassion, love (v)
17:36

רחם womb (n)
7:28, 30; 12:31; 17:30

רחמים compassion (n)
2:27; 4:23, 29; 5:34; 6:14, 34; 7:18, 29; 8:27; 9:33; 12:33, 37, 38; 13:4; 14:12; 15:30, 33 = 4QpapH[f] frg. 12 1; 15:38 = 4QH[b] frg. 10 2; 17:3, 8, 30, 34; 18:16, 23; 19:12, 21 = 4QH[a] frg. 1 2; 19:32, 35; 21:11 = 4QH[a] frg. 10 1; 23:15; [26:18] = 4QH[a] frg. 7 1:22; [26:18] = 4QH[a] frg. 7 1:23; [26:32] = 4QH[a] frg. 7 2:14; [26:34] = 4QH[a] frg. 7 2:16; C1 2

רחק to be far (v)
6:32

ריב to strive, contend (v)
17:23; 25:15

ריב strife, dispute (n)
10:16; 13:24, 32 = 4QH[c] frg. 3 2; 13:37; 15:26; 17:15, 19, 23; 18:37

רכיל slander, gossip (n)
13:27

רמה to deceive (v)
4:19

רמה height (n)
24:14

רמה worm (n)
4:31; 20:28

רמיה deceit, negligence (n)
6:25; 9:29; 10:18, 36; 12:8, 11, 18, 22; 20:19; 21:29, 30, 35; [26:22] = 4QH[a] frg. 7 2:4

רמס to trample (v)
14:35

רנה shout of joy, song, exultation (n)
2:14; 7:21; 11:24; 13:15; 19:8, 17, 29 = 4QH[b] frg. 12 1:2; [26:13] = 4QH[a] frg. 7 1:17

רנן to sing for joy (v)
2:15; 7:17 = 4QH[a] frg. 8 1:9; [25:30] = 4QH[b] frg. 20 1; [26:10] = 4QH[a] frg. 7 1:14

רע bad, evil (adj)
5:20 = 4QH[b] frg. 2 2; 6:29, 30; 15:6; 25:7; [26:3] = 4QH[a] frg. 7 1:6 = 4QH[e] frg. 1 2

רע friend, companion, fellow (n)
12:10; 13:25; 17:15; 18:30; [26:6] = 4QH[a] frg. 7 1:10 = 4QH[e] frg. 1 6

רע evil (n)
15:6

רעד to tremble (v)
11:36

רעד trembling (n)
12:34

רעדה trembling (n)
18:35

רעה to shepherd, pasture, feed (v)
16:9

רעם to thunder (v)
11:35

רענן green (adj)
18:27

רעע to break (v)
12:34

רפש mire (n)
10:14; 11:33; 16:16

רצה to accept, be pleased with (v)
7:31; 17:10; 27:13

רצון favor, will (n)
4:35; 6:21, 24, 38; 7:28, 39; 8:22, 28, 30, 31, 32; 9:10, 12, 17, 22; 12:34; 13:6; 18:4, 8, 11, 21, 24; 19:12; 23:28; 24:13; 26:38 = 4QH[a] frg. 7 2:19; C6 4

רק only, still, however (part)
5:33; 6:39; 7:27; 18:14

רקיע expanse, sky (n)
5:25; 6:41; 11:32 = 4QH[b] frg. 5 6

רשם to inscribe (v)
8:28

רשע to be wicked, condemn, transgress (v)
5:33; 15:15; 17:9; 24:14, 26, 27 (2x); 25:15 = 4QH[b] frg. 18 5

רשע wicked, guilty (adj)
4:33; 5:38; 6:23, 35; 7:30; 10:12, 14, 26, 38; 12:35, 39; 13:19; 15:15

רשע wickedness, wicked deed (n)
6:20, 25, 27; 9:4; 24:24

רשעה wickedness (n)
4:22; 6:30; 7:37, 38; 10:10; 11:25, 27; 14:25 = 4QH[c] frg. 4 1:12; 14:32, 33; 15:10; 20:19; 21:28; 22:9; 25:6, 7 = 4QH[b] frg. 17 1; 25:9; [25:25] = 4QH[b] frg. 19 5; [26:20] = 4QH[e] frg. 2 1

רשת net (n)
10:31; 21:21 = 4QH[b] frg. 13 4; 21:24 = 4QH[a] frg. 11 2

רתח to boil (v)
11:16 = 4QpapH[f] frg. 5 3

רתק to bind (v)
16:36

רתת trembling (n)
12:34

שׂבע to satisfy, fill (v)
23:16

שׂגב to be exalted, high, strong (v)
14:28; 15:11

שׂדה field (n)
16:6

שׂוג to grow (v)
16:10

שׂוך to hedge, enclose, protect (v)
10:23; 13:35; 16:12

שׂושׂ to rejoice (v)
18:32

שׂטן Satan (?), adversary, accuser (n)
22:25; 24:23

שׂיבה gray hair, advanced age (n)
12:31; 17:34

שׂיח to meditate, speak (v)
9:37; 14:14; 17:7; 19:8

שׂים to put, set, make (v)
3:28; 9:30; 10:6 = 4QpapH[f] frg. 3 2; 10:11, 15, 20, 22, 35; 11:7; 12:16 = 4QH[d] frg. 1 3; 13:9 = 4QH[c] frg. 1 1:1; 14:29; 15:11, 23, 37; 16:17; 18:25; 19:36

שׂכל to be wise, prudent, understand (v)
5:31; 6:20, 22; 7:12, 34; 8:32; 15:29; 17:16; 18:6, 8, 9; 19:7, 13; 20:23, 36; 25:13 = 4QH[b] frg. 18 2; 26:33 = 4QH[a] frg. 7 2:14

שׂכל understanding (n)
3:26; 4:33; 5:30; 6:14, 30; 7:15; 9:33; 17:26, 31, 41; 18:29; 19:28, 31; 20:16, 25; 23:22

שׂמח to rejoice (v)
19:33; 26:10

שׂמחה joy (n)
5:23; 10:7; 17:24; 19:26; 20:5; 22:24; 23:16; [26:13] = 4QH[a] frg. 7 1:17; [26:23] = 4QH[a] frg. 7 2:14 = 4QH[e] frg. 2 3; 26:30 = 4QH[a] frg. 7 2:11

שׂנא to hate (v)
4:15, 36; 6:36; 7:32

שׂפה lip, speech, edge (n)
9:30, 31; 10:9, 13, 20; 12:17; 13:26 = 4QH[b] frg. 7 1; 15:14, 15; 16:26, 37; 19:8; [26:5] = 4QH[e] frg. 1 5; [26:12] = 4QH[a] frg. 7 1:16; [26:41] = 4QH[a] frg. 7 2:22 = 4QH[b] frg. 21 4

שׂר prince, chief (n)
14:17; 18:10

שׂרפה burning (n)
11:32

שׂשׂון joy (n)
17:24

שׁאול Sheol (n)
4:25; 11:10, 17 = 4QpapH[f] frg.

5 4; 11:20; 14:20; 16:29; 17:4; 18:36; 25:14 = 4QH[b] frg. 18 4

שאון mire (n)
13:24

שאון roar, clamor (n)
10:29; 14:10

שארית remnant (n)
14:11, 35; 15:25; 26:27 = 4QH[a] frg. 7 2:8 = 4QH[e] frg. 2 7

שבול path (n)
15:18

שבועה oath (n)
6:28

שביב flame (n)
11:31 = 4QH[b] frg. 5 5 = 4QpapH[f] frg. 6 5; 14:21; 16:21

שבע seven (adj)
13:18; 15:27

שבר to break (v)
13:9, 39; 14:31; 15:5; 16:34

שבת to cease, rest (v)
7:16; 9:38; 14:15; 15:18; 16:33; 17:40; 19:27; 20:17; 21:14; 23:3; [25:31] = 4QH[b] frg. 20 2; [26:13] = 4QH[a] frg. 7 1:18; [26:21] = 4QH[e] frg. 2 2; [26:24] = 4QH[a] frg. 7 2:5 = 4QH[e] frg. 2 4; [26:25] = 4QH[a] frg. 7 2:6 = 4QH[e] frg. 2 5; [26:30] = 4QH[a] frg. 7 2:11

שגה to stray (v)
8:23

שד breast (n)
17:30

שדד to devastate (v)
25:8 = 4QH[b] frg. 17 2

שוא worthlessness, deception, destruction (n)
10:24, 30; 14:8; 15:37

שואה devastation (n)
13:32; 17:6

שוב to turn, return, repent, restore (v)
5:35, 36; 6:32, 35, 39; 7:13; 8:35, 36; 9:2, 28; 10:11; 11:28, 37; 13:20 = 4QH[c] frg. 1 2:5; 14:9, 16, 17, 26 = 4QH[c] frg. 4 2:3; 15:32; 16:25; 17:8; 18:9, 14; 20:23, 26, 29, 30, 33, 34; 22:8, 16, 30; 23:10, 32; [26:15] = 4QH[a] frg. 7 1:20; 26:37 = 4QH[a] frg. 7 2:18

שוה to be like, compare (v)
7:36; [26:4] = 4QH[e] frg. 1 3

שוח to sink down, gesture (v)
16:33; 17:9

שוחה pit (n)
10:19; 21:21 = 4QH[b] frg. 13 4

שוט to spread, roam about (v)
11:31 = 4QpapH[f] frg. 6 5; 11:37

שוט flood (n)
14:38

שועה cry for help (n)
13:14

שושנה lily (n)
18:33

שחד bribe, gift (n)
6:30, 31; 7:37

שחק cloud, sky; layer of dust (n)
11:14; 14:19 = 4QH[b] frg. 8 4; 26:14; [26:27] = 4QH[a] frg. 7 2:9 = 4QH[e] frg. 2 8

שחר dawn (n)
12:7

שחת to destroy, corrupt, be spoiled (v)
10:29; 11:39; 22:25; 24:22, 23

שחת pit, destruction, perdition (n)
5:22; 10:23, 40; 11:13 = 4QH[b] frg. 4 2; 11:17 = 4QpapH[f] frg. 5 5; 11:19, 20, 27, 28 = 4QH[b] frg. 5 1; 13:8; 16:30

שטף to overflow, rinse (v)
14:38; 16:16, 18

שיר to sing (v)
[26:9] = 4QH[a] frg. 7 1:13

שיר song (n)
7:21; [25:34] = 4QH[a] frg. 3 4

שית thorn (n)
16:26

שכב to lie down (v)
14:37

שכול bereavement (n)
10:33

שלהבת flame, blade (n)
16:31

שלוה prosperity, tranquility (n)
20:5

שלום peace, welfare, completeness (n)
5:22, 34; 7:29; 10:8 = 4QpapH[f] frg. 3 4; 15:18; 17:11, 33; 19:30 = 4QH[b] frg. 12 1:3; 20:5 = 4QH[a] frg. 3 2; 20:6 = 4QH[a] frg. 3 2; 21:16, 23; [26:23] = 4QH[a] frg. 7 2:5 = 4QH[e] frg. 2 4

שלום recompense (n)
9:19

שלח to send, allow (v)
16:8, 11, 35; 24:14, 24

שלך to throw, fling, cast (v)
4:27

שלם to be complete, be sound, pay, make peace (v)
8:29

שלם whole, completed, perfect (adj)
8:25, 35

שם there (part)
13:10; 20:30

שם name (n)
3:32; 4:26, 32; 9:32; 10:32; 11:24; 17:39; 19:9, 28 = 4QH[a] frg. 1 6 = 4QH[b] frg. 12 1:1; 20:6 = 4QH[a] frg. 3 3; 21:18; 22:36; 23:9; 26:12 = 4QH[a] frg. 7 1:16; A6 2

שמד to destroy (v)
6:27; 7:38

שמועה report (n)
10:8; [15:41] = 1QH[b] frg. 1 13; 23:7

שמים heavens, sky (n)
8:10, 21; 9:11; 11:23, 36, 37; 14:33; 16:18; 18:37; 22:5; 23:30; 24:11; 25:26; [26:36] = 4QH[a] frg. 7 2:18; [26:41] = 4QH[a] frg. 7 2:23

שמיר thorn (n)
16:26

שמם to be desolate, appalled (v)
15:6; 21:6; 25:7

שממה desolation (n)
20:20

שמע to hear, obey (v)
2:14; 7:16 = 4QH[a] frg. 8 1:8; 9:25, 36; 10:7; 11:18; 12:25; 13:14; 15:6; 18:36; 19:28 = 4QH[b] frg. 12 1:2; 20:15; 21:5; 23:8, 12, 21; 24:34; 26:13 = 4QH[a] frg. 7 1:17; 26:26 = 4QH[a] frg. 7 2:7 = 4QH[e] frg. 2 6; [26:38] = 4QH[a] frg. 7

2:20a = 4QH[b] frg. 21 1; [26:41] = 4QH[a] frg. 7 2:22

שׁמר to keep, watch, preserve (v)
7:28; 8:31, 35; 10:6 = 4QpapH[f] frg. 3 2; 21:10, 25 = 4QH[b] frg. 13 8; 21:27; 22:10

שׁמשׁ sun, sunlight (n)
16:23; C2 2

שׁן tooth, rocky crag (n)
10:13; 13:12, 16

שׂנאב vegetation (n)
11:30

שׁנה to change, pervert (v)
6:26; 7:27; 13:38 = 4QH[c] frg. 3 10; 24:9

שׁנה year (n)
3:24; 9:21, 26

שׁנן to sharpen (v)
13:15

שׁנן to repeat (v)
12:11

שׁען to lean, depend on (v)
12:37; 14:28; 15:21; 18:19; 19:35; 22:12, 32

שׁעע to be blind (v)
15:5

שׁעע to delight (v)
15:24; 17:8, 13, 32; 18:18, 33; 19:10

שׁער gate, horizon (n)
11:18; 14:27, 30, 34

שׁפט to judge, rule (v)
5:24; 12:19; 13:8; 14:12; 15:31 = 1QH[b] frg. 1 2; 17:34; 19:21; 25:13 = 4QH[b] frg. 18 3; 25:14 = 4QH[b] frg. 18 4; [26:17] = 4QH[a] frg. 7 1:21

שׁפט judgment (n)
7:32

שׁפך to pour out, attack (v)
10:35

שׁפל to be low, abased (v)
26:16 = 4QH[a] frg. 7 1:20; [26:26] = 4QH[a] frg. 7 2:8

שׁפלה low (n)
4:13

שׁקה to provide drink, irrigate (v)
12:12

שׁקוי drink (n)
13:36 = 4QH[c] frg. 3 7 = 4QpapH[f] frg. 11 1; 13:37 = 4QH[c] frg. 3 9

שׁקט quiet (n)
20:5 = 4QH[a] frg. 3 2

שׁקר lie, falsehood (n)
13:29; 15:15

שׁררות stubbornness (n)
12:16

שׁרשׁ to take root (v)
16:8

שׁרשׁ root (n)
11:32; 12:15; 14:19 = 4QH[b] frg. 8 4; 16:8, 11, 24

שׁרת to minister, serve (v)
7:37; 13:23; 20:26; 23:34; 24:12; 25:29

שׁתה to drink (v)
11:31; 13:9; 16:14 = 1QH[b] frg. 2 2

תאשׁור cypress tree (n)
16:6

תבל world, earth (n)
6:17; 7:36; 9:17; 11:34, 37; 14:18 = 4QH[b] frg. 8 3; 14:20 = 4QH[b] frg. 8 5; A3 2

תדהר elm (n)
16:6

תהו formless, empty, chaos (n)
3:29; 9:2; 15:35

תהום deep (n)
5:26; 9:16; 11:16 = 4QpapH[f] frg. 5 3; 11:18, 32, 33; 13:40; 14:19, 27 = 4QH[c] frg. 4 2:4; 18:35

תהלה praise, psalm (n)
19:8, 26, 36

תוחלה expectation, hope (n)
17:14

תוך midst (n)
7:19 = 4QH[a] frg. 8 1:11; 13:8; 14:14; 16:7; 19:9; 20:6 = 4QH[b] frg. 12 2:2; 20:16 (2x)

תוכחת reproof (n)
15:32; 17:9, 24, 33; 20:24, 34; 22:28

תולעת worm, crimson (n)
14:37; 19:15

תועבה abomination (n)
19:14

תועה error (n)
9:24

תור to spy, follow (v)
12:16

תורה law, instruction (n)
12:11; 13:13; 14:13

תחלאים diseases (n)
21:36

תחנה supplication (n)
17:11; 19:37; [26:18] = 4QH[a] frg. 7 1:22

תחת under, instead of (prep)
11:18 = 4QpapH[f] frg. 5 6

תחתי lower (adj)
4:25; 25:14 = 4QH[b] frg. 18 4

תירושׁ new wine (n)
18:26

תכון rank, plan, arrangement, measure, precept (n)
20:8, 11, 12

תכמים filth, bowels, inner self (n)
4:37; 13:30; 15:7; [16:2] = 4QH[b] frg. 10 8; 16:40; 22:28

תכן to weigh, regulate, put right, apportion (v)
2:28, 29; 9:17

תלמוד teaching (n)
10:19

תלנות grumbling (n)
13:25, 32

תם integrity, perfection (n)
12:31

תמיד continually (part)
3:28; 19:9; 20:7, 10; 22:36; 23:26

תמים blameless, perfect (adj)
9:38

תמך to hold, support (v)
10:23; 12:2 = 4QpapH[f] frg. 7 4; 12:23; 15:23; 22:14

תמם to end, be complete (v)
4:33; 10:34; 11:30 = 4QH[b] frg. 5 5 = 4QpapH[f] frg. 6 5; 12:33; 13:30 = 4QH[c] frg. 2 12; 14:31 = 4QH[c] frg. 4 2:12; 16:32; 21:29; 22:34; [26:16] = 4QH[a] frg. 7 1:21; [26:20] = 4QH[e] frg. 2 1

תנין serpent, dragon, monster (n)
13:12, 29 = 4QH[c] frg. 2 9

תעב to abhor (v)
6:21, 32, 37; 7:31; 8:28; 18:31; 23:37, 38

תעה to err, wander (v)
12:8 (2x), 26

תעודה ordained time, assembly, testimony (n)
6:12; 9:21; 10:39; 14:22; 20:12; 25:13 = 4QH[b] frg. 18 2

תעות error, aberration (n)
10:16; 12:13, 17 = 4QH[d] frg. 1 4; 12:21; C1 4

תענוג delight (n)
6:18

תער razor, sheath (n)
13:17

תפל stupid, dull, insane (adj)
14:39

תפלה prayer (n)
20:7

תפשׂ to seize (v)
12:13, 20

תקוה hope (n)
11:28 = 4QpapH[f] frg. 6 2; 14:35; 17:12

תקופה turn, circuit, course, season (n)
9:26; 20:8, 9, 11 = 4QH[a] frg. 8 2:14

תקן to straighten, order (v)
21:13

תרן signal post (n)
14:37

תשׁובה return, response, repentance (n)
18:6; 19:23 = 4QH[a] frg. 1 3; 20:29; 23:31; C4 1; C4 3

CPSIA information can be obtained at www.ICGtesting.com
Printed in the USA
BVOW020732280612

293845BV00006B/1/P